THE PRESENCE OF THE PAST, THE PASTNESS OF THE PRESENT

History, Time, and Paradigm in Rabbinic Judaism

JACOB NEUSNER

CDL PRESS
Bethesda, Maryland

Library of Congress Cataloging-in-Publication

Neusner, Jacob, 1932-
    The presence of the past, the pastness of the present : history, time and
paradigm in rabbinic Judaism / Jacob Neusner.
        p.   cm.
    Includes bibliographical references and index.
    ISBN 1-883053-22-6
    1. Rabbinical literature — History and criticism. 2. Jews — History — To
70 A.D. — Historiography. I. Title.
BM504.2.N494 1996
296.1'206—dc20   95-46770
                                                                              CIP
                                                                               r96

ISBN 1-883053-22-6

TABLE OF CONTENTS

PART THREE

THE PRESENCE OF THE PAST, THE PASTNESS OF THE PRESENT

PART FOUR
FROM HISTORY TO PARADIGM

PART FIVE
TRANSCENDING THE BOUNDS OF TIME

PREFACE

> A major part of any course in Old Testament is the study of the history of Israel...the fact that [the history of the Israelite people] constituted the context out of which the Scriptures of the Old Testament emerged gives it special significance... How can we really appreciate the messages of the Old Testament authors unless we are familiar with the situations which produced them and to which they were addressed?
>
> George W. Ramsey[1]

Even without familiarity with the historical situations that produced them and to which they are addressed, the Judaic and Christian faithful have had no difficulty whatsoever in appreciating the messages of Scripture, which, in their eyes, were and are addressed to the faithful of all times. Contemporary exegetes have lost sight of the quite other-than-historical approach to history and time that governs throughout the entire corpus of Judaic and Christian reading of Scripture, indeed, governs in the Hebrew Scriptures themselves. History provides one way of marking time. But there are others, and the Judaism of the dual Torah, set forth in the Rabbinic literature from the Mishnah through the Talmud of Babylonia, ca. 200-600 C.E., defines one such alternative, one in which no boundary distinguishes past from present—the past forms a perpetual presence, the present takes place on the plane of the past, and no lines of structure or order distinguish the one from the other.

If we wish to understand Judaism, we shall have to set aside the forms of consciousness we today find self-evident and explore those other forms that defined perception for "our sages of blessed memory" and all who made themselves their disciples through the ages. This book tells the story of how a historical way of thinking about past, present, and future, time and eternity,

---

1. George W. Ramsey, *The Question for the Historical Israel. Reconstructing Israel's Early History* (London: SCM Press, 1982), p. xii.

the here and now in relationship to the ages, that is, Scripture's way of thinking, gave way to another mode of thought altogether, replacing history with a different model for the organization of experience, one constructed around a pattern or paradigm to impose meaning and order on events. Paradigmatic thinking, with a conception of time that elides past and present and removes all barriers between them, governed the reception of Scripture in Judaism and Christianity until nearly our own time. In this book I present, through the single case of Rabbinic Judaism, precisely how that other way of reading Scripture, the paradigmatic and, to be sure, also ahistorical way, did its work, and why, for so many centuries, that reading of the heritage of ancient Israel governed.

I shall present [1] a conception of time different from the historical one and [2] premises on how to take the measure of time that form a legitimate alternative to those that define the foundations of the historical way of measuring time. It follows that I mean to regain that way of reading and responding to Scripture that, for nearly the whole of the history of Judaism and Christianity, governed the encounter between today and that other time portrayed in the Hebrew Scriptures.

Throughout the book, I quote verbatim but a small selection of the documents required to sustain my thesis, since I have already published an extensive set of selections of the Rabbinic literature's presentation of what we should call "history." My survey in these pages then depends upon already-available evidence. Specifically, though moving in a quite new direction, this work depends upon the research reports contained in my following studies:

> *From Text to Historical Context in Rabbinic Judaism: Historical Facts in Systemic Documents. I. The Mishnah, Tosefta, Abot, Sifra, Sifré to Numbers, and Sifré to Deuteronomy.* Atlanta, 1993: Scholars Press for South Florida Studies in the History of Judaism.

> *From Text to Historical Context in Rabbinic Judaism: Historical Facts in Systemic Documents. II. The Later Midrash-Compilations: Genesis Rabbah, Leviticus Rabbah, Pesiqta deRab Kahana.* Atlanta, 1994: Scholars Press for South Florida Studies in the History of Judaism.

> *From Text to Historical Context in Rabbinic Judaism: Historical Facts in Systemic Documents. III. The Latest Midrash-Compilations: Song of Songs Rabbah, Ruth Rabbah, Esther Rabbah I, and Lamentations Rabbah.* Atlanta, 1994: Scholars Press for South Florida Studies in the History of Judaism.

In the biting cool of a Finnish spring, I wrote this book in my term as Visiting Research Professor at Åbo Akademi Forskningsinstitut and in association with my colleagues at Åbo Akademi's Theologisk Fakultetet. My dual position as Research Professor in the Research Institute and also Theological Faculty member brought me into contact with a variety of Finnish professors and students, from whom I received not only a warm welcome but also much stimulating conversation. I express thanks to the Åbo Akademi Forskningsinstitut for a very generous research stipend for April through August, 1993, and for providing comfortable living and working conditions.

Among many valued Finnish friends, both Finnish- and Swedish-speaking, I thank most especially my host and friend, Professor Karl-Johan Illman, for inviting me and making the visit memorable and happy. He made specific contributions to this book by calling to my attention important works in the area of ancient Israel's history that I might otherwise have missed. He gave me the benefit of his opinion on a variety of controverted scholarly questions in Tanakh studies, which is not my field. Not only so, but the many long walks we took around Åbo/Turku, enriched by his wise reflections about life in Finland and about our shared scholarly interests led, by circuitous paths sometimes, to the pages of this book and the companions produced in my Finnish sojourn. Fortunate indeed are the Americans invited to pursue their scholarship in that sturdy and welcoming country.

During this same span of time, I was invited to lecture at the fifth congress of the Scandinavian Congress for Jewish Studies, at Lund, and also for the Theological Faculty, University of Lund. I express my thanks to my colleagues at Lund and also those in Judaic studies throughout Scandinavia, who received me very cordially and responded to my lectures with penetrating and stimulating questions. During this same period I lectured for the Jewish communities of Stockholm, Uppsala, Helsinki, and Åbo, and express appreciation for the warm hospitality my wife and I received there. The lectures I gave in Finland and in Sweden are published in *Åbo Addresses. And Other Recent Essays on Judaism in Time and Eternity.* Atlanta, 1993: Scholars Press for South Florida Studies in the History of Judaism.

Since I used the opportunity to improve my Swedish and to undertake the most elementary Suomi (Finnish) as well, I express my appreciation, also, to many patient Finns, both Finnish- and Swedish-speaking, who formed a language laboratory without walls for my continuing education in one or another of their languages. It was certainly one of the most interesting summer terms I can remember, and one of the most pleasant and productive as well.

No work of mine can omit reference to the exceptionally favorable circumstances in which I conduct my research as Distinguished Research Professor in the Florida State University System at the University of South Florida. I wrote this book as part of my long-term labor of research scholarship, expressed through both publication and teaching at the University of South Florida, which has afforded me an ideal situation in which to conduct a scholarly life. I express my thanks for not only the advantage of a Distinguished Research Professorship in the Florida State University System, but also of a substantial research expense fund, ample research time, and some stimulating and cordial colleagues.

Jacob Neusner

Visiting Research Professor
Åbo Akademi Forskningsinstitut
FIN 20700 Turku/Åbo, Suomi/Finland
and
Distinguished Research Professor of Religious Studies
University of South Florida

July 28, 1993. My sixty-first birthday.

INTRODUCTION

> History writing answers to the needs to account for social change and to provide a basis for new meaning, new authority, and new legitimation for those traditional forms that have become dysfunctional in changing social circumstances.
>
> John van Seters[1]

The Hebrew Scriptures of ancient Israel ('the written Torah', to Judaism and 'the Old Testament' to Christianity), all scholarship concurs, set forth Israel's life as history, with a beginning, middle, and end; a purpose and a coherence; a teleological system. All accounts agree that Scriptures distinguished past from present, present from future, and composed a sustained narrative, made up of one-time, irreversible events. All maintain that, in Scripture's historical portrait, Israel's present condition appealed for explanation to Israel's past, perceived as a coherent sequence of weighty events, each unique, all formed into a great chain of meaning.

But this is not how for most of the history of Western civilization the Hebrew Scriptures have been read by Judaism and Christianity. The idea of history, with its rigid distinction between past and present and its careful sifting of connections from the one to the other, came quite late onto the scene of intellectual life. Both Judaism and Christianity for most of their histories have read the Hebrew Scriptures in an other-than-historical framework. They found in Scripture's words paradigms of an enduring present, by which all things must take their measure; they possessed no conception whatsoever of the pastness of the past. In due course, we shall consider an explanation for how and why, in Judaism, paradigmatic thinking replaced the historical kind. But first, let us explore the full and detailed character of the paradig-

---

1. John van Seters, *In Search of History. Historiography in the Ancient World and the Origins of Biblical History* (New Haven and London, 1983), p. 4.

I

matic approach to the explanation of Israel's condition, viewed (to state the negative side of matters) atemporally, ahistorically, episodically, and not through sustained narrative or its personal counterpart, biography, composed of connected, one-time and unique, irreversible events, in the manner of history.

Visually, we grasp the ahistorical perception in the union of past and present that takes place through representation of the past in the forms of the present: the clothing, the colors, the landscapes of the familiar world. But this is mere anachronism, which history can tolerate. Conceptually, we understand their mode of receiving Scripture when we understand that, for our sages of blessed memory of Judaism, as for the saints and sages of Christianity, the past took place in the acutely present tense of today, but the present found its locus in the presence of the ages as well. And this is something historical thinking cannot abide. Not only so, but it contradicts the most fundamental patterns of explanation that we ordinarily take for granted in contemporary cultural life.

A paradigmatic conception of marking time differs so radically from our own that reading Scripture in the way in which, for nearly the whole of its reception, it has been read proves exceedingly difficult. Our conception of history forms a barrier between us and the understanding of time that defined the Judaic and the Christian encounter with ancient Israel. The givenness of the barrier between time now and time then yields for us banalities about anachronism, on the one side, and imposes upon us the requirement of mediating between historical fact and religious truth, on the other.

Receiving those Scriptures and systematically reviewing them, the Judaism of the dual Torah—represented by the canonical writings of rabbis from the Mishnah, ca. 200, through the Talmud of Babylonia, ca. 600—recast this corpus of historical thinking, substituting paradigm or pattern for narrative sequence, by redefining the received notion of time altogether. This transformation of ancient Israel's Scripture from history to paradigm defines the conception of history of Rabbinic Judaism—calling into question the notion that this Judaism possessed a conception of history at all.[2] For what we shall see in these pages is how, when, where, and why an alternative conception of time took over and replaced the historical conception of time altogether—and with what consequences.

2. Chapter Eight goes over this question in its own terms, dealing with allegations that Rabbinic Judaism is a historical religion, examining the most current formulation, and showing its profound misunderstanding of Rabbinic literature.

In the Judaism set forth by principal documents that record the oral part of the dual Torah, particularly those that reached closure from ca. 200 to ca. 600 C.E., both documents of law such as the Mishnah and Tosefta, and documents of Scriptural exegesis, such as Sifré to Deuteronomy, Genesis Rabbah, Leviticus Rabbah, and Song of Songs Rabbah, concepts of history, coming to expression in the categories of time and change, along with distinctions between past, present, and future utterly give way to a conception of recording and explaining the social order different from that of history. It is one that sets aside time and change in favor of enduring paradigms recapitulated in each succeeding age. The concept of history as we know it, and as Scripture knows it, surrenders to an altogether different way of conceiving time and change as well as the course of noteworthy, even memorable social events. The past takes place in the present. The present embodies the past. And there is no indeterminate future over the horizon, only a clear and present path to be chosen if people will it. With distinctions between past, present and future time found to make no difference, and in their stead, different categories of meaning and social order deemed self-evident, the Judaism of the dual Torah transforms ancient Israel's history into the categorical structure of eternal Israel's society, so that past, present, and future meet in the here and now.

In this construction of thought, history finds no place, time, change, the movement of events toward a purposive goal have no purchase, and a different exegesis of happenings supplants the conception of history. No place in Rabbinic thought, portrayed in successive documents examined severally and jointly, accommodates the notions of change and time, unique events and history, particular lives and biography. All things are transformed by this other way of thinking, besides the historical one that Scripture uses to organize the facts of social existence of Israel.

Here we deal with a realm in which the past is ever present, the present a recapitulation and reformulation of the past. When people recapitulate the past in the present, and when they deem the present to be no different from a remote long ago, they organize and interpret experience in an other-than-historical framework, one that substitutes paradigms of enduring permanence for patterns of historical change. Instead of history, thought proceeds through the explanation of paradigms, the likenesses or unlikenesses of things to an original pattern. The familiar modes of classifying noteworthy events, the long ago and the here and now, lose currency. Memory as the medium of interpretation of the social order falls away, and historical thinking ceases to serve. Universal paradigms govern, against which all things,

now, then, anytime, are compared; events lose all specificity and particularity. The characterization of this Judaism as a historical religion and of the
medium of this religion as memory in no way conforms to the facts of the
Judaism that is studied here.

In this Judaism, with the past very present, the present an exercise in recapitulation of an enduring paradigm, therefore, time and change signify nothing. It follows, too, that there also is nothing to remember; the exegesis of
events invokes a different hermeneutics. The category of memory is null,
containing nothing, forming no source of meaning. Rabbinic Judaism is
ahistorical because it forms meaning in other than historical ways; it is ahistorical because it is paradigmatic in its structure and sensibility. So, with the
loss of the experience of memory in favor of a different kind of encounter
with time past, present, and future, time as a conception in the measurement
of things ceases to serve. Time is neither linear nor cyclical; it simply is not
a consideration in thinking about what happens and what counts.[3] Instead,
paradigms for the formation of the social order of transcendence and permanence govern, so that what was now is, and what will be is what was and is.

The ideas set forth in these pages prove so unfamiliar that a measure of
patience is required to understand and appreciate this other way of seeing
things. I found this study extremely challenging and the going hard. The
fact that at the start and finish I turn for metaphors to the mathematics of
our own time (however imperfectly grasped to be sure) indicates the difficulties I have faced. If I have succeeded, the reader will not find quite so
dense and difficult the ideas that, when they came to me, proved alien and
tough to express.

PART I – HISTORY, TIME, AND PARADIGM IN SCRIPTURE: My opening
question is, what gives me reason to speak of history at all, and what do I
mean by history? The answer derives solely from context. I do not deal with

---

3. Mircea Eliade's formulation of a perfect time—then, not now—to which we repair,
which defines the norm, and recovery of which secures eternity, certainly intersects with
the conceptions set forth in these pages. "That time" as paradigm corresponds in a rough way
to the outcome of the ahistorical thinking characteristic of our sages of blessed memory. But
when we look more closely at the claim set forth here that time plays no role, we see an
important point of difference. For our sages, the operative mantra is, "what was, was,"
meaning, "was and is no more, makes no difference, need not be taken into account." This
strikes me as quite contrary to Eliade's program of a perfect time then. For our sages, reality
takes place on a plane of continuities and takes shape through the realization in the here and
now of permanent paradigns that set beyond time altogether.

abstract definitions but only with accepted and conventional ones, not with history in general but only in the setting of the Hebrew Scriptures themselves. By 'history' in the context of the religion of Israel through time, scholarship universally refers to the Hebrew Scriptures ('Old Testament') and identifies the books of Genesis through Kings as a standard history, the story of Israel from creation to the expulsion from the Land of Israel.[4] Therefore by 'history', I mean, writing that exhibits the indicative traits of those books of Hebrew Scripture that learning in general classifies as history.

To establish the credentials of my later argument, I survey a wide variety of opinion on the traits of those writings, simply to establish some obvious facts. Writing history requires [1] narrative that in a teleological framework or pattern links [2] unique and meaningful events involving [3] singular persons, with traits of individuality. History tells what has happened so as to demonstrate propositions concerning the fate and faith of the community; it is a medium of explaining the social order and bears messages concerning how this order should be shaped and reformed. I mean to show that these simple indicators of historical writing, therefore of conceptions of history, characterize the Hebrew Scriptures' historical books.

CHAPTERS ONE AND TWO: Chapter One begins with a brief survey of the universal consensus that the Hebrew Scriptures present history and that what marks writing as historical is defined in terms of teleology given expression in narrative, of events as singular and also significant, and of persons (both women and men) as distinct and individually defined. Then I show the negative side, that the Rabbinic literature of late antiquity viewed in the aggregate and also document by document contains no evidences of historical thinking or indications of a concept of history comparable to that of Scripture: no sustained narrative, no biography, no conception of historical time defined whether teleologically or otherwise, whether cyclically or

---

4. I am much influenced by the scholarship of David Noel Freedman and my colleague Sara Mandel, whose work is cited in specific contexts, but upon whom I draw even when I do not explicitly cite their work. Their account of the structure and coherence of the Authorized History strikes me as definitive for the purpose of this book. Their insistence on reading the Hebrew Scriptures as a cogent statement by a small group at a determinate time, based on the internal evidence of the document itself, justifies my treating Genesis through Kings as a single coherent statement, as I do. I am also influenced by the newest work of Philip R. Davies, *In Search of Ancient Israel* (Sheffield, 1993: Journal for the Study of the Old Testament Supplement Series 148), and I find striking the complementary results produced by the two scholars. But in the relevant chapters I cite and quote a great many other Old Testament scholars, all of whom concur on the historicity of Scripture as a principal medium of thought and expression.

as linear in direction. My argument, hence my categories, works out four
distinct points. We start with an overview of the requirements of historical
thinking and writing that the Hebrew Scriptures define and exemplify. My
account derives entirely from current biblical scholarship. Reviewing how
accounts of history-writing in ancient Israel was carried on, I am able to give
a definitive account of the indicators that historical thinking has generated
historical writing in documents that are set forth as continuous with those
Scriptures. Chapter Two then proceeds to the heart of matters: the conception of time (and space) that animates historical thinking, including that of
Scripture, contrasted with the conception of time that governs paradigmatic
thinking.

I attempt to prove through a negative, then a positive, demonstration,
that Rabbinic Judaism formulated time through paradigm, which accounts
for the atemporality of this Judaism. My survey covers a sequential reading
of Rabbinic literature down to, but not including, the two Talmuds. We
survey the Mishnah and its continuators (Tosefta, Tractate Abot, Sifra and
the two Sifrés), ca. 200-300, then the Rabbinic amplifications of Scripture,
read in two groups, Genesis Rabbah, Leviticus Rabbah, and Pesiqta deRab
Kahana, ca. 400-500, and Lamentations Rabbah, Song of Songs Rabbah,
Ruth Rabbah, and Esther Rabbah I, as well as the Fathers According to
Rabbi Nathan, ca. 500-600. Proceeding through the sequence of documents, we examine three issues, addressed in Parts Two, Three, and Four.

PART II – THE ABSENCE OF HISTORY: sets forth the testing of two null-
hypotheses aimed at showing through negative evidence that the Rabbinic
documents do not resort to the media of historical thinking and do not
contain the most fundamental messages of historical thinking.

1. I formulate the first null-hypothesis in these terms: if the
    Rabbinic documents conformed to historical modes of thought
    and yielded historical writings, they would yield writing compa-
    rable to the historical writing of Scripture. That is to say, we
    should find resort to the media that express historical thinking:
    a linear narrative of one-time events for social history, on the
    one side, biography, on the other. In Chapter Three we conduct
    a test of this null-hypothesis, asking for evidence of narrative,
    on the one side, biography, on the other.

2. A second null-hypothesis requires testing. Once more, in the
    model of the Scripture's message yielded by historical thinking,
    if the Rabbinic documents yield the results of historical modes

of thought, then we should find in them a clear representation of the past as past, the present as distinct from the past, and of time as linear or cyclical (in the terms defined in the present chapter). In Chapter Four we seek evidence that Rabbinic literature recognizes the past as over and done with, the present as distinct and separate therefrom.

PART III – THE PRESENCE OF THE PAST, THE PASTNESS OF THE PRESENT moves from the theory that paradigmatic, not historical, thinking generates the kind of writing characteristic of Rabbinic documents and defines in great detail precisely the model that governed throughout. This model comprises four fundamental components. Each is defined and shown in practice.

PART IV – FROM HISTORY TO PARADIGM accomplishes that positive demonstration that corresponds to Part Two's negative one. Here I show how narrative, on the one side, and biography, on the other, find their counterparts in the paradigmatic conception that governs in Rabbinic documents. Narrative in a paradigm serves the purpose of the paradigm, selecting a topic and expounding that topic within the model's rules; and the same is so for biography. So we find ourselves able to explain not only what we do not find, but also what we do have at hand. The result is that time is treated as divisible, even as historical or natural time is subject to taxonomic analysis: differentiated in accord with a specified set of indicators. But the taxonomy of time—my 'temporal taxonomies'—takes place under the aspect of God's perspective on things, here called 'the aspect of eternity'. This 'aspect of eternity' in theological language corresponds to the 'paradigm' in secular formulation.

Historical differences hardly attracted the sages' attention, because their minds were shaped in accord with a different model from the historical one, the premises of historical thinking finding no place in their consciousness. When we have examined the negative evidences—the absence of historical thinking—and the positive—the model that took the place of history, we shall grasp how an altogether different conception of time and change, order and chaos, provoked for sages a reading of Scripture that, in their deepest conviction, accorded with God's purpose in revealing it. And this leads me to Part Five, where I propose to explain what is at stake in Judaism's paradigmatic thinking, and how the historical modes of thought characteristic of the received, and definitive, Scripture gave way to a different pattern altogether.

PART V – TRANSCENDING THE BOUNDS OF TIME concludes with a contrast between how historical and paradigmatic thinking yields each its own formulation of intellectual and emotional life. Since Rabbinic Judaism is often defined as historical, I therefore address the further allegation that Rabbinic Judaism is a traditional religion and ask whether traditionality necessarily signals the presence of historical thinking. I then turn to an important and current statement of the position contrary to the one treated here, spelling out views and systematically analyzing them. At the end I restate the contrary view, the conception of thinking by appeal to models rather than linear sequences of events. This leads me to ask why, when, and where did our sages of blessed memory make the shift from historical to paradigmatic thinking, and the explanation that I offer also permits me to account for the principles of selection that governed the meanings conveyed by the particular paradigm at hand.

OMITTING THE TWO TALMUDS: Readers will rightly ask why I have not surveyed the two Talmuds in examining documentary evidence of the historical and paradigmatic modes of thought characteristic of, dominant in Rabbinic Judaism. The reason is that I took for myself a more difficult challenge than is represented by the two Talmuds, with their now-well-documented traits of ahistorical thinking. It is the fact that earlier research[5] has already shown me how those two documents deal with the explanation of the social order formed by Israel, and it is an entirely ahistorical mode of thought. Paradigmatic thinking is fully exposed in the Mishnah, and the two Talmuds closely link their statements to the Mishnah. But in the nature of its work of setting forth the principles of Israel's natural and social existence, the Mishnah is ahistorical and appeals instead to enduring paradigms. I took for granted (and also, as a matter of fact, have demonstrated) that writings closely tied to the Mishnah do not present occasions for the exploration of historical thinking. There, I reasoned, I was not going to find distinctions among time past, present, and future.

Specifically, focusing upon the exposition of the Mishnah, an utterly ahistorical document, the two Talmuds set forth a conception of Israel that

---

5. See *The Foundations of Judaism. Method, Teleology, Doctrine*. Philadelphia, 1983-5: Fortress Press. I-III. II. *Messiah in Context. Israel's History and Destiny in Formative Judaism*. Second printing: Lanham, 1988: University Press of America. Studies in Judaism series; *Judaisms and their Messiahs in the beginning of Christianity*. New York, 1987: Cambridge University Press; and *The Christian and Judaic Invention of History*. Atlanta, 1990: Scholars Press for American Academy of Religion. Studies in Religion series.

subordinates history to law and presents the Messiah as a sage and an ahistorical figure, who comes in response to the condition of Israel's soul and heart, not in the aftermath of a sequence of historical events. I preferred for this exposition to focus most of my attention on the documents that, in the Rabbinic literature, take a position closest to that of Scripture, citing the Torah and the prophets throughout. Here, I theorized, if I am going to find a historical mode of thought, distinguishing among past, present, and future as the prophets do, it will be in the Midrash-compilations. There, I imagined, I should find a past clearly differentiated from the present and a perspective upon a distant future, not one time for all time.

So too, I supposed, I should find in the exposition of the past tense of the written Torah, such as the Midrash-compilations provide, a clear formulation of the distinction between past and present. I wanted to center interest on the Midrash-compilations because they take as their focus the history of Scripture. If I was going to find any writings that bore the marks of historical thinking, they would be within those compilations in particular. Having failed in prior inquiries to find a conception of history of any kind in Rabbinic Judaism, I assumed that I had best formulate the problem so as to focus on the very writing closest to the most historical of the parts of the Torah. These are Midrash-compilations of exegeses of the Pentateuch, for one major example, and, as in the case of the books of Esther, Lamentations, and Ruth, in Esther Rabbah, Lamentations Rabbati, and Ruth Rabbah, on the one side, and Pesiqta deRab Kahana, on the other, treatments of themes defined by historical events (Esther, Lamentations), the Messiah-theme (Ruth), or commemorative occasions (Pesiqta deRab Kahana). Here, I imagined, if a concept of history governed the exegesis of Scripture and a clear pattern of time formed the principal mode of thought, I should find it.

So far as the marks of historical thinking are defined as narrative, a conception of linear events with beginnings, middles, and ends, and biographies cast along those same lines—let alone a clear perception of the pastness of the past and the acute distinction of present from past that history requires in order to accomplish its tasks—I have not found those traits of mind: not only no narrative and no biography, no evidence of a sustaining history, but a different conception of time altogether. In these pages I show I have found the very opposite. At the very passages in which Scripture records one-time events and imputes meaning to them, finding hope for the future in the rules yielded by the past, distinguishing among past, present, and future as the generative problematic of discourse, our sages of blessed memory serenely make their way, drawing their own conclusions concerning paradigmatic reality, not those invited by Scripture's historical reality. This accounts for the selection of documents that are subjected to close analysis in this book.

❧ *Part One* ❧

HISTORY, TIME, AND PARADIGM IN SCRIPTURE

CHAPTER I

HEBREW SCRIPTURE
AND THE REQUIREMENTS OF HISTORICAL THINKING

The confessional use of the Bible is fundamentally ahistorical. It makes of Scripture a sort of map, a single, synchronic system in which the part illuminates the whole, in which it does not matter that different parts of the map come from divergent perspectives and different periods. The devotee uses it to search for treasure: under the X lies a trove of secret knowledge; a pot of truths sits across the exegetical rainbow, and with them one can conjure knowledge, power, eternity. Worshipers do not read the Bible with an intrinsic interest in human events. Like the prophet or psalmists or, in Acts, the saint, they seek behind the events a single, unifying cause that lends them meaning and makes the historical differences among them irrelevant. In history, the *faithful* seek the permanent, the ahistorical; in time, they quest for timelessness; in reality, in the concrete, they seek Spirit, the insubstantial. Confessional reading levels historical differences—among the authors in the Bible and between those authors and church tradition—because its interests are life present (in the identity of a community of believers) and eternal.

Baruch Halpern[1]

i. Historical vs. Paradigmatic Thinking in Judaism

Halpern characterizes what is under study in these pages, that alternative to the historical reading of Scripture that both Judaism and Christianity selected and faithfully followed for eighteen hundred years, until the advent of historical learning in the nineteenth century and its transformation of a powerful instrument of exegesis of Scripture in the twentieth. Until that time another way of reading and responding to events, besides the historical one, governed the way in which the historical writings of ancient Israel were received.

---

1. Baruch Halpern, *The First Historians. The Hebrew Bible and History* (San Francisco, 1988: Harper & Row), pp. 3-4.

What is at stake is a different conception of time. Specifically, I propose
to explain precisely how an other-than-historical reading of Scripture
worked, identifying its premises and showing its results. For at issue is something different from indifference to whether or not things really happened
as they are portrayed, and 'timelessness' obscures that vastly different
conception of time that comes into play in the Judaic and Christian reception of ancient Israel's Scripture, especially its history.

For nearly the whole of the history of Judaism and Christianity, a mode
of reading Scripture predominated that today is scarcely understood and only
rarely respected. In Halpern's description, it is characterized as 'confessional',
and dismissed as ahistorical. But 'confessional' tells us only that faithful practitioners of Judaism and Christianity come to Scripture with reverence and
seek there to find what God has told to humanity. The faith of Judaism and
Christianity need not insist upon the reading of Scripture as a single,
synchronic system—but it does, so the pejorative, 'confessional', is both
beside the point and accurate. The 'ahistorical' reading means to overcome
the barriers of time and space and address Scripture in an unmediated
present.

The key to the uncomprehending caricature lies in the contrasts, with
the climax, 'insubstantial'. Militant, ideological historicism in this word
makes its complete and final statement.[2] Faith admittedly is in things unseen,
but not in what is 'insubstantial'. Still, scholarship for a century and a half
has appealed to secular rules for reading documents of religions, Judaism and
Christianity, that read the Hebrew Scriptures as the written Torah and the
Old Testament, respectively.

During the now-protracted spell since the advent of historicism, the holy
books of Judaism and Christianity have been asked to tell us everything but

---

2.   I ignore the institutional foundations for the historicistic reading of sacred Scripture,
the conduct of this reading under mostly secular auspices. In fact, the Bible is a privileged
document, enjoying a central position in the academic study of religion that secular
considerations alone will not have accorded it. The result is that academic scholarship on
Scripture enjoys the sponsorship of the faithful and takes as its task the imposition of secular
norms upon the documents of the faith—in the name of the rational labor of the academy.
This is why I regard as critical to my venture here the demonstration of the rationality,
within the norms of the academy, of the ahistorical, atemporal reading of Scripture that
Judaism and Christianity have for most of their histories adopted for themselves, and this
means I show the intellectual power of paradigmatic, as opposed to historical thinking. It is
not enough to describe how people saw things, I have also to explain their modes of thought
within the norms of academic rationality. The issue then is theological, though the
evidence, argument, and thesis merely academic.

that to which they are devoted: about human events, not about God's perspective on and dealings with humanity. And, in this same long period of time, the reason people have taken up these books and read and studied them—the quest for the written record of God's intervention into human history (for the Torah of Judaism) or of God's footsteps on earth (for the Bible of Christianity)—has been dismissed. After such a long span of time people have forgotten the religious rules for reading those same holy books and, as Halpern's statement makes clear, they even have lost the capacity to understand those same rules. But for nearly eighteen centuries those norms governed, and whether or not we accept their discipline, we owe it to ourselves to try to make sense of them. In the pages of this book I shall not only attempt to explain, but also to advocate the rationality of, a different model of reading from that of historicism.

The historical way, so long dominant in the West's reception of its own holy books, proves no longer a secure path to knowledge. For history's premise—the self-evidence of the linearity of events, so that, first came this, then came that, and this 'stands behind' or explains or causes that—contradicts the now-articulated experience of humanity. Chaos governs, while from history's perspective, order should reign. Sometimes 'this' yields 'that', as it should, but sometimes it does not. To the contrary, what happens in ordinary life yields not events that relate to one another like pearls on a necklace, first this, then that, then the other thing, in proper procession. Not at all. Life is unpredictable; if this happens, we cannot securely assume that that must occur in sequence, in order—at least, not in the experience of humanity. This is proven by the irregularity of events, the unpredictability, by all and any rules, of what, if this happens, will follow next. Knowing 'this', we never can securely claim to predict 'that' as well.

History's inexorable stopping point, the present moment, calls into question the rationality of the past that history portrays for us. The iron wall between past and present for historical thinking marks the outer limit of rationality. This is expressed by the French philosopher of historiography, Jacques LeGoff, in the following language:

> The opposition between past and present is fundamental, since the activity of memory and history is founded on this distinction...[3]

3. Jacques LeGoff, *History and Memory* (N.Y., 1992: Columbia University Press). Translated by Steven Randall and Elizabeth Claman, p. xii.

This distinction, commonplace and fundamental in every current account of history-writing, indeed, is given the status of a psychological norm, when LeGoff cites Piaget in this language (p. 3):

> For the child, "to understand time is to liberate oneself from the present' not only to anticipate the future in relation to the regularities unconsciously established in the past, but to deploy a series of states, each of which is different from the others, and whose connection can be established only by a gradual movement without fixation and stopping point."...In societies, the distinction between past and present (and future) also implies this ascent into memory and this liberation from the present.

But what psychology may we impute to a civilization that makes no such distinction, that manages memory in a different way altogether, finding the present a chapter of the past, defining the past as a component of an enduring present? And how shall we reconstruct the mentality of an entire group that denies what many maintain characterizes the normal, as does LeGoff in the following words:

> The pathology of individual attitudes toward time shows that 'normal' behavior maintains an equilibrium between the consciousness of the past, the present, and the future, but with a slight predominance of the orientation toward the future...The orientation toward the present, characteristic of very young children (who even "reconstitute the past in relation to the present," as Piaget has noted), of mentally defective or insane persons...is encountered fairly commonly among old people...

This characterization of the incapacity of distinguishing past from present as an indicator of insanity or senility hardly prepares us to understand the many, long centuries in which Western civilization, Judaic and Christian, in no way conceded the pastness of the past or the barrier between past and present.

Here we address a vast corpus of writing that contains no sustained narrative, concedes no gap or barrier to separate present from past, views the present as autonomous of past and future, and, it goes without saying, finds sustained story-history a useless medium for the making of its statement. Here we deal not with non-literate but highly literate sages; not with a world of myth and ritual that relates past and present in such a way that history is both separated from the present and joined with it (Levi-Strauss cited by LeGoff). The mode of telling time so profoundly intimate to both Judaic and Christian conceptions of the social order lies beyond the power of theory of history not only to explain, but even to comprehend, except in primitive terms.

That matter must remain a puzzle, as I establish that, for our sages of blessed memory history as defined by the Authorized History of Scripture yielded an altogether different form of consciousness, a quite ahistorical, atemporal, but profound and powerful mode of confronting and manipulating the historical record received in Scripture. The entire program of this book rests upon the certainty that historical thinking requires the distinction between past and present, and a mode of representing the social order of a group in such a way that the past forms a vivid presence, but the present also takes place in the past, is a mode of thought and re-presentation of matters that is simply not historical.

The distinction between past and present is not the only indicator of historical modes of organizing experience. A further trait of historical thinking is the linearity of events, a sense for the teleology of matters, however the goal find its definition. Past was then but leads to now. It is not now but it guides us into the acute present tense, and onward to the future. For what may happen is not to be predicted; linearity presupposes predictability, regularity, order,—and therefore contradicts the unpredictability of the world. Historical study correlates this to that, ideas to events, always seeking reasonable explanation for what has come about. Its very premise is that of the Enlightenment, concerning the ultimate order awaiting discovery. History then forms a subset of the quest for order—a persuasive one, one that enjoys the standing of self-evidence.

But all premises concerning order, except the one that insists upon the ultimate chaos of things, lose plausibility. In turning to another way of receiving Scripture, besides the historical way, we update our approach to the problem of defining how we shall identify what matters therein. If not historical explanation, resting on linear sequences of events, which we assume we really can recover in their fullness, then what? The end of history's self-evident power of description, analysis, and explanation requires us to review other approaches and their logic. And among them, the received, religious approach (Halpern's 'confessional' one) demands attention, not because it served for so long with such power, but because it appeals to a different logic, one more current than the historical.

Unlike history, religion takes into account the failure of linear logic, with its regularities and certainties and categorical dismissal of chaos. In its reading of Scripture, Judaism (along with Christianity) posits instead a world that may be compared to that of fractal shapes, in the language of mathematics, or classified as paradigms, models, or patterns, in the language of this book. These fractals or paradigms describe how things are, whether large or small, whether here or there, whether today or in a distant past or an unimaginable future. Fractal thinking finds sameness without regard to scale, from small to large—and so too in the case of events. Fractal thinking therefore makes possible the quest for a few specific patterns, because out of acknowledged chaos it isolates points of regularity or recurrence and describes, analyzes, and permits us to interpret them.[4]

Paradigms describe the structure of being without regard to scale, therefore in complete indifference to the specificities of context. They derive from imagination, not from perceived reality. They impose upon the world their own structure and order, selecting among things that happen those few moments that are eventful and meaningful. Paradigms form a different conception of time from the historical, defining a different conception of relationship from the linear. Stated very simply, while historical thinking is linear, religious thinking corresponds to mathematics' fractal thinking.

Whether we draw our analogy from mathematics or from structures, the result is the same. To call the religious way of reading Scripture ahistorical is both accurate and monumentally beside the point; it is only to say what it is not, not what it is. I claim it is paradigmatic thinking, in place of linear thinking. Here I shall set forth precisely what this way of thinking is, so far as the Judaism of the dual Torah exemplifies paradigmatic thinking, i.e., how history and time give way to a different order of being altogether.

The shift from historical to paradigmatic models of thinking is set forth in these pages in the contrast between two conflicting conceptions of how the social experience of Israel is to be organized, written down, and formed into patterns of meaning. The one, Hebrew Scripture, is linear, the other, Rabbinic literature, fractal. Hebrew Scripture sets forth its theological statement through the medium of history; all scholarship from the nineteenth century forward concurs on this simple statement. It is a linear statement of

---

4. I invoke the analogy of fractal mathematics only to introduce external evidence in support of my insistence upon the rationality of paradigmatic thinking. I find the points of analogy in fractals in particular in [1] the dismissal of considerations of scale; [2] the admission of chaos into the data out of which order is selected; [3] the insistence that a few specific patterns are all that we have, but that these serve in a variety of circumstances and can be described in a reliable and predictable way. The starting point is chaos, the goal, the discovery of order. The givenness, for historical thinking, of linearity then defines a different starting point, one of order, not chaos, and this strikes me as lacking all rationality, when measured against the perceived experience of humanity. As I shall argue in a moment, historical thinking forms the last remnant of the Enlightenment's pious optimism, and paradigmatic thinking offers a more plausible way of ordering the chaos of nature and society alike.

things, a mode of thinking which came to compete with another which defined a model or paradigm and selected among happenings those events that conformed to the paradigm or that identified the paradigm in the here and now of ordinary persons' lives and the nation's alike, without regard to time or change. Time meant something else than it had in Scripture, and change meant nothing whatsoever.

Rabbinic literature makes its statement through a different, quite ahistorical medium, one that explicitly rejects distinctions among past, present, and future, and treats the past as a powerful presence, but the present as a chapter of the past, and the future as a negotiation of not time but principle. A paradigm governs, all events conforming to its atemporal rule. Consequently, the two conflicting conceptions of social explanation—the historical, the paradigmatic—appeal to two different ways of conceiving of, and evaluating, time. Historical time measures one thing, paradigmatic time, another, though both refer to the same facts of nature and of the social order. It follows that, at stake in this study is a detail of the much larger problem of what we mean by 'time', but here I offer only a footnote to the study of this protean question.

For its exposition of the cogency and meaning of Israel's social experience, Rabbinic Judaism possesses no concept of history and therefore produces as its statements of the sense of the life of the people neither historical narrative nor biography. The negative of course is to be matched by a positive conception. That Judaism sets forth a concept of paradigm and produces its own counterparts to historical writing: stories about what it deems worth narrating, chapters, not 'lives', it identifies as worth emulating. People generally concur that ancient Israel organized its social experience in historical terms: unique events formed into continuous narrative, biography, all formed into an account of what has happened and its meaning—and therefore where matters are heading.

While taking over the heritage of ancient Israel, "our sages of blessed memory," who produced the Mishnah, Tosefta, tractate Abot, and the score of Midrash-compilations surveyed here, made sense of the social experience of Israel in terms unrelated to conceptions of past, present, and future, composed into narrative formed out of distinctive events and distinct biographies.

Rabbinic Judaism formulates its conception of the social order—of the life of its 'Israel' and the meaning of that life through time and change—in enduring paradigms that admit no distinction between past, present, and future. All things take form in a single plane of being; Israel lives not in

historical time, moving from a beginning, to a middle, to an end, in a linear
plan. Nor does it form its existence in cyclical time, repeating time and again
familiar cycles of events. Those familiar modes of making sense out of the
chaos of change and the passage of time serve not at all. Rather, Israel lives
in accord with an enduring paradigm that knows neither past, present, nor
future. Appealing to a world of timeless myth, that Judaism accounts for how
things are not by appeal to what was and what will be, but by invoking the
criterion of what characterizes the authentic and true being of Israel, an idea
or ideal defined by the written Torah and imposed upon the chaos of time
and change. The pattern that controls recapitulates, without regard to time
or change, the paradigmatic lives of the patriarchs and matriarchs, so that a
single set of patterns governs. Here history gives way to not eternity but
permanence, the rules of the paradigm telling us not how to make sense of
what was or how to predict what will be, but only what it is that matters.

In the context of a Judaism what is at stake in all explanation, whether
historical or paradigmatic, is the same thing, namely, accounting for the here
and now of 'Israel', that social entity that a particular group of Jews conceives
itself as constituting. Now 'Israel's' existence may be explained in diverse
ways. It is a people that has evolved through a series of events, progressing
through time and through its actions in relationship to God, writing a history
for itself. So to be 'Israel' means: to have come from somewhere and to be
en route to some other place, and to explain this 'Israel' we tell the story of
the journey. People then may join the trip, take up the burden of history,
and assume the hope for the future destination as well. Shared memory
(fabricated or otherwise) forms the medium for the social message.

Paradigmatic thinking defines and explains 'Israel' in a different way.[5]
To be 'Israel' means to conform to a pattern of actions and attitudes set forth
for all time and without distinction in time. This pattern, or paradigm, comes
to definition in the lives of the patriarchs and matriarchs. It is then recapitulated in a social world that knows not change but conformity to paradigm.
Since the paradigm endures, we explain happenings by appeal to its rules,
and the event is not what is singular and distinctive but what conforms to
the rule: we notice what is like the paradigm, not what diverges from it. To

---

5. On the negotiability, the systemic particularity, of 'Israel' or the concept of Israel, see
my *Judaism and its Social Metaphors. Israel in the History of Jewish Thought*. N.Y., 1988:
Cambridge University Press, and now, also, Philip R. Davies, *In Search of Ancient Israel*
(Sheffield, 1993: Journal for the Study of the Old Testament Supplement Series 148), who
did not know of my work when he pursued exactly the same problem within precisely the
same premises—the indeterminacy of 'Israel'—though in a different temporal setting.

the paradigm matters of memory and hope prove monumentally irrelevant, because they explain nothing, making distinctions that stand for no important differences at all.

To explain what it means to be 'Israel', we appeal not to time and change but to eternity and permanence. Or rather, the conception of the category, time—what is measured by the passage of the sun and moon in relationship to events here on earth—altogether loses standing. In place of distinguishing happenings through the confluence of time, measured by the passage of the sun and moon, and event, distinguished by specificity and particularity, paradigmatic thinking takes another route. It finds an event in what conforms to the paradigm; what is meaningful in what confirms the paradigm. In our own setting, we make this distinction when we speak of nominalism as against realism, or the humanities as against the social sciences, or the individual and singular as against the general and the uniform, or the exception as against the rule. How these various modes of making sense of the social order pertain here is now clear. In historical thinking we ask the distinctive event and its consequences out of the past to deliver its meaning to the present and its message concerning the future: if this, then that. In paradigmatic thinking we examine the norms for an account of how things ought to be, finding the rule that tells us how things really are. Then past, present, future differentiate not at all, the pattern of an eternal present taking over to make sense of the social order.

It follows that in the paradigmatic mode of thinking about the social order, the categories of past, present, and future, singular event and particular life, all prove useless. In their place come the categories defined by the actions and attitudes of paradigmatic persons, Abraham and Sarah, for instance, or paradigmatic places, the Temple, or paradigmatic occasions, holy time. We identify a happening not by its consequence ('historical') but by its conformity to the appropriate paradigm. We classify events in accord with their paradigms as not past, present, or future, therefore, because to the indicators of eventfulness—what marks a happening as eventful or noteworthy—time and change, by definition, have no bearing at all. Great empires do not make history; they fit a pattern.

To this way of thinking, apocalypse, with its appeal to symbol to represent vast forces on earth, makes its contribution; but paradigmatic and apocalyptic thinking about Israel's social being scarcely intersect. The paradigmatic excludes the historical, the indicative, the categorical pattern, the possibility of noteworthy change. Matters are just the opposite, indeed: paradigmatic thinking accommodates historical thinking not at all, since the beginning of history, in the notion of the pastness of the past, contradicts the generative conception of the paradigm: the very paradigmatic character of the happening that bears meaning.

In this context, therefore, the governing categories speak of not time and change, movement and direction, but the recapitulation of a given pattern, the repetition of the received paradigm. Being then moves from the one-time, the concrete, the linear and accumulative, to the recurrent, the mythic, and the repetitive: from the historical to the paradigmatic. These modes of identifying a happening as consequential and eventful then admit no past or present or future subject to differentiation and prognostication, respectively. Time therefore bears no meaning, nor the passage of time, consequence. If, therefore, the historical mode of organizing shared experience into events forming patterns, its identification of events as unique and persons as noteworthy, of memory as the medium for seeking meaning, and narrative as the medium for spelling it out, paradigmatic thinking will dictate a different mode of culture, one in which shared experience takes on meaning when the received paradigms of behavior and the interpretation of the consequence of behavior come to realization once again: the paradigm recapitulated is the paradigm confirmed. What takes place that is identified as noteworthy becomes remarkable because today conforms to yesterday and provokes, too, tomorrow's recapitulation as well. We notice not the unlike—the singular event—but the like, not what calls into question the ancient pattern but what reviews and confirms it. If, then, we wish to make sense of who we are, we ask not where we come from or where we are heading, but whom we resemble, and into which classification of persons or events we fit or what happens appears to repeat. The social order then finds its explanation in its resemblances, the likenesses and the unlikenesses of persons and happenings alike.

The meaning of shared experience, such as history sets forth in its categories of past, present, future, and teleology through narrative of particular events or through biography of singular lives, emerges in a different way altogether. In the formulation of the social order through paradigm, past, present, future, the conception of time in general, set forth distinctions that by definition make no difference. Events contradict the paradigm; what is particular bears no sense. Then remarkable happenings, formed into teleology through history-writing, or noteworthy persons' lives, formed into memorable cases through biography, no longer serve as the media of making a statement bearing intelligible, cultural consequence.

Paradigmatic thinking is never generalized; it is a mode of thought that is just as specific to the case as is theological thinking in the historical medium. Specific paradigms come into play. They define the criteria for the selection as consequential and noteworthy of some happenings but not others. They further dictate the way to think about remarkable happenings, events, so as to yield sense concerning them. They tell people that one thing bears meaning, while another does not, and they further instruct people on the self-evident meaning to be imputed to that which is deemed consequential. The paradigms are fully as social in their dimensions, entirely as encompassing in their outreach, as historical categories. We deal not with the paradigms of universal, individual life, taking the place of those of particular, social existence, such as history, with its unique, one-time, sequential and linear events, posits. The result of paradigmatic thinking is no different from that of the historical kind.

Before us is not a random sequence of entirely personal recapitulations of universal experiences, for instance, birth, maturing, marriage, love, and death; these modes of permanence in change, these personal paradigms that form a counterpoint to one-time, public moments play no role in the formation of what endures, whether past, whether past, whether future, in the eternal now. The definition of the consequential, permanent paradigms that replace the conception of history altogether will emerge in due course. At the outset what is at stake must be clear. The shift from historical to paradigmatic thinking represents a movement from one kind of thinking about the social order to another kind. The particularity of history finds its counterpart in the particularity of the paradigm of thought.

This paradigmatic thinking—ahistorical, and, I claim, utterly anti-historical and dismissive of particularities of time or circumstance, but rather philosophical and generalizing—characterizes Rabbinic writing. Here the past is present, the present is past, and time contains no delineative future tense at all; eschatological teleology gives way to paradigmatic teleology, and biography abdicates in favor of highly selective paradigms of exemplarity in the lives of persons, events to patterns. Sustained narrative is abandoned because it is irrelevant; biography, because it is filled with useless information. The concept of organizing the facts (real or fabricated) of the social world of Israel into history as the story of the life and times of Israel, past, present, and future, is succeeded by the concept of organizing the received and now perceived fasts of the social world of Israel into the enduring paradigm in which past, present, and future fuse into an eternal now.

When recapitulative paradigms of meaning obliterate all lines between past, present, and future, writing too changes in character, for with the loss of historical thinking perish three kinds of writing:

[1] Narrative, the tale of a singular past leading to present and pointing toward the future, the concretization therefore of teleology.

[2] Biography, the notion of an individual and particular life, also with its beginning, middle, and end.

[3] The formulation of events as unique, with close study of the lessons to be derived from happenings of a singular character.

The loss of these three types of writing, commonplace in the standard history, Genesis through Kings, signals a shift in categories, from the category of history, resting on the notion of time as a taxonomic indicator, to a different category altogether. For the concept of history generates its conception of time, made concrete through the writing of narrative and biography, the formulation of things that have taken place into the formation of consequential, singular events, comparable to the identification of particular persons as events of consequence, worthy of preservation; time starts somewhere and leads to a goal, and lives begin, come to a climax, and conclude as well.

With the end of linear, cumulative, and teleological-historical thinking, the realization of history in narrative, event, and biography loses currency. Narrative strings together one time events into meaningful patterns, with a beginning, middle, and end; this is the medium of history, and this medium bears history's self-evident messages (whatever they may be). Biography then does for individuals what narrative accomplishes for remarkable moments in the existence of the social entity; the narrative takes its measure in different dimensions, but the mode of thought is identical, and the medium for explanation the same. So too the conception of time, that is, a sequence of distinct moments, whether cyclical, following a pattern of recurrence, or linear, pursuing a single line from start to finish, also loses all self-evidence. In place, the passage of the fixed stars and planets, the moon and sun, cease to mark off ages and signify periods in human events—this year, this event, next year, that event—and instead measure something else altogether. Just as the passage of a person's life from birth to death takes place outside of historical, that is, public, shared, eventful time, only rarely intersecting with the historical and the consequential, so the paradigms marked off something other than the cumulative passing of public time, or of any time that people ordinarily would measure at all.

With the past eternally present, with the present simply another form of the immediate realization of times past, and with the future predetermined by rules long known and also formed as a recapitulation of the eternal paradigm, the conception of history as we know it from the Holy Scriptures of ancient Israel—'the Old Testament', the Written [part of the] Torah—loses all standing. Whether in the form of the view that what has been is what will be, that is, cyclical time, or in the version of the history from Genesis through Kings that posited linear time, the concept of history simply gives way to another way of thinking altogether. Before we can proceed, we have now to establish that historical thinking did predominate in the Scriptures inherited by our sages of blessed memory and recast by them in the writings of legal, exegetical, and theological character through which they mediated Scripture into the(ir) Torah.

ii. Historical Thinking in Ancient Israel

The Hebrew Scriptures of ancient Israel are nearly universally described as historical.[6] Accordingly, the paramount position, "considerations of priority or posteriority do not apply to the Torah" (*én muqdam ume'uhar battorah*),[7] which characterizes the conception of history, time, and the eternal present of the Rabbinical literature, contradicts the deepest premise of the scriptural historian-theologians. The writings that attest to how ancient Israel organized and interpreted experience form a systematic history from creation to the destruction of the Temple of Jerusalem in 586 B.C.E. This history, composed at ca. 560 B.C.E., is, if not wholly continuous (leaving gaps as it does), quite coherent, beginning to end.[8] It is formulated within a cogent theology of Israel's life and experience, from the beginning to the present,

6. I have concentrated on writings in English, German, and, to a less extent, Swedish, but, of course, wherever the Hebrew Scriptures are studied in the academy, these same conclusions are set forth, and I could have included in these notes items in Hebrew, French, Spanish, Italian, and Portuguese, not to mention Danish and Norwegian. The consensus is universal for Protestant, Judaic, and most Roman Catholic scholarship. I do not have access to Orthodox Christianity's exegetical traditions or to its mode of reading Scripture, which accounts for the 'nearly'.

7. The relevant source is given at the head of Chapter Four.

8. This assertion is based upon the work of David Noel Freedman; see his *The Unity of the Hebrew Bible* (Ann Arbor, 1991: The University of Michigan Press). This work is cited presently. See also Philip R. Davies, *In Search of Ancient Israel*, who assigns this cogent and systematic work to the same period as does Freedman, though for different reasons.

and it expresses a clear sense of closure—past distinct from present, present separate from future.

From the perspective of the final formation and closure, it is systematic and orderly and cogent from Genesis through Kings. This Primary History, as it has been called,[9] narrates and accounts for the existence of Israel, i.e., how this people came into being and what happened to them over time. The narrative sets forth the meaning and message of its social existence. My purpose now is to demonstrate three facts.

[1] All learning concurs that the Scriptures organize experience in a linear, historical way.

[2] All learning concurs on the literary requirements for making a historical statement, which are a sustained, continuous narrative of specific, unique events, and the premise that the past leads into the present and adumbrates the future.

[3] Scripture's representation of historical thinking not only follows a linear course but also posits a clear and present distinction between past and present, present and future, future and past. The beginning of its historical thinking lies in the recognition of an abyss and a barrier between now and then; the circumstance, as Freedman and Davies (among many) insist, is the age beyond the destruction of the first Temple in ca. 586 B.C.E.

A succinct account of the received scholarly tradition on this matter begins with an account of why Israelite Scripture takes the path of history. The reason that the critical mass of the Hebrew Scriptures is set forth in the medium of coherent history is stated in the language of G. Ernest Wright, "Biblical theology is the confessional recital of the redemptive acts of God in a particular history, because history is the chief medium of revelation."[10] What marks Scripture's treatment of history as distinctive is that while in the cultures surrounding Israel, the various types of history-writing are preserved in discrete form, "raw materials of history rather than history proper," "...in the Old Testament, all these elements, as far as the

9. Sara Mandell and David Noel Friedman, *The Relationship between Herodotus' History and Primary History* (Atlanta, 1993: Scholars Press for South Florida Studies in the History of Judaism).

10. G. Ernest Wright, *God Who Acts. Biblical Theology as Recital* (London, 1952), p. 13, cited in J.R. Porter, "Old Testament Historiography," G.W. Anderson, *Tradition and Interpretation* (Oxford, 1979: Clarendon Press), p. 125. Porter's survey of the matter is a good starting point throughout.

Pentateuch and the Former Prophets are concerned, are embedded in a chronologically added narrative. It is this that provides their setting, it is only in this framework that they have eventually been preserved, and it is the narrative which is intended to determine their significance."[11]

What is essential in the characterization of the Hebrew Scriptures as history is, first, the provision of a sustained and continuous narrative of distinct, sequential, and unique events. It would be difficult to improve upon James Barr's concise statement, "...in Hebrew thought the sequence of historical events, or of some historical events, is a purposive movement towards a goal; it is certainly not cyclic in the sense of something recurrent, but is non-recurrent, non-reversible, and unique."[12] The requirement for historical thinking in ancient Israel is the conviction that events are unique, bear meaning, come from an unrecoverable past, and point toward specific traits of the immediate. Hence history is a composition of events aimed at explaining how things now are by appeal to how they came about. The conception of history may carry with it the idea of eternity, that is, beyond history; but then eternity is as distinct from history as is present from past time. The entire program adumbrated at the outset is covered in Barr's statement.

The importance of historical thinking in ancient Israel hardly requires extended exposition. The nearly universal conviction is stated very simply:

> ...almost any standard work on Old Testament religion or theology written in the last decades will agree, more or less explicitly, that the 'knowledge of God was an inference from what actually had happened in human history' and that 'Yhwh is the God of history and history is his foremost means of revelation.'[13]

We need not debate whether or not "revelation through history" accurately conveys the Hebrew Scriptures' mode of thought. It suffices to observe that a broad consensus assigns to history a considerable place in the formulation of the world-view of ancient Israel, and any later development of an ahistorical mode of organizing experience, resting on the foundations of the Hebrew Scriptures, is going to require considerable attention.

---

11. Porter, op. cit., pp. 120-21.

12. James Barr, *Biblical Words for Time* (London, 1969). Second, revised edition, pp. 146-47.

13. Bertil Albrektson, *History and the Gods. An Essay on the Idea of Historical Events as Divine Manifestations in the Ancient Near East and in Israel* (Lund, 1967: CWK Gleerup), p. 11. The comparison of Israelite historiography to history-writing in other ancient Near Eastern settings is not germane to my argument, which concerns only Israel's scriptures in their Judaic (and Christian) setting.

The historical mode of thought in the biblical history identifies boundaries between past, present, and future, and at the same time points to the
paths that lead from the one to the next. Conventional and accepted statements take priority. That this brazen wall between past and present marks
the presence of historical thinking comes to expression in the premise of
Umberto Cassuto's picture of why people want to know history. Cassuto's
somewhat florid passage serves to state definitively the premise of the present
study—the pastness of the past marks the presence of historical thinkings:

> ...there is not a person who does not feel in his heart the constant desire
> to know what is taking place around him—what is happening, what has
> already happened, and what will happen in the future. He strives to over-
> come distance of place and time, and to rend the veil that separates him
> from the facts that cannot be ascertained by his senses at the moment and
> the locality in which he finds himself. The wish to know what is occurring
> at a distance of place led to the technical inventions that were made in the
> course of the generations and which have reached a high level of devel-
> opment and success in our own times. It was harder to tear asunder the
> veil that hides the past from us; and it was still more difficult, if at all possi-
> ble, to rend the curtain that conceals the future from us. Nevertheless,
> despite the inherent difficulty, men constantly endeavored, in every place
> and time, in various ways and with varying degrees of skill and success, to
> tear apart the veil of the one and of the other. To the people of Israel are
> to be credited unique achievements in piercing the veil in both direc-
> tions...As for the past, Israel has the distinction of being the first of the
> civilized peoples to create historiography, in the full and precise meaning
> of the word...
>
> In the days of Solomon, in the period of Israel's political and social pros-
> perity, there was created, for the first time, historiography in the sense with
> which modern scholarship invests the term, historical writing whose aim
> is to determine the facts as they are, and to explain how they originated
> and developed according to the laws of causality.[14]

Cassuto stands for an entire literature on biblical history, which begins
with the premise that history records times past, which are distinct from
times present and future. The further premise, that an account of what
happened, joined to an explanation of how things originated and developed,

---

14. Umberto Cassuto, *Biblical and Oriental Studies* (Jerusalem, 1973: Magnes Press of the
Hebrew University). Translated by Israel Abrahams. I. *Bible*, pp. 11, 16.

yields an example of the workings of the laws of causality.[15] Along these same lines, we find the formulation of John L. McKenzie:

> ...we speak of the experience of God in history as the experience of God in events, but in discussing the theology of history in the Old Testament, we mean the theology of the record of the events.[16]
>
> [What is required is that] a series of events [is] seen to have an intelligible unity...The consciousness of history means the realization that the past lives in the present because the past has determined, antecedent to the decision of the present generation, the character of the group which makes the present decisions. The past has endowed the group with its peculiar strengths and weaknesses and at the same time has limited the options available to the group. A consciousness of history means that the group knows that it can affirm its identity only by affirming what it has been...[17]

Once more it is taken for granted that the past is over and done with, but also that the past bears power over the present. That power then serves to explain the character of the present and to set forth the choices confronting those who look toward the future.

The Israelite scriptural history—the Official or Authorized History—speaks of past, present, and future, clearly delineating the boundaries that mark the one off from the other, at the same time carefully pointing to the orderly connections between the one and the other. Specifically, the story of Israel, encompassing the creation of the world, begins with Eden and the fall of humanity, then begins again with Abraham and the formation of Israel, and concludes with the exile of Israel from its land. The past yields its lessons, but it is carefully distinguished from the present; the present

---

15. Among many works that state the same premises, note G. E. Wright, cited above, and William Foxwell Albright, *From the Stone Age to Christianity. Monotheism and the Historical Process* (Baltimore, 1946: The Johns Hopkins Press). The same views are broadly circulated in biblical scholarship in French, German, and Swedish. These instances suffice to make the point important for my argument: the pastness of the past, the power of the past to explain the present. But paradigmatic thinking will soon show us the very opposite: the power of the present to explain the past, along with the removal of any barrier between present and past. And, I shall claim in due course, that other way of thinking—a historical and explicitly anti-historical—more fully conforms to perceived experience ("Now I understand...") than the historical, not only in the reversibility of time, but also in the conception of a governing paradigm that imposes itself on matters large and small, here and there, now and then. Certainly within psychology and chaos-theory, paradigms, not sequential and linear patterns, take priority in explaining how things are.

16. John L. McKenzie, *A Theology of the Old Testament* (London, 1974: Geoffrey Chapman), p. 131.

17. Ibid., p. 132.

points toward the future, but the future is conceived as an autonomous realm of being. Time is sequential and differentiated. This is why Genesis through Kings tells that story, a coherent account of a past that is differentiated from the present yet connected to it, yielding a future that can be conceived out of the lines of order extended outward from the present moment. The standard history set forth by Scripture then accounts for a specific moment by appeal to what was and furthermore explains this same moment by prognosis concerning what will be. The lessons of the past then explain the present and dictate the shape of the future.

To think historically in the model of Scripture, then, is to recognize [1] the pastness of the past, [2] the difference between present and past, and [3] the linear, teleological lines that guide into the perceived future. It is a way of organizing experience by appeal to how things have been in explanation of how they now are and how they will, or ought to, be. Any mode of thinking other than the historical will have to find its own way to deal with the same intellectual tasks: to render plausible account of how things are. History chooses the past as the arena for the explanation of the present.

The definition of history as a mode of social organization that animates these remarks derives from Jan Huizinga: "History is the intellectual form in which a civilization renders account to itself of its past."[18] This definition presents an obvious difficulty, since when 'history' is defined as "account ...past," that which is to be defined turns out to form part of the definition; we find ourselves left with "past is past," or "history is history." By reference to a systematic, continuous, narrative story of how things were before now, a group of people may well explain who and what the group is. This view is underlined by van Seters when he states (p. 19):

> The notion of a people or nation rendering account to itself has a dual connotation...on the one hand, to render account has a forensic sense of assessing responsibility for, and passing judgment upon, a nation's past actions and their consequences for the present state of affairs.... However, another aspect of a civilization rendering account to itself has to do with corporate identity. A national history expresses what a nation is, and what principles it stands for.

18. John van Seters, *In Search of History. Historiography in the Ancient World and the Origins of Biblical History* (New Haven and London, 1983), p. 1.

Now let us first address in some detail what we anticipate in the historical mode of thinking about the social order.[19] What are the distinctive traits of historical explanation of a group's existence? History as a mode of social explanation takes the form of writing and only this form. Events may be preserved in a variety of ways, but formed into history only through narrative, and, for the case at hand, narrative is accomplished through the writing of sustained history, first this, then that; because of this, that happened. The narrative form realizes the conception of history. The components of this conception are, first, a clear sense of a division between past and present, second, an equally clear conception of the connection between what was and what is, and third, a conception of the self-evidence of the explanation contained in this connection. There must be a conception of the past, that which is over and done with; the present, that out of contemporary social existence that is seen continuous with, and explained by, what has gone before; and the meaning of what has been and what is, which is contained in an account of the future, the direction indicated by the course of past events that continue in the present.

The whole takes the form of a story, a narrative that is continuous but also broken up into chapters, covering

[1] once upon a time...,

[2] therefore now..., and

[3] on that account, moreover in time to come....

Without a clear conception that some events took place once upon a time, at a point clearly differentiated from the present, we do not have history, and narrative in the sense of sequence and order of past time, continuing into the differentiated present, does not take place. The differentiation of past from present requires also a clear perception that today is not the same as yesterday or tomorrow. If we do not know that what happened last week is not the same as what is happening today, there can be no historical mode

---

19. This is not to exclude the historical mode of thinking about the individual's life, which yields biography. History is to society what biography is to the individual; just as much as history proves a social construction, so, obviously, does biography. But then, where we have a different mode of account for the social order from the historical, then we also must expect a quite distinct way of addressing the individual, other than the biographical one. This is to say, a different concept of time will produce neither history nor biography; it will account in a different way for the character of the social order, and it also will take up the topic of the individual that merits attention in a way different from the standard biographical 'life'.

of explaining how things now are, only a present-tense description. It must follow, therefore, that where we do not find a clear conception of the difference between the present and the past, we have an other-than-historical mode of explaining the life of the group. And let me state with heavy emphasis: *that is so, even when events perceived to form part of the past are addressed and encompassed within that explanation.* Where we find a recognition of what has happened in the past as consequential, it need not follow that historical thinking is in play. Only when the past is understood as separate from the present but critical in the formation of the present do we have historical thinking.[20]

It is important to differentiate historical thinking, fully realized in history-writing, from a variety of other approaches to taking account of what has happened. Recording facts out of the past, whether genealogies or events such as battles or great personalities now dead, need not and commonly does not yield history. Such records supply information, but that information is organized and interpreted in other-than-historical ways as commonly as in historical ones. The key to the matter lies in van Seters' statement that stands at the head of this chapter. History as a mode of thought and organization of social experience answers a specific set of questions; there are other ways to deal with these same questions, to accomplish the same intellectual tasks in the service of the social order. This is why clear indicators require specification, and van Seters's account serves:

> ... I would propose the following criteria by which to identify history writing in ancient Israel:
>
> 1. History writing is a specific form of tradition in its own right...
>
> 2. History writing is not primarily the accurate reporting of past events. It also considers the reason for recalling the past and the significance given to past events.
>
> 3. History writing examines the causes of present conditions and circumstances...
>
> 4. History writing is national or corporate in character...

20. Note that I have not introduced the word 'tradition' into this discussion of history and its definition as a cultural artifact. The reason is that in the context at hand I cannot say I know the meaning of the word. I find van Seter's treatment of this matter, pp. 2-3, difficult to penetrate. Nothing in the Rabbinic writings we survey justifies the identification of 'tradition' with 'the past' or with history-writing. So when he says, "History writing is also a genre of tradition" and when he speaks of "the functions of tradition—the uses of the past" treating these as one and the same thing, I simply do not know what he means.

5.   History writing is part of the literary tradition and plays a significant role in the corporate tradition of the people...[21]

To these indicators I have already added a premise that van Seters found unnecessary to list: history writing takes for granted the pastness of the past. It begins with the conviction that today is different from yesterday and from tomorrow, but also connected to both, and it takes as its task the identification of the connection between what is to begin with distinct and separate: yesterday, today, tomorrow. This I take to be the point of nos. 2, 3, 4 above and, given the teleology implicit therein, no. 5 as well.

iii. Historical Writing in Ancient Israel

A brief account of how, in ancient Israel, history accomplished the task of accounting for the character of the social group—in the language of van Seters, "...assessing responsibility for, and passing judgment upon, a nation's past actions and their consequences for the present state of affairs ...express[ing] what a nation is, and what principles it stands for..."—suffices. What concerns us is not the origin of historical writing in Israel, let alone the various components that comprise the cogent history that Scripture sets forth in its final form in Genesis through Kings. These issues of the history of historical writing have no bearing upon our problem. What we wish to know is how, seen whole and completed, the official history of Israel set forth its message. For this purpose, we begin with the brief summary provided by van Seters in his account of the Deuteronomistic history:

> ...The history moves from the founding of the nation under Moses, through the conquest under Joshua and the rule of the judges, to the rise of the monarchy under Saul and David. The fortunes of the monarchy are traced from its height under Solomon through its subsequent division and the unfolding fate of the two kingdoms, down to the exile and the author's own day...Dtr's purpose, above all, is to communicate through this story of the people's past a sense of their identity...The form of this national or corporate identity in Dtr's work is quite simple. It is expressed, first and foremost, in the Mosaic (Deuteronomic) covenant by which Israel became the people of Yahweh and Yahweh became their God. The birth of the nation was the exodus from Egypt, and the conditions for its life in the land of promise were the laws of Moses. Violations of those conditions and of loyalty to Yahweh could only result in death as a nation and expulsion from the land—which happened in the exile.[22]

21. Van Seters, op. cit., pp. 4-5.

22. Ibid., p. 359.

To fill out this definition, one further point is required. History is made up of stories. For stories to serve for historical purposes, they must prove unitary, as distinct from separate anecdotes denied all specific context; the story also will be given a chronological framework that sets it against a time scale.[23]

It follows that the requirements of history-writing implicit in this account are these familiar items:

1. Narrative continuity among stories as just now defined, set forth on a grand scale, with a starting point and a coherent narrative extending from that point;

2. Systematic attention to the lives of consequential persons, the interplay of their distinctive personalities and policies with the history of the nation as a whole;

3. Sustained concern with the story of Israel the people, the covenant between Israel and God, the occasions that bring the covenant to realization.

Yet a fourth requirement is set forth by Edmond Jacob, in his stress on the uniqueness of events: their non-repetitive character. He states, "...the nature of history is its inability to repeat itself. If, therefore, God reveals himself in history, he does so through very precise events in time, the historicity of which is in no way weakened by the typological meaning acquired by those events."[24] Jacob makes a further point important in this survey: history is made up of not only raw facts but also their interpretation (p. 184): "one's idea of an event...assures for it its quality as an historical fact, that is, as a decisive fact in the course of events." We may then add two further items to our catalogue of requirements:

4. The conviction that events are unique and not subject to repetition, exemplary but not typological;

5. The intention so to portray a selection of happenings set forth as eventful as to convey a coherent account of things, to tell a story, once more, yielding a beginning and a middle and an end.

23. James Barr, "Story and History in Biblical Theology," in his *Explorations in Theology* 7, London, 1980: SCM), pp. 6-7. But note that Barr distinguishes story from history: "story belongs to literary form," and Barr will not regard stories as tantamount to history; that position governs here as well, as what follows indicates.

24. Edmond Jacob, *Theology of the Old Testament* (London, 1958: Hodder and Stoughton), translated by Arthur W. Heathcote and Philip J. Allcock, p. 183.

This coherence, in Jacobs' language, derives from faith in one God (p. 194): "Faith in a single god who directs events according to the laws of justice for the purpose of establishing his kingdom was the basis of all presentations of Israel's history and produced methods and results whose originality and value historians of antiquity are pleased to stress." So the coherence of narrative, effected through a selection of happenings deemed to bear consequence and to form a statement of sense, proportion, balance, and cogency, forms an expression of a deeper conviction about the meaning of perceived experience, a theological conviction. We need not spell out the substance of this conviction, e.g., election, covenant, mission, miracles, providence and the like; such matters carry us far beyond the limits of our interest in the character of historical writing in the Hebrew Scriptures. This interest is defined by the requirement that we compare and contrast the character of history in ancient Israelite writing with the counterpart modes of organizing experience and explaining the social order that characterize the Rabbinic heirs of Scripture. But one point does demand close iteration.

This concerns narrative, the composition out of this and that of a sustained and systematic account. The importance of sustained narrative in any definition of historical consciousness is underlined by Jacob Licht, when he states:

> Reconstructing history means to narrate it…historians of ancient Israel did what all historians are basically doing: finding out as much as possible about past events and showing how they make sense… . It was indeed quite an achievement to impose a more or less coherent single line of narrative on such a lot of events, beginning with the Creation and ending with the renewal of hope under Nehemiah….[25]

> The paramount requirement of history in Scripture is to show how one thing lead to another.[26]

This yields a theological point, e.g., divine reward, punishment, or mercy, or a theory of theodicy. But the main trait of history-writing is the narrative that is continuous and that bears a clear proposition. It is that the past explains the present, again Licht: "…everything becomes at least partially comprehensible when measured on the twin scales of chronology and development." These two matters—chronology and development—then form the center of interest. The latter poses few problems. It is simply the claim that one thing leads to another, 'develops' from another. In

---

25. Jacob Licht, "Biblical Historicism," in H. Tadmor and M. Weinfeld, eds., *History, Historiography, and Interpretation. Studies in biblical and cuneiform literatures* (Jerusalem, 1983: Magnes Press), pp. 108-9.

26. Ibid., p. 112.

extreme form, of course, the notion of historical sequence yielding historical explanation replicates in a crude way the logical error, *post hoc, ergo propter hoc*. This is to say, it is an error to suppose that merely because one event followed another, the earlier of the two events brought about, and therefore explains, the later of the two. That may be so, but it cannot be assumed to be so, and historical explanation appealing to development may well depend upon this assumption. But this problem need not detain us, since it scarcely captured the interest of the scriptural historians. But the issue of chronology—the very conception of what is measured by 'the logic of time'—demands close consideration, as we shall see presently.

Not all scholarship concurs on the proposition that narrative continuity yields history. We should err were we to ignore the important caveat of James Barr, who insists that we distinguish story from history:

> ...the Old Testament tells acts, events, speeches, thoughts, conversations, and all sorts of varied information, in a highly varied complex. Within this complex, however, certain relations receive particularly clear marking, and one of the clearest is that of temporal sequence. The narrative material has clear...marking of temporal sequence. It is characterized by chronological data, by family genealogies, by references back to earlier events, and by an unmistakable progression. It is thus like history, in that it reads in a temporal progression and tells a story which is cumulative from the beginning along a temporal scale. The nearness to history, however, should not be exaggerated. From some points of view what is related is rather a story than a history...[27]

At issue for Barr is whether we may say that history forms a medium of revelation, and Barr argues that this is not the case. Nonetheless, his position requires a clear statement of not only what we require to have history, such as van Seters provides, but also of what we mean by history.

What, specifically, is the substance of the ancient Israelite history? To answer this question we turn, finally, to David Noel Freedman, whose picture of historical writing in ancient Israel, encompassing the whole of the Hebrew Scriptures, suffices for our purposes. His is both the most current and also the most compelling picture we have of Scripture's history as a whole. This he calls "the Primary History," covering the Torah and Former Prophets, Genesis through Kings; these books form exactly one half of the Hebrew Scriptures.[28] Freedman's characterization will now form the definitive statement of the cogent narrative, made up of unique and irreversible

---

27. James Barr, *Old and New in Interpretation* (London, 1966: SCM Press), p. 81.

28. Freedman, *The Unity of the Hebrew Bible*, pp. 4-5.

events, that taken all together defines history in practice, therefore also in theory, in the received Scriptures.

Freedman has demonstrated that the four parts of the Hebrew Scriptures—Torah, Former Prophets, Latter Prophets, Writings, form a symmetrical pattern. Divided in the middle, attaching the former prophets (Joshua, Judges, Samuel, Kings) to the Torah to form a single, continuous narrative, Genesis through Kings, we have precisely one half of the words of the entire Hebrew Scriptures. These nine books—Genesis through Kings, which Freedman calls "the Primary History," reveal "the true nature of the initial main and central content of the Bible" (pp. 6-7). Freedman's reading of the Primary History is contained, *in nuce*, in the following (p. 6):

> For the Hebrew Bible as a whole, the center comes at the end of the Primary History and at the beginning of the Latter Prophets—at which point the Bible tells of the captivity of the people of Judah, the loss of nationhood, and the destruction of the capital city of Jerusalem and the Temple. In a similar way, if we look at the corpus of the Latter Prophets, the same melancholy series of events is at the center, in the latter part of Jeremiah and the first part of Ezekiel. Even in the Writings, with its great diversity of materials, the central point is held by the Book of Lamentations...We can say, therefore, that the entire Hebrew Bible revolves around that point in time, that historical moment when the life of the nation came to an end, when tragedy struck in multiple blows at the kingdom, its ruling dynasty, and at the sacred center of worship and service of their God. Such a decisive event and its enveloping circumstances must have had a powerful effect and pervasive influence over the literature as a whole, and most of what is written in the Bible reflects this unquestioned fact of Israel's (or Judah's) experience.

Now, lest we forget our starting point, which was Halpern's characterization of the confessional reading of Scripture as ahistorical, we must take notice of how Freedman provides out of this historical reading, this Primary History, a clear statement of precisely those propositions that the ahistorical approach is meant to attain (p. 8):

> ...what do these stories tell us about the humans in the picture? Briefly put, they tell successive stories of human disobedience and depravity, of resistance to the will of the Lord god, and of the necessary consequences in punishment and, more specifically, in banishment and exile. These stories are, simply put, successive parables about Israel's experience, its relationship to its God and the consequences of its rebellion against the will of the sovereign Lord. For those writing and reading the finished version of the story, which was published shortly after the last entry at the end of Kings, the linkage would be unmistakable. Adam and Eve in the Garden of Eden is a story of disobedience and rebellion against the

commandment of God. The upshot is banishment from the Garden to the life of exile in the world. How could those in captivity in Babylon...miss the point or fail to compare the story in Genesis with theirs?

In due course, we shall see that our sages of blessed memory read precisely the same stories in precisely the same manner and drew identical conclusions. But they formulated their reading and set forth their conclusions in a different way, one that transforms the Primary History into a statement of another sort altogether. It is this same Primary History that yielded for them precisely the meaning that they sought. But no less than for the framers of the Primary History, they came with an intrinsic interest in human events, and, as Freedman makes clear, the Primary History is so framed as to yield precisely the conclusions that this other-than-historical reading Halpern sets forth at the head of this chapter is meant to produce.

I have now to ask about the premises of the Primary History: what makes that history historical? And then I have to spell out the nature of those other premises that underlie the paradigmatic reading of Scripture's history, the reformulation of Israel's being in other than historical terms that takes place in Rabbinic Judaism. It suffices to define the historicity of the Primary History through Freedman's language (pp. 9-10):

> ...it is the first and perhaps the most important and influential prose narrative every written, preceding...Herodotus and his History of the Persian Wars by at least a century. The Primary History may be compared with such a historical work because it constitutes historical writing....it is clearly interested in real people, real places, and real events...

> The Primary History offered both an account of the origin, rise, ascendance, decline, and fall of Israel, and an interpretation of that prolonged and ultimately agonizing experience...

These brief observations suffice to complete an account of historical writing in ancient Israel. The indicators of the presence of historical thinking, deriving from the concrete evidence of the character of historical writing, now are fully exposed. One need not follow all of Freedman's theory to concur on his basic proposition, that the Primary History forms the center and unifying point of the Israelite Scriptures, and that the traits of this Primary History are historical in precisely the sense in which Halpern (among many) defines historical thinking and writing at the head of this chapter. So much for the surface of matters. Now we move to the deeper layers of thought, both historical and paradigmatic.

CHAPTER II

HISTORY, TIME, AND PARADIGM

"And the Lord spoke to Moses in the wilderness of Sinai in the first month of the second year after they had come out of the land of Egypt, saying, ['Let the people of Israel keep the passover at its appointed time. On the fourteenth day of this month, in the evening, you shall keep it at its appointed time; according to all its statutes and all its ordinances you shall keep it."]" (Num. 9:1-14):

Scripture teaches you that *considerations of temporal order do not apply to the sequence of scriptural stories.*

For at the beginning of the present book Scripture states, "The Lord spoke to Moses in the wilderness of Sinai in the tent of meeting on the first day of the *second* month in the second year after they had come out of the land of Egypt" (Num. 1:1).

And here Scripture refers to "the *first* month," so serving to teach you that *considerations of temporal order do not apply to the sequence of scriptural stories.*

Sifré to Numbers LXIV:I.1

i. *Historical Writing and the Conception of Time*

Nature and humanity mark time in distinctive ways. Geological time takes as its outer limit the five billion years of earth's existence (the planet's 'history'), while human time may be delineated in units of, say, the seventy years of a human life, or the two or three or four centuries of an empire's hegemony. Religion—Judaism and Christianity in particular—means to bridge the gap between creation's and humanity's time, speaking of time in aggregates that vastly transcend the limits of historical, that is, human time, and extend outward to nature's time, that is, God's evanescent moment. Scripture makes explicit the contrast between humanity's time and God's, "A day in your sight...," and the task of religion, mediating between God's creation's time and humanity's, defines the way in which Scripture is taken over by the paradigms that govern the Judaic and Christian reading thereof.

History serves as a means of telling time: measuring, evaluating and differentiating within spans of time and their sequence in passage. But there are other ways of doing so. So to identify what is at issue between historical and paradigmatic thinking about events—in other language, linear vs. fractal thinking—we have, therefore, to identify the premises concerning time and its measurement that define the basis for historical thinking and history-writing, on the one side, and paradigmatic thinking and reading of Scripture, on the other.

What, exactly, do we mean by 'time'? The word, 'time', standing on its own of course baffles us by its abstraction. Defining the term without appealing for assistance to the term itself in our definition presents formidable difficulties. But in this setting, these need not form obstacles to our goal. Once we recognize that the word can be defined, if not only, then at least best in context and for a concrete purpose, we may accomplish that provisional task that makes possible the accomplishment of our goal. That is, time as an abstraction defies my powers of definition, but time understood in the context of history, or for the purposes of cosmology, or in the setting of geology is readily defined. Utterly different units of time point to variables in context, from nano-seconds to aeons or ages measured in hundreds of millions of solar years.

That is to say, in some disciplines of learning, cosmology, for example, time is measured in aggregates so vast as to defy our capacities of understanding and imagining. The units of time found indicative in history, days, months, years, and those treated as consequential in geology, multiples of millions of years, or in astronomy, light-years and beyond, show what is at stake. Historical time, by contrast to time required for the natural sciences and cosmological ones appears trivial and inconsequential. This is for an obvious reason. 'The ages' for humans, who live perhaps for seventy, perhaps for eighty years, and 'the ages' for life on earth scarcely correlate. Not only so, but in other disciplines of learning, time, while measurable, is divided into units with no bearing upon the life of humanity—geology is a good instance. This is what makes the definition of 'time' in abstraction parlous.

Let us define time in the setting of humanity and of history. For history takes for its arena of analysis that ephemeral moment out of cosmological or geological time in which humanity's actions take place. But time even in the context of the life of humanity must be defined in both historical and also other than historical terms altogether. History takes as its premise definitions of time and its divisions that derive from nature. History then further divides these divisions or characterizes them, imposing upon them history's own indicators. So historical time forms a construct in which nature's time (defined in a moment) and history's time coincide.

LeGoff expresses this same conception in a slightly different way:

> The basic material of history is time. For a long while, therefore, chronology has played an essential role as the armature and auxiliary of history. The main tool of chronology is the calendar, which goes back far beyond the historian's field, since it is the fundamental temporal framework within which societies function. The calendar shows the effort made by human societies to domesticate "natural" time, the natural movement of the moon or the sun, the cycle of the seasons, the alternation of day and night. But its most effective articulations, the hour and the week, are linked to culture and not to nature....The past/present opposition is is essential to an acquisition of the consciousness of time.[1]

LeGoff underlines the interplay of nature's time and history's time, and this union is precisely what is at stake here.[2]

Nature marks day and night through light and darkness. Then, according to the most common human understanding of things, a set, a unit of light and a unit of darkness, forms one day.[3] This is a convention that commonly serves to define the smallest whole unit of time, the complete cycle of a 'day'. The solar day is not the sole natural unit of time. Nature moreover marks sets of such units of day and night by the phases in shape and size of the moon. The lunar unit of subunits of light and darkness then measures what we call a month. Here again, we find a complete sequence that is orderly and fixed, from new to full to waning size and shape. These too mark time, which then may be defined as a solar day or a lunar month. That is to say,

---

1. Jacques LeGoff, *History and Memory*, (N.Y., 1992: Columbia University Press), pp. xix, xx.

2. LeGoff does not adequately address systems of dealing with the past that are not historical and also not cyclical or mythical. He sees an effort "made by human societies to transform the cyclical time of nature and myths, of the eternal return, into a linear time, punctuated by groups of years...centuries, eras, etc. Two important advances are intimately connected with history: the definition of the chronological starting point (the foundation of Rome, the birth of Christ, the Hegira...), and the search for a periodization, the creation of equal, measurable units of time" (p. xx). But we deal with a set of thinkers who inherited out of Scripture linear, historical time and utterly reshaped and recast this conception.

3. This is not to suggest the ubiquity of the conception of 'a day' as a complete cycle of light and darkness. Indeed, even the Talmuds know the *'onah*, which is the smallest whole unit of time and is not equivalent to a solar day, light and darkness, ending with the next light. But it is sufficiently conventional to regard the smallest whole natural unit of time as a solar cycle of light and darkness that we may confidently define matters in this setting. I ignore the conception of 'hours', which nature on its own does not yield but form a social convention, all the more so minutes, seconds, and so on. These play no role in my exposition.

'time' is the spell marked from one sunset to the next; or 'time' is the spell marked from one new moon to the next. This definition hardly is ideal, leaving vague the sense of 'spell'. But for our purposes it suffices.

Matters do not conclude (for the purpose of this exposition) with the solar day and the lunar month. Nature furthermore marks sets of such aggregates of light and darkness as the passage of the moon denotes. This is supplied through observations of the positions of the sun in the southern sky (from the perspective of the northern hemisphere), with the sun at noon high in summer, low in winter; with the shadows long in winter, short in summer; and so on. The solar year then marks off in a natural way still larger aggregates of time. These, then, form the simplest natural boundaries of time: the interplay of light and dark, the fixed sequence of lunar phases or appearances, and the equally fixed sequence of solar ones, further differentiated (in temperate climates) by the passage of the seasons. Now nature gives us three spans, units of time, and all three are correlated: the solar day, the lunar month, the solar year. (If we wish to ignore the solar year, of course, we may claim that a fixed sequence of months denotes a lunar year.)

Nature's time is repeated—cyclical—since in each solar year the same events of nature repeat themselves. And the cyclicality of nature's time bears a further consequence. It is reversible, in that what happens this year happened last year, as much as it will happen next year. Indicators of time in nature repeat themselves, by definition moving in any direction, forward or backward, equally naturally. Nature's 'events'—that is, points of differentiation of otherwise undifferentiated passages—are not unique but gain their signification through their points of commonality; one month is the same as the one before and the one to follow, so too the day (unit of light, unit of darkness), so too the year. So much for time as nature defines matters on its own: the interval between sunset and sunset, new moon and new moon, sun at apogee and sun at apogee. The earliest monuments of humanity attest to the widespread definition of these intervals by appeal to solar time (at Stonehenge, for instance), and lunar time is equally broadly attested as well. So for the purpose and in the context of nature as humanity perceives matters, time finds its definition through the taxonomy of natural phenomena: day, month, year.

Now that simple digression into obvious matters is necessary to permit us to proceed to the question that is urgent here: the conception of time in history, which guides us in differentiating historical from paradigmatic thinking. Precisely what do we mean by 'time' in the setting of history, and how does historical time relate to natural time?

We commence with the simple question, How, in history, is time to be defined and measured? History recognizes natural time and imposes its taxic indicators, its points of differentiation, upon it. History knows days, months, years, but proposes to differentiate among them, treating this day as different from that because on this day, such and such happened, but on that day, it did not.[4] So historical time is a way of cutting down to human size the eternities of nature's time. History takes over nature's measures of matters and, making them its own, further marks them in its own way. The heritage of nature's time is clear. Now, history—historical thinking, in its conception of time—takes over nature's time and imposes upon it a second set of indicators or points of differentiation. History takes for granted the facticity of days, months, years, as indicating fixed points in time. But these spans of time are further differentiated by history, made into something that, in nature, they are not.

Specifically, the power of history to measure time lies in its capacity to differentiate what in nature is uniform. Nature's time is uniform, history marks unit off from unit; nature's time is repeated and may be reversed; history's events, the indicators of difference, have the power to mark off undifferentiated units of time by the very definitive fact of their uniqueness; and nature's time is reversible, but, for the same reason history's indicators are unique, history's time is irreversible, moving in only one direction. Nature knows no past that makes a difference from the present, no present that moves inexorably into the future.

History's time begins with the recognition that what is past is past, but leads to the present; what is present is here and now, separate from the past, also prelude to, but not part of, the future. History's time is linear, marking past, present, future; history's time can conceive of eternity, when time is past altogether. History does its work by recasting nature's time into humanity's dimensions, marking time in such a way that the human understanding can encompass and make sense of matters. History's time forms humanity's

4. The same may description serves for astrology, with its interest in correlating the stars with human events. In this sense, astrology and history compete as modes of explanation of time and change. Appealing to the same kind of logic, linearity and the uniqueness of events, for instance, they propose different bases of explanation spun out of one logic. They differ in history's insistence on the pastness of the past, a matter to which astrology finds itself indifferent. Admittedly, astrology invokes paradigms, but these derive from its alleged observations of natural and historical correlations, while religion's paradigms (those of Christianity and Judaism) derive from God's revelation of them, not humanity's discovery.

perspective on the dimensions of nature, cutting down to human size the enormous dimensions of nature's markings.

How does history's time impose itself upon nature's time? As I have already indicated, history both depends upon, identifies the natural units of time—day, month, year—but further differentiates among them—beyond nature's own points of differentiation—by reference to this-worldly events in the here and now. In such and such a year (however enumerated), in such and such a month (as indicated by its position in the sequence of months within a solar year), on such and such a day (as indicated, e.g., by the position of the moon within the lunar month), something noteworthy happened. This happening then marks the day, the month, the year, differentiating it from all other days and months and years. History's way of marking time, then, is to differentiate among the units of time indicated by nature, and its medium of differentiation is the event that takes place and imparts its distinctive character on one day, month, year, rather than on another.

History therefore defines and measures time through two intersecting indicators, the meeting of [1] the natural and [2] the human. As is clear in the foregoing remarks, the context in which 'time' is now defined is [1] the passage of days, weeks, months, and years, as marked by the movement of the sun and the stars in the heavens and [2] the recognition of noteworthy events that have taken place in specific occasions during the passage of those days and months and years. 'Time' then refers to the passage of days, months, years, as marked off by natural phenomena and as differentiated, also, by human activity. For purposes of history, 'time' is defined as the making of distinctions between and among days or weeks or months or years, and 'history' refers to the utilization, for indicators of the difference between one day and the next or one year and the next, of noteworthy events.[5]

Let me spell out this mode of marking time, since the identification of its premises will lead us deep into the definition of the alternative mode. We know that in the course of nature, one season differs from the other by reason of the position of the sun and fixed stars in the firmament, with corresponding changes in the character of the weather on earth, the sun high over the horizon, the heat, or low, the cold, for instance. One form of differen-

5. Barr's discussion in *Biblical Words for Time*, pp. 170-284, provides as ample a survey of opinion on the conception of time as this work requires. The study of words for 'time' and the like proves to have no bearing upon the discussion that follows, for reasons that will quickly become obvious.

tiation of day from day, hence one way of measuring time, then, will derive from events of nature, dry days, wet days, and the like.

But there is another form of differentiation, and this concerns the correlation of the passage of the indicators of the natural world—in Israel's context, the moons in their phases, the sun in the seasons—and chosen indicators of the social world. These, in the Israelite history, are simple enough to identify. King X ruled for so-and-so-many years, and he did such and such, with the specified consequences. In this setting, then, natural time (divisions of, distinctions among days, weeks, months, years) and social time (divisions of, distinctions among days or years) are made to intersect. The advent of a king marks the counting of solar or lunar years; what happens in that sequence of days, weeks, months, years, then is treated as a coherent whole—a reign—and a set of such reigns then may be laid out in sequence.

The sequence of reigns or other social significations of the differentiation of days, weeks, months, years already differentiated by natural indicators (position of the moon, shape of the sun, and the like) then forms the centerpiece of interest. For natural indicators left by themselves yield no sequential narrative, with a beginning, middle, and end, for the simple reason that nature on its own—once more, the sun or the moon in passage through the skies—differentiates days, weeks, months, or years, in only a single way. When we know the position of the sun or the shape of the moon, we know where we stand in the natural sequence of time, but in the nature of things, we also know that last year at this time, or next year at this time, we shall be precisely where we are now. So natural time yields no conception of beginnings, middles, and endings.

It is only when the correlation between natural time and the condition of a this-worldly entity, a social group for instance, assumes self-evidence that beginnings, middles, and endings come under consideration. Then, and only then, questions of origins emerge: who are 'we'? when did 'we' come into being? where are 'we' heading? By appeal to the analogy of the 'I', the individual's birth, life, and death, the social entity made up of individuals is given this same life-course, if not the same life-span. And this is the point at which the social world intervenes in the notation of the passing of the natural indicators of things; time is no longer differentiated, day from day, week from week, month from month, year from year, by appeal to the course of the sun and the moon and the fixed stars. Time now is differentiated by two indicators, not one, the natural in correlation with, in response to, the social. In this lunar cycle, or in this solar cycle (in Israel: month, year, respectively), such and such happened. Then the cycle is indicated not only by reason of the natural difference, with its recurrence, but also of the social difference, with its trait of individuality and even uniqueness.

Concretely, we note the confluence of occasion in the social world—the noteworthy event—and of season (day, week, month, year) in the natural world. And this permits us to define the premises of historical definitions of time:

[1] human events (however defined), viewed as unique happenings, by contrast to the recurrent happenings of natural time, form givens, as much as natural events form givens, in the measurement of time; but these markers differ, being of a quite opposite character from the natural divisions of aggregates of time, the human events being unique, natural events common, human events particular, natural ones general;

[2] and nature's time is cut down to size by history's time. This is accomplished by recasting nature's time, which finds points of differentiation in cyclical events (lunar months, solar seasons), and is therefore marked off by recurrent points of differentiation. Since human events have the power to differentiate one unit of natural time from some other (whether day, month, or year), these events must be viewed as unique, irreversible, irrecoverable, and linear; for if not, they would not have the power to differentiate from one another the common, repeated, and cyclical units of measurement that operate in natural time

[3] consequently, history's premise is that nature's time subordinates itself to history's time; time is itself linear, marked off by unique events, irreversible in direction from past to future, clearly differentiated (for the same reason) into past, present, and future.

Above all, history's time differentiates past from present, present from future, future from past. The reversibility of nature's time once lost, history's time, its linearity above all, takes over. Chaos does not govern when events move in a line, that is to say, in order—in an order we can discern through close study of what has gone before. Kept in line, the sequence of events yields that order through its linearity. Events then can be strung together on a line, like pearls on a necklace.

Linear history is not the only way of formulating this view of time and its meaning; cyclical history, to which we now turn, bears the same potential of ordering and explaining affairs. Neither linear nor cyclical time takes account of the irregularity of events; both accomplish the goal of demonstrating their regularity. Neither can accommodate itself to chaos or admit to the unpredictability of things. The logic of history—linearity, division of past from present together with linkage of past to present—and the regularity of cyclical time contradict the disorder of the world yet fail to recognize what is orderly in the world, which, for mathematics, is expressed through fractals, and, for religion, as we shall see, through paradigms.

Nature divides time by appealing not to unique events but to common ones. Nature marks the aggregates of time by reference to indicators that are reversible, recurrent, and not restricted by considerations of past, present, and future. Is there a way of dividing time in accord with dimensions humanity can accommodate, yet also congruent to nature's divisions? That is, are there media for the division of time that humanity may adopt and that are reversible, recurrent, and unrestricted by lines of division between past and present, present and future? The answer is, there are two such ways, one familiar, the other represented here by the Rabbinic literature and at the same time unfamiliar and absolutely routine in the history of Scripture's reception in Western civilization, Judaic and Christian alike.

ii. From Historical Time to Time Cyclical and Time Paradigmatic

Time is understood in Scripture in a historical way: separated into past, present, future; irreversible; marked off by singular events; yet a powerful continuum into the present. If mythic time aims at the recovery of a primordial perfection, historical time in Scripture organizes reality in a different way. This is described by Brevard S. Childs in the following language:

> The Biblical understanding of reality in contrast to the mythical can be described as "three-stage." There was a state of non-being pictured as chaos in the Old Testament. This was overcome by God's gracious acts of creation which brought world reality into being. A third factor was introduced by man's disobedience...A history of sin began which was not a continuation of god's creation but a perversion of reality. The Old Testament recounts the struggle between reality and the perversion of reality...The myth looks to the past, the Old Testament to the future. The reality which the myth wishes to maintain is understood by the Old Testament as part of the "old age" and therefore transitory.[6]

History is not the only way of thinking about natural time. History solves the existential problem posed by the enormous disproportion between

6. Brevard S. Childs, *Myth and Reality in the Old Testament* (London, 1960: SCM Press), pp. 83-84.

humanity's experience of time, which is by definition brief (a life-span or five successive life-spans) and ephemeral (here now, gone tomorrow), and natural time, from the perspective of mortal man and transitory, even ephemeral society, endless in its farthest limits. But this same problem may be worked out in another way of thinking about time altogether. Time is to be differentiated not only by events, unique, linear, irreversible, deemed to differentiate units of time by imposing their definitive character upon said units. Another way of measuring time within the human ambiance, besides nature's way, may be formulated, in which humanly-sensible aggregates of time may be formulated in their own terms but not made to intersect with natural time at all.

Defining this other way is made easy by finding the answer to a simple question. Can we differentiate nature's time for humanity's purposes not by appeal to indicators that contrast with nature's indicators for dividing time but that cohere in character with them? Can we find indicators of the division of time that are human but also comparable to the natural ones? If we can find a way of thinking about time that both remains well within the dimensions of humanity's sensibility and intellect (ephemeral, brief, yet encompassing) and also retains the character of consubstantiality with nature's time, then we can answer the question in an affirmative way.

TIME CYCLICAL: One such way, entirely familiar in our context, is the cyclical one. This is the view of time that notes recurrent patterns, or cycles, repeated sequences of specific events that conform to a general pattern. Cyclical time differentiates natural time by marking of sequences of years or months or days marked by a given pattern of events, then further sequences of years or months or days that recapitulate that very same pattern of events. So time is viewed as forming not only natural but also social or historical aggregates, distinct from one another as much as one year is distinct from another, and yet repetitive of a single pattern throughout. The conception of cyclical time takes over from nature that uniformity of day, month, or year, but recasts the terms of uniformity to encompass humanity's, not only nature's, repetitions.

Then history is the discovery of the cycles in an endless sequence. And profound historical thought will require the close study of cycles, with the interest in differentiating cycle from cycle, the discovery, for example, of when the cycles run their course (if they do). All of this intellectual labor is carried on well within the framework of natural differentiation of time. Nature's time and history's time then correspond in that both are differentiated by the appeal to the same recurrent indicators, though the indicators for natural time and those for historical time will differ. So the mode of differentiation is the same, but each said of differentiating indicators conforms to its setting, the human then corresponding to the natural one.

Whence the sense of the cyclicality of time, such as *Qohelet* (Ecclesiastes) expresses in saying what has been is what will be? An answer drawn from human existence serves. Cyclical time extends to the human condition the observed character of natural time—or reverses the process, assigning to nature the orderly character of human life; the correspondence is what counts. Just as natural time runs through cycles, so humanity marks time through corresponding cycles. For instance, in the aggregates of humanity formed by family, village, or territorial unit ('kingdom', 'nation' for example), just as the seasons run from spring through summer to fall to winter, and the human life from youth to middle age to old age to death, so social aggregates prove cyclical.

The territorial unit may be accorded a cycle of time, from birth through maturity, old age, and death, and its 'history' may form a chapter in the cyclical patterns of human time, corresponding to natural time. Humanity's mode of differentiating the time marked off by nature, then, accords with the natural indicators of differentiation: the life of the human being forming a metaphor for the life of the social unit. Then humanity's indicators correspond in character to nature's—the cyclicality of the one matching the character of cyclicality revealed by the other. Yet humanity's indicators also prove natural to the human condition, with the life-cycle forming one (among a variety to be sure) means of differentiating humanly among the divisions of nature's time.

TIME HISTORICAL: If, now, we revert to the characterization of historical time offered just now, how shall we read the cyclical, as distinct from the historical, mode of formulating a human counterpart to nature's time? Here are the point by point correspondences:

[1]   human events form givens, as much as natural events form givens, in the measurement of time; but these events correspond in character to those of nature, because, like those in nature, they recur in a fixed and predictable pattern, just as nature's events do; human events, like natural divisions of aggregates of time, are not unique, not particular, not one-time only; they are recurrent and mark of an eternal return of the pattern set forth *ab initio* (whether from creation, whether from the formation of the social order);

[2] but the problem of a human formulation of the nature of time is
solved as much as it is by history, though in a different way; specifically, nature's time is cut down to human size by cyclical time,
but this is done in nature's way. Cyclical time recasts nature's
time. As the latter finds points of differentiation in cyclical events
(lunar months, solar seasons), so the former—historical time
viewed cyclically—is marked off recurrent points of differentiation, but these are, in the nature of things, measured in the dimensions of the human life.

[3] consequently, nature's time does not subordinate itself to history's
time; time is itself not linear, not marked off by unique events,
reversible in direction from past to future, and not at all clearly
differentiated (for the same reason) into past, present, and future.

It follows that nature provides the metaphor for cyclical time. This
explains why cyclical time is coherent with nature in a way in which historical time is not. Specifically, nature in humanity is expressed through a cycle
of birth, youth, maturity, old age, death. The next step, for cyclical time
given the form of historical narrative (for example) is then readily to be
predicted. How nature divides the time of a human life then is translated
into, or raised to the level of, the social order. Then society (e.g., the territorial unit, the city, the community, the kingdom, the empire) is born,
matures, grows old, dies, with a further cycle to follow, onward into time.
This is how human time, like nature's time, is deemed to conform to a cycle
corresponding to the natural and the individual. The events of the social
order viewed as comparable to the natural one are not unique, irreversible,
irrecoverable, and linear, but common, recurrent, recoverable, and, of
course, cyclical.

TIME PARADIGMATIC: We see, therefore, two media for the taxonomy of
humanity's time, in response to the classification of nature's time, the historical and the cyclical. But there is a third, which I call, the paradigmatic classification of humanity's time; it is not historical, and it also is not cyclical.
This is what has now to be defined. Time paradigmatic refers to a pattern,
or a model, or a paradigm (the words are interchangeable here) that provides
yet another way of defining time in human terms, which is to say, of taking
the natural divisions of time and correlating with them aggregates of time
that express time in human terms. But paradigmatic time takes a different
measure altogether from historical and cyclical time; it deems nature's time
as being merely integral to its own.

iii. Paradigmatic Time: A Definition

By paradigm time is marked off by indicators that are utterly free-standing, in no way correlated with natural time at all; rather, time is defined in units that are framed quite independently of the epiphenomena of time and change as we know it in this life. Paradigms may be formed on a variety of bases, but all paradigmatic formulations of time have in common their autonomy of nature, on the one side, and events beyond their own pattern's definitions, (whether by nature or by historical events), on the other. In Judaism and Christianity it is God who in creation has defined the paradigms of time, Scripture that conveys those paradigms, and humanity that discovers, in things large and small, those paradigms that inhere in the very nature of creation itself.

Reverting to matters set forth in Chapter One, these fractals (in mathematical language) or paradigms describe how things are, whether large or small, whether here or there, whether today or in a distant past or an unimaginable future. The paradigm identifies the sense and order of things, their sameness, without regard to scale; a few specific patterns, revealed in this and that, hither and yon, isolate points of regularity or recurrence. We know those 'fractals' or paradigms because, in Scripture, God has told us what they are; our task is so to receive and study Scripture as to find the paradigms; so to examine and study events as to discern the paradigms; so to correlate Scripture and time—whether present time or past time then matters not at all—as to identify the indicators of order, the patterns that occur and recur and (from God's perspective) impose sense on the nonsense of human events.

A paradigm forms a way of keeping time that invokes its own differentiating indicators, its own counterparts to the indicators of nature's time. I cannot overstress the fictive, predetermined character of time as measured in the paradigmatic manner, that is, time as formulated by a free-standing, (incidentally) atemporal model, not appealing to the course of sun and moon, not concerned with the metaphor of human life and its cyclicality either. Paradigms are set forth by neither nature (by definition) nor natural history (what happens on its own here on earth); by neither the cosmos (sun and moon) or the natural history of humanity (the life cycle and analogies drawn therefrom). In the setting of Judaism and Christianity, paradigms are set forth in revelation; they explain the Creator's sense of order and regularity, which is neither imposed upon, nor derived from, nature's time, not to be discovered through history's time. And this is why to paradigmatic time, history is wildly incongruous, and considerations of linearity, temporality, and historical order beyond all comprehension. God has set forth the paradigms that measure time by indicators of an other-than natural character: supernatural time, which of course is beyond all conception of time.

Paradigms derive from human invention and human imagination, imposed on nature and on history alike. Nature is absorbed, history recast, through time paradigmatic; that is, time invented, not time discovered; time defined for a purpose determined by humanity (the social order, the faithful, for instance), time not discovered by determined and predetermined, time that is not natural or formed in correspondence to nature, or imposed upon nature at specified intersections; but time that is defined completely in terms of the prior pattern or the determined paradigm or fabricated model itself: time wholly invented for the purposes of the social order that invents and recognizes time.

I refer, for time paradigmatic, to perfectly familiar ways of thinking about the passage of time. Once I define time paradigmatic as time invented by humanity for humanity's own purposes, time framed by a system set forth to make sense of a social order, for example, the examples multiply. The use of B.C./B.C.E. and A.D./C.E. forms one obvious paradigm: all time is divided into two parts by reference to the advent of Jesus Christ. Another paradigm is marked by the history of humanity set forth in Scripture: Eden, then after Eden; or (as Freedman states matters, and, as we shall see, Rabbinic paradigms define matters), Adam vs. Israel, Eden vs. the Land; Adam's fall vs. Israel's loss of the Land. The sages will impose a further, critical variable on the pattern of Eden vs. Land of Israel, Adam vs. Israel, and that is, Sinai. A pattern then will recognize the divisions of time between before Sinai and afterward.

iv. Paradigmatic Time: An Example in Rabbinic Literature

These general definitions should be made still more concrete in the setting of Rabbinic Judaism. Let me give a single example of time paradigmatic, in contrast to the conceptions of time that govern in the Hebrew Scriptures. The character of paradigmatic time is captured in the following, which encompasses the entirety of Israel's being (its 'history' in conventional language) within the conversation that is portrayed between Boaz and Ruth. (The following passage is abbreviated to highlight the critical components.)

Ruth Rabbah Parashah Five

XL:i

1.A. *And at mealtime Boaz said to her, 'Come here and eat some bread, and dip your morsel in the wine.' So she sat beside the reapers, and he passed to her parched grain; and she ate until she was satisfied, and she had some left over.*

   B. R. Yohanan interpreted the phrase "come here" in six ways:

   C. "The first speaks of David.

   D. "'Come here' means, to the throne: *That you have brought me here* (2 Sam. 7:18).

   E. "'...and eat some bread': the bread of the throne.

   F. "'...and dip your morsel in vinegar': this speaks of his sufferings: *O Lord, do not rebuke me in your anger* (Ps. 6:2).

   G. "'So she sat beside the reapers': for the throne was taken from him for a time."

   I. [Resuming from G:] "'and he passed to her parched grain': he was restored to the throne: *Now I know that the Lord saves his anointed* (Ps. 20:7).

   J. "'...and she ate and was satisfied and left some over': this indicates that he would eat in this world, in the days of the messiah, and in the age to come.

2.A. "The second interpretation refers to Solomon: 'Come here': means, to the throne.

   B. "'...and eat some bread': this is the bread of the throne: *And Solomon's provision for one day was thirty measures of fine flour and three score measures of meal* (1 Kgs. 5:2).

   C. "'...and dip your morsel in vinegar': this refers to the dirty of the deeds [that he did].

   D. "'So she sat beside the reapers': for the throne was taken from him for a time."

   G. [Reverting to D:] "'and he passed to her parched grain': for he was restored to the throne.

H.   "'...and she ate and was satisfied and left some over': this indicates that he would eat in this world, in the days of the messiah, and in the age to come.

3.A.   "The third interpretation speaks of Hezekiah: 'Come here': means, to the throne.

B.   "'...and eat some bread': this is the bread of the throne.

C.   "'...and dip your morsel in vinegar': this refers to sufferings: *And Isaiah said, Let them take a cake of figs* (Isa. 38:21).

D.   "'So she sat beside the reapers': for the throne was taken from him for a time: *Thus says Hezekiah, "This day is a day of trouble and rebuke"* (Isa. 37:3).

E.   "'...and he passed to her parched grain': for he was restored to the throne: *So that he was exalted in the sight of all nations from then on* (2 Chr. 32:23).

F.   "'...and she ate and was satisfied and left some over': this indicates that he would eat in this world, in the days of the messiah, and in the age to come.

4.A.   "The fourth interpretation refers to Manasseh: 'Come here': means, to the throne.

B.   "'...and eat some bread': this is the bread of the throne.

C.   "'...and dip your morsel in vinegar': for his dirty deeds were like vinegar, on account of wicked actions.

D.   "'So she sat beside the reapers': for the throne was taken from him for a time: *And the Lord spoke to Manasseh and to his people, but they did not listen. So the Lord brought them the captains of the host of the king of Assyria, who took Manasseh with hooks* (2 Chr. 33:10-11)."

K.   [Reverting to D:] "'and he passed to her parched grain': for he was restored to the throne: *And brought him back to Jerusalem to his kingdom* (2 Chr. 33:13).

N.   "'...and she ate and was satisfied and left some over': this indicates that he would eat in this world, in the days of the messiah, and in the age to come.

5.A.   "The fifth interpretation refers to the Messiah: 'Come here': means, to the throne.

B.   "'...and eat some bread': this is the bread of the throne.

C.   "'...and dip your morsel in vinegar': this refers to suffering: *But he was wounded because of our transgressions* (Isa. 53:5).

D.   "'So she sat beside the reapers': for the throne is destined to be taken from him for a time: *For I will gather all nations against Jerusalem to battle and the city shall be taken* (Zech. 14:2).

E.   "'...and he passed to her parched grain': for he will be restored to the throne: *And he shall smite the land with the rod of his mouth* (Isa. 11:4)."

I.   [reverting to G:] "so the last redeemer will be revealed to them and then hidden from them."

The paradigm here may be formed of five units: [1] David's monarchy; [2] Solomon's reign; [3] Hezekiah's reign; [4] Manasseh's reign; [5] the Messiah's reign. So paradigmatic time compresses events to the dimensions of its model. All things happen on a single plane of time. Past, present, future are undifferentiated, and this is why a single action contains within itself an entire account of Israel's social order under the aspect of eternity.

The foundations of this paradigm, of course, rest on the fact that David, Solomon, Hezekiah, Manasseh, and therefore also the Messiah descend from the union of Ruth and Boaz. Then, within the framework of the paradigm, the event that is described here—"And at mealtime Boaz said to her, 'Come here and eat some bread, and dip your morsel in the wine.' So she sat beside the reapers, and he passed to her parched grain; and she ate until she was satisfied, and she had some left over"—forms not an event but a pattern. The pattern transcends time; or more accurately, aggregates of time, the passage of time, the course of events—these are all simply irrelevant to what is in play in Scripture. Rather we have a tableau,[7] joining persons who lived at widely separated moments, linking them all as presences at this simple exchange between Boaz and Ruth, imputing to them all the shape and structure of that simple moment: the presence of the past, for David, Solomon, Hezekiah, and so on, but the pastness of the present in which David or Solomon—or the Messiah for that matter—lived or would live.

7.   For the notion of the representation of Israel's existence as an ahistorical tableau, see my *Judaism. The Evidence of the Mishnah*. Chicago, 1981: University of Chicago Press. Paperback edition: 1984. Second printing, 1985. Third printing, 1986. Second edition, augmented: Atlanta, 1987: Scholars Press for Brown Judaic Studies.

Taking account of both the simple example of B.C.E. and C.E. and the
complex one involving the Israelite monarchy and the Messiah, we ask
ourselves how time has been framed within the paradigmatic mode of
thought. The negative is now clear. Paradigmatic time has no relationship
whatsoever to nature's time. It is time invented, not discovered; time predetermined in accord with a model or pattern.

Here the points of differentiation scarcely intersect with either nature's
or history's time. Time is not sequential, whether in natural or historical
terms; it is not made up of unique events, whether in nature or in the social
order; it is not differentiated by indicators of a commonplace character.
Divisions between past, present, and future lie beyond all comprehension.
Natural time is simply ignored here; years do not count, months do not
register; the passage of time marked by the sun, correlated with, or ignored
by, the course of human events, plays no role at all. All flows from this
model—in the present instance, the model of time divided into chapters of
Davidic dynastic rulers, time before the Messiah but tightly bound to the
person of the Messiah. The division of time here can take the form of before
Boaz's gesture of offering food to Ruth and afterward; before David and
after the Messiah; and the like. A variety of interpretations of the passage
may yield a range of paradigms; but the model of paradigmatic time will
remain one and the same.

The case now permits us further to generalize. The paradigm takes its
measures quite atemporally, in terms of not historical movements or recurrent cycles but rather a temporal units of experience, those same aggregates
of time, such as nature makes available through the movement of the sun
and moon and the passing of the seasons, on the one hand, and through the
life of the human being, on the other. A model or pattern or paradigm will
set forth an account of the life of the social entity (village, kingdom, people,
territory) in terms of differentiated events—wars, reigns, for one example,
building a given building and destroying it, for another—yet entirely out
of phase with sequences of time.

A paradigm imposed upon time does not call upon the day or month or
year to accomplish its task. It will simply set aside nature's time altogether,
regarding years and months as bearing a significance other than the temporal
one (sequence, span of time, aggregates of time) that history, inclusive of
cyclical time's history, posits. Time paradigmatic then views humanity's
time as formed into aggregates out of all phase with nature's time, measured
in aggregates not coherent with those of the solar year and the lunar month.
The aggregates of humanity's time are dictated by humanity's life, as much

as the aggregates of nature's time are defined by the course of nature. Nature's time serves not to correlate with humanity's patterns (no longer, humanity's time), but rather to mark off units of time to be correlated with the paradigm's aggregates.

It remains to reconsider those systematic comparisons between history's time and other modes of keeping time that have already served us well. Since the comparison of historical and cyclical time is now in hand, let us turn directly to ask how we shall read the paradigmatic, as distinct from the cyclical mode of formulating a human counterpart to nature's time? Here are the point by point correspondences:

[1] in time paradigmatic, human events do not form givens, any more than natural events form givens, in the measurement of time; while both of those definitions of the eventful correspond in character to the course of nature, paradigmatic events find their definition in the paradigm, within the logic of the system, in accord with the predetermined pattern, and not in response to the givens of the natural world, whether in the heavens or in the life cycle; paradigmatic time also follows a fixed and predictable pattern, but its identification of what is eventful out of what happens in the world at large derives from its own logic and its own perception; nothing is dictated by nature, not nature's time, not history's time, not the linear progress of historical events, not the cyclical progress of historical patterns;

[2] as we shall see much later—the matter is scarcely adumbrated in the case before us—nature's time plays no independent rule in paradigmatic time; cut down to human size by cyclical time in nature's way, nature's time in paradigmatic thinking is simply absorbed into the system and treated as neutral—nature's time is marked, celebrated, sanctified, but removed from the entire range of history, which is wholly taken over and defined by the paradigm.

[3] consequently, nature's time plays no role in paradigmatic time; time is neither cyclical not linear, it is not marked off by unique events, it is simply neutral and inert. Time is inconsequential; the issue is not whether or not time is reversible in direction from past to future, or whether or not time is to be differentiated (for the same reason) into past, present, and future.

Nature's time, with its sense of forward movement (within the natural analogy supplied by the human life, from birth to death) is simply beyond the paradigmatic limits, for the paradigm admits of neither past nor present nor future, differentiated but also linked; nor cycle and recurrence. These conceptions contradict its very character. A paradigm predetermines, selects happenings in accord with a pattern possessed of its own logic and meaning, unresponsive to the illogic of happenings, whether chaotic, whether orderly, from the human perspective. A model is just that: there to dictate, there to organize, there to take over, make selections, recognize connections, draw conclusions. To characterize paradigmatic time as atemporal therefore proves accurate but tangential, since atemporality is not a definitive taxic trait, merely a byproduct of that trait. Indeed, the very phrase, "paradigmatic time," standing by itself presents an oxymoron. Paradigms admit to time— the spell that intervenes between this and that, the this and the that beyond defined within the paradigm. In that sense, time pertains, as much as the spell between sunset and sunset or new moon and new moon pertains in nature's time.

But in situating the events in the scale of human time, as history would have matters, to the model of Ruth and Boaz, David, Solomon, and the Messiah, captured in the little gesture, "and he passed to her parched grain; and she ate until she was satisfied, and she had some left over," the matter of time simply does not pertain. For the action was not one-time (even for all-time) nor cyclical, but altogether out of history's and nature's time time. Time is contingent, within the model. The paradigm serves to select events; model to endow events with order and meaning, structure and familiarity. Rich in time-sequences, the scene is a tableau, full of action but lacking temporality. Paradigmatic time organizes events in patterns, invokes a model that everywhere pertains; the atemporality then is a byproduct of the very character of thinking about time and change that governs.

v. Past, Present, Future Time and Eternity vs. Time Undifferentiated by Event

Clearly, in paradigmatic existence, time is not differentiated by events, whether natural or social. Time is differentiated in another way altogether, and that way so recasts what happens on earth as to formulate a view of existence to which any notion of events strung together into sequential history or of time as distinguished by one event rather than some other is not so much irrelevant as beyond all comprehension. To characterize Rabbinic Judaism as atemporal or ahistorical is both accurate and irrelevant. That Judaism sets forth a different conception of existence, besides the historical one that depends upon nature's and humanity's conventions on the definition and division of time.

Existence takes on sense and meaning not by reason of sequence and order, as history maintains in its response to nature's time. Rather, existence takes shape and acquires structure in accord with a paradigm that is independent of nature and the givens of the social order: God's structure, God's paradigm, our sages of blessed memory would call it; but in secular terms, a model or a pattern that in no way responds to the givens of nature or the social order. It is a conception of time that is undifferentiated by event, because time is comprised of components that themselves dictate the character of events: what is noteworthy, chosen out of the variety of things that merely happen. And what is remarkable conforms to the conventions of the paradigm.

Since we commenced this account of history, time, and paradigm, with a brief formulation of how ancient Israel's historical thinking took place and how historical writing unfolded, let us consider how the conceptions of time laid out here compare with the initial formulation of matters. Explaining what Judaic and Christian readings of Scripture do not do but unable to account for what they do accomplish, Halpern's statement contains these important components:

1.   The confessional use of the Bible is fundamentally ahistorical.
2.   Worshipers do not read the Bible with an intrinsic interest in human events. Like the prophet or psalmists or, in Acts, the saint, they seek behind the events a single, unifying cause that lends them meaning and makes the historical differences among them irrelevant.
3.   In history, the *faithful* seek the permanent, the ahistorical;
4.   in time, they quest for timelessness;
5.   in reality, in the concrete, they seek Spirit, the insubstantial.
6.   Confessional reading levels historical differences—among the authors in the Bible and between those authors and church tradition—because its interests are life present (in the identity of a community of believers) and eternal.

What we have found certainly conforms to Halpern's observations, but hardly for his reasons. He stresses the ahistorical character of the religious reading of Scripture, and his stress is sound. But he has not explained this ahistorical reading, he has only described its components. The one point of explanation comes at the end. But the "because" clause strikes me as monumentally irrelevant to the matter at hand, since the ahistorical character of the religious reading of Scripture in Judaism and Christianity finds its explanation merely in the motive for reading Scripture. But this same explanation can serve for any number of readings of Scripture besides the ahistorical, and it is not particular to the data at hand. The explanation offered just now, the appeal to paradigmatic time as against historical or cyclical time, by contrast addresses a particular phenomenon and no other. The ahistorical character of the religious reading of Scripture turns out to derive from a conception of time quite different from that of history. And the rest follows.

❧ *Part Two* ❧

THE ABSENCE OF HISTORY

CHAPTER III

MISSING MEDIA OF HISTORICAL THINKING:
THE SUSTAINING NARRATIVE OF ONE-TIME EVENTS, BIOGRAPHY

> In many major currents of Judaism what I have here called story, unitary
> and cumulative, broke down into anecdote and annotation. The sense of
> temporal distance was lost, for in much rabbinic discourse persons of
> remote antiquity are depicted as living and thinking in the terms of...rabbis
>
> James Barr[1]

i. General Considerations

The survey of the requirements of historical thinking and writing identifies as indicators of history an interest in the formation of narratives out of
the presentation of singular ("unique") events. Along these same lines,
historical thinking yields not only anecdotes but biography, not only incidents but a whole life, with a beginning, middle, and end. Scripture validates
defining indicators in just this way. It follows that the next step is to formulate
a null hypothesis. If our sages were to carry forward Scripture's modes of
historical thought and writing, then they ought to give us if not whole narratives (like those of Josephus) then at least fragments of a sustained narrative.
They ought, furthermore, to give evidence of telling stories not to exemplify
virtue or norm or conviction but to portray a singular moment, which is
the opposite of narrative for exemplary purposes. It is now our task to characterize the writings' formulation of events, on the one side, and incidents
in lives of persons, on the other. How are events portrayed and for what
purpose are they utilized? How are persons characterized, and to what end
is the characterization employed?

In setting forth the character of thought on the way to explain the present
condition of Israel—an account of the social order and its meaning—we
have to consider both how our sages of blessed memory set forth the results
of their thinking. Since Scripture provided models, the character of those

---

1. James Barr, "Story and History in Biblical Theology," in his *Explorations in Theology*
7, (London, 1980: SCM), p. 15.

models—sustained narrative of events, "lives" of persons (e.g., Samson, Samuel, David, Solomon, Elijah)—defines one part of our work: do we find in Rabbinic literature any evidence of thinking comparable to the historical modes of thought that, in Scripture, yielded "story, unitary and cumulative," or lives of important persons? The fact is that we find little sustained narrative or biography.

The uniformity that characterizes the various compilations, respectively, most of which exhibit distinctive and internally consistent traits of formal rhetoric, logic of coherent discourse, and topical and even propositional program, makes a limited survey quite feasible. Since each compilation is uniform, we can accurately characterize the types of writing the respective documents set forth and on this basis draw reliable inferences concerning various composites' authors' conceptions and modes of thought.

But what about that which we do *not* find in Rabbinical writings, which (for this part of my argument) is the marks of historical thinking—methods of presentation, messages alike? While superficially an argument from silence, in fact it is an argument resting on substantial evidence. First, Scripture tells us what our sages could have done[2] and chose not to do: narrative history, biography. When we maintain, then, that the absence of a particular kind of writing bears consequence, it is because, on the basis of the documents sages themselves deemed authoritative, we have reason to expect this kind of writing to make an appearance. Second, we may draw inferences from not only what people do not do anywhere but also what people do everywhere, and this too then serves to indicate what they choose not to do anywhere in their writings. For, in a literature of such consistency and uniformity, the choices people always make inform us, also, about what they have chosen never to do. If sages tell stories as illustrative anecdotes but not as part of strings of meaningful events that point to a given proposition, that means they choose to supply anecdotes and not narratives thereof. If they treat chapters of lives of sages in isolation from the entire life of a given sage, telling stories but providing no biography, this is because they choose to give us episodes but not biography.

---

2. I could draw evidence from other Jewish documents, e.g., the writings of Josephus or of Jewish writers in Greek. But since our sages recognize and cite as authoritative only Scripture (excepting Ben Sira), we deal solely with the writings they themselves acknowledged as authoritative. They treat with perfect silence every other document held by scholarship to derive from Jews and to stand for (a) Judaism, and we must therefore do the same if we wish to understand our sages in particular.

The demonstration that historical thinking does not govern in the documents under study here requires two steps. We have first to characterize the one-time events that the documents under study do set forth, and, second, with the sequences of one-time events portrayed in Genesis or Kings in mind, ask about how these events serve the program of the framers of documents. So we both survey what we find and, along the way, take note of what we do not find. At issue are the matters of presentation and use of one-time events for historical purposes and the comparable narrative of lives of persons for biography. We examine the documents in sequential groups, and we consider a minimum of representative passages from each.

ii. The Mishnah, Tosefta, Abot, Sifra, Sifré to Numbers, and Sifré to Deuteronomy

A. ONE-TIME EVENTS

One-time events in the Mishnah mainly comprise precedents, hence not historical incidents of a singular character but exemplary ones, speaking of a pattern and not an incident. These may occur in narrative form, but, in the Mishnah, are meant to exemplify, rather than to characterize, to move from the particular to the general, rather than vice versa. Here, for example, Gamaliel's report of the practice of his father's household hardly constitutes an historical narrative:

A. Said Rabban Gamaliel, "In my father's household, they used to designate one [portion of produce as] *peah* for all of the olive trees that they owned in every direction [all that they had together].

B. "But as regards carob trees, all that are within sight of each other [constitute a single orchard, and *peah* is designated for all of them together]."

M. Peah 2:4

The item is best classified not as a singular incident but as an exemplary one; it is preserved in context not to show what is unique or personal but the very opposite, providing a precedent. Here, then, we have not evidence of historical thinking but an example of the annotation of a law code with cases serving as precedents. Precedents, stating the law in the form of a case, are represented by the following:

A.   There was a case involving a boy who sanctified his spade to Heaven, and his father brought him before R. Aqiba.

B.   And R. Aqiba interrogated him.

C.   He said to him, "My son, to what did you sanctify it? Perhaps it was to the sun or to the moon or to the stars and the planets, because they are pretty?"

D.   He said to him, "I sanctified it only to Him to whom iron belongs, blessed be He."

E.   R. Aqiba said, "This one has been interrogated and found in good order."

M. Nedarim 5:16

A.   There was the case involving a certain child.

B.   They were traveling on a ship, and a sea-storm rose against them, and they were crying to their god, as it is said, *And the sailors feared and cried, each to his god* [Jonah 1:5].

C.   That child said to them, "How long are you going to act foolishly? Cry out to him who created the sea!"

D.   And the case came before the sages and they said, "This one has been interrogated and found in good order."

M. Nedarim 5:17

Items like these provide the opposite of one-time, unique events; what makes these items important is that they are not remarkable or eventful in a historical sense but authoritative in a legal context and only there.

Where, moreover, we are told what sages did on some particular occasion, the little tale merely forms a setting for what matters, which is a report of an action that validates like actions. Here is a chapter that serves both as a precedent and as an allusion to an event in the life of several sages, that is, a trip that they made.

A.   One whose produce is unavailable to him [when the time for removal arrives]

B. must make an oral declaration [designating the required agricultural gifts and transferring them to their proper recipients]—

C. M'SH B: Rabban Gamaliel and the elders were traveling on a ship [when the time for removal occurred]. Said Rabban Gamaliel, "The tenth I intend to measure out [and designate as first tithe] is given to Joshua [who is a Levite], and the place [in which it is located] is rented to him. The other tenth which I intend to remove [and designate as poor man's tithe] is given to Aqiba ben Joseph, who will make it available to the poor and the place [in which it is located] is rented to him."

D. Said R. Joshua, "The tenth I intend to measure out [of the first tithe I will receive from Rabban Gamaliel and which I intend to designate as heave offering of the tithe for the priest], and the place [in which it is located] is rented to him."

E. And they received rent payment from one another.

M. M.S. 5:9

The fact that sages were traveling on a ship is included not in order to tell us how sages went somewhere, for some singular purpose; it is only to explain why the actions that they took bear special interest.

A final item suffices to prove that, for the document at hand, singular incidents served no role, and where we do find anecdotes, they are presented for an other-than-historical purpose; they are not preserved as the raw materials of either history or biography. They point toward what I call, the missing media of historical thinking. That at stake is the search for precedents becomes clear when two versions of a given incident are preserved. This allows us to identify the purpose of preserving the incident, and, it is clear, the reason is to preserve the law in narrative form. In this instance, the practice of Gamaliel's household is recorded, but two versions are available, each to serve its respective legal position:

A. "He who dwells in the same courtyard with a gentile,

B. "or with [an Israelite] who does not concede the validity of the *erub*—

C. "lo, this one [the gentile or nonbeliever] restricts him [from using the courtyard]," the words of R. Meir.

D.   R. Eliezer b. Jacob says, "Under no circumstances does any one prohibit [the believer in the *erub* from making use of the court-yard] unless two Israelites prohibit one another."

M. Erubin 6:1

A.   Said Rabban Gamaliel, M'SH B: "A Sadducean lived with us in the same alleyway in Jerusalem.

B.   "And father said to us, 'Make haste and bring all sorts of utensils into the alleyway before he brings out his and prohibits you [from carrying about in it]."

C.   R. Judah says it in another version, "Make haste and do all your needs in the alleyway before he brings out his utensils and prohibits you [from using it]."

M. Erubin 6:2

These compositions, and many like them, find a place in the Mishnah because they stand not for singular events but for the opposite, exemplary ones; all of them are readily translated into abstract language for the presentation of normative rules. The cases at hand serve for nearly the whole of the Mishnah. We do find narratives of a sustained order, but these have nothing to do with an effort to record a story that forms the counterpart to the Authorized History from Genesis through Kings or any part of it; and the narrative I shall portray later in no way conforms to the indicators of historical thinking that are set out in the Authorized History. As to the Tosefta, its still richer collection does not materially change the picture these items provide.

What about stories about sages outside of the legal setting? A great many of these turn out to supply a narrative setting for a set of sayings, not an anecdote in any way resembling a "one-time event." A single example of how a narrative setting is provided for what is in fact an encounter of talking heads suffices:

Sifré to Deuteronomy XLI:II

4.A.   And it says, *Thus says the Lord, 'For three transgressions of Judah, yes, for four, I will not reverse it, because they have rejected the law of the Lord and have not kept his statutes'* (Amos 2:4).

5.A. R. Tarfon, R. Aqiba, R. Yosé the Galilean were reclining [at a meal] in the house of Aris in Lydda. This question was presented to them: "What is more important, learning or action?"

B. Said R. Tarfon, "Action is more important."

C. R. Aqiba says, "Greater is learning."

D. All responded, saying, "More important is learning, for learning brings about action."

E. R. Yosé the Galilean says, "Learning is more important, for the religious duty to learn [and study the Torah] came prior to the religious duty to separate dough-offering by forty years, to separate tithes by fifty-four years [the conquest of the land requiring fourteen], the obligation of the taboo of the years of release by sixty-one years, and prior to the requirement to observe the jubilee years by one hundred and three."

Here again, "they were reclining at such and such a place..." in no way marks the anecdote as a historical account of a one-time event; true, the discussion is assumed to have been singular; but the inclusion of details of where and how it took place has no bearing on what happened; and the interest of the story for time to come derives solely from what was said. The contents, of course, concern enduring philosophical issues; this anecdote forms a counterpart to a Platonic dialogue *in nuce*, not to an event (of an other-than-intellectual character) in the lives of the persons portrayed; any other names will have served equally well; anybody else's venue will have sufficed; and it goes without saying, even if we concede the validity of every detail, we have no more history than if we denied them all.

This is not to suggest sages make no allusions to important events of their times. But from what they say, we can scarcely reconstruct those events. And more to the point, sages make no effort at forming a narrative made up of singular happenings, telling the whole tale and conveying its implications and meaning. One example suffices. We have a clear reference to the siege of Betar and other events connected to the war of 132-135. But these matters serve only to illustrate the workings of the law, bearing no profound implications for the study of either history or the law.

A. Said Rabban Simeon b. Gamaliel, "There was this precedent: A band of prisoners went to Antioch, and upon their return they

said, 'Of our group only So-and-so, a Jew, was killed.' And the
case came before sages, who permitted his wife to remarry."

Tosefta Yebamot 14:7

A.   SWB M'SH B: Sixty men went down to the fortress at Betar
     and not a single one of them came back. And the matter came
     before sages, who permitted their wives to remarry.

B.   They give testimony concerning him [the deceased] only by
     mentioning his name and the name of his father, his name and
     the name of his town.

C.   But if one said, "So and so has gone forth from such and such
     a town," and they searched in that town—

D.   if only he went forth from that town, his wife may remarry.

Tosefta Yebamot 14:8

The circumstances of the precedent invoke the catastrophe of Betar; sages
knew perfectly well what was happening around them. This makes all the
more striking their failure to put together a sequence of events into a coherent picture, or even to compose coherent anecdotal accounts of events one
by one.

Even stories that clearly record one-time, specific incidents, set forth not
principally as precedents, still point toward normative behavior; we have a
variety of instances in which the law is given a history. But ordinarily, the
substance of this history, that is, the appeal to concrete events to explain the
formation of the law, serves in context in the same familiar way, that is, as
an account for why the law is one way, rather than another. So even when
the narrator claims to tell us things that have actually taken place, the context
of the account remains the same. More to the point, out of incidents such
as these, no sustained narrative emerges, nor, indeed, an account of an event
exemplary in any context other than that of the law that the Mishnah
proposes to set forth. The point remains the same throughout, namely,
where we do find writing that purposes to tell us how things were, the
purpose of the narrative is very rarely other than the exposition of the law,
its logic and its context in the enduring social order. Here is a set of such
one-time narratives that yield an explanation for why the law is what it is:

A.   M'SH S: More than forty pairs of witnesses came forward.

B.   But R. Aqiba kept them back at Lud.

C.   Rabban Gamaliel said to him, "If you keep back the people, you will turn out to make them err in the future."

M. Rosh Hashanah 1:6

A.   A father and his son who saw the new moon should go [to give testimony].

B.   It is not that they join together with one another [to provide adequate testimony], but so that, if one of them should turn out to be invalid [as a witness], the other may join with someone else [to make up the requisite number of witnesses].

C.   R. Simeon says, "A father and his son, and all relatives, are valid to give testimony about the new moon."

D.   Said R. Yosé, "M'SH B: Tobiah, the physician, saw the new moon in Jerusalem—he, his son, and his freed slave. And the priests accepted him and his son [as witnesses to the new moon], but they invalidated the testimony of his slave. But when they came before the court, they accepted his [testimony] and that of his slave, but they invalidated that of his son."

M. Rosh Hashanah 1:7

We need not survey the entire repertoire of the first layer of the Rabbinic writings to make the point that, even when one-time events are set forth, they ordinarily serve an other-than historical purpose, and rarely account for the law by appeal to a specific, one-time event. The Mishnah's authors have no interest in explaining the law as the response to episodes or ad hoc situations.

Historical narrative in a legal context, while rare, provides important evidence that, in the formation of law, one-time concrete incidents were taken into account and did form the basis for law transcending the occasion. These are not many, but they provide evidence that historical thinking does form an occasion for transforming a singular situation and ad hoc law pertaining to it into an exemplary case and a fixed norm emerging there-from. So far as I am able to discern, for the Mishnah, all such cases pertain to the Temple,[3] which is the only locus in which singular events yield

3. This fact will take on meaning in Part Four, below.

enduring, legal consequences. The Temple is the only locus of history, and the cult the only focus of sustained narrative, for the Mishnah. Here are a historical events or facts accorded normative consequence:

A. [At one time] all blessings in the Temple concluded with "forever."

B. When the heretics corrupted [the practice] and said, "There is but one world [but no world to come]," they ordained that they should say, "forever and ever" [thus suggesting the existence of a world to come].

C. And they ordained that an individual should greet his fellow with [God's] name,

D. in accordance with what is said, *And behold Boaz came from Bethlehem; and he said to the reapers, "The Lord be with you!" And they answered, "The Lord bless you"* (Ruth 2:4).

E. And it says, *The Lord is with you, you mighty man of valor* (Judges 6:12).

F. And it says, *Do not despise your mother when she is old* (Prov. 23:22).

G. And it says, *It is the time for the Lord to act, for thy law has been broken* (Ps. 119:126).

M. Ber. 9:5

What is important here is the allegation that in response to a particular event or set of events, sages made the law different from what it had been. Comparable cases include these:

A. Nittai and Teqoan brought dough offering from Beitar [to the Land of Israel to give it to a priest], and [the priesthood] would not accept [it] from him.

B. People from Alexandria brought their dough offering from Alexandria [to the Land of Israel to give it to a priest], and [the priesthood] would not accept [it] from them.

C. People from Mount Sevoim brought their firstfruits [to Jerusalem to give to a priest] before Pentecost [too early (M. Bik. 1:3)], and [the priesthood] would not accept [the firstfruits] from them...

M. Hal. 4:10

A.   The son of Antines brought firstborn [animals] up from Baby-
     lonia [to the Land of Israel to give to a priest], and [the priest-
     hood] would not accept [them] from him.

B.   Joseph the priest brought the first of the wine and oil, [to the
     land of Israel to give to a priest], and [the priesthood] would not
     accept [it] from him.

C.   He even brought his children and the members of his household
     up [to Jerusalem] to celebrate Minor Passover,[4] and they sent
     him away,

D.   so that the matter would not be established as obligatory.

E.   Ariston brought his firstfruits from Apamea [to Jerusalem to give
     to a priest] and [the priesthood] accepted [the firstfruits] from
     him, because they said, "One who acquires [land] in Syria is like
     one who acquires [land] in the outskirts of Jerusalem."

M. Hal. 4:11

These episodes hardly qualify as paragraphs in a historical chapter. Another
fine example of the focus upon the Temple in the narrative of specific incidents that affected the formation of the law is the case in which the Boethusians made troubles for sages in the determination of the lunar calendar,
a matter critical to the conduct of the cult in the Temple:

A.   *At first they would accept testimony concerning the new moon from*
     everybody [M. R.H. 2:1B].

B.   One time the Boethusians hired two witnesses to come and fool
     the sages.

C.   For the Boethusians do not concede that Pentecost should come
     at any time except on the day following the Sabbath.

D.   One of them came along and gave his testimony and went his
     way.

E.   Then the second one said, "I was coming up at Ma'aleh
     Adumim, and I saw it crouching between two rocks,

---

4.   The festival on the fourteenth of Iyyar for those who were in a state of uncleanness
on the fourteenth of Nisan, the date of Passover (Num. 7:3-11) in Jerusalem.

F.   "its head looking like a calf, and its ears looking like a lamb, and its horns looking like a deer, and its tail lying between its thighs.

G.   "I saw it, I was astonished, and I fell backward.

H.   "And lo, [I found] two hundred *zuz* tied up for me in my purse."

I.   They said to him, "The two hundred *zuz* are given over to you as a gift. The one who hired you will be laid out on the post.

J.   "Why did you get involved in this matter?"

K.   He said to them, "I heard that the Boethusians were planning to confuse sages. I said to myself, 'It's better that I should go and tell sages.'"

Tosefta Rosh Hashanah 1:15

The determination of the calendar provides one fine instance of how the interests of the cult determined the inclusion of a historical explanation for a matter of law. And once historical circumstance enters into deliberations on the law, then the circumstance will be preserved and described. But it is, we see, in the setting of not narrative history but legal exposition—and therefore underlines the negative result of this survey: history in the form of unique events set forth in sustained narrative is a neglected medium of expression. Linear thinking is replaced here by thought about the discovery and presentation of recurrent norms or patterns. So the very formulation of historical materials underscores the paradigmatic character of the thought behind the writing.

A still weightier case than the foregoing concerns major changes in Temple procedures by reason of historical events of a formidable character. When the Temple was destroyed, various ordinances were made to take account of the loss of the Temple, and these responded to a specific, historical incident:

A.   On the festival day of the New Year which coincided with the Sabbath

B.   in the Temple they would sound the shofar—

C.   But not in the provinces.

D.   When the Temple was destroyed, Rabban Yohanan ben Zakkai made the rule that they should sound the shofar in every locale in which there was a court.

E.   Said R. Eleazar, "Rabban Yohanan b. Zakkai made that rule in the case of Yabneh alone."

F.   They said to him, "All the same are Yabneh and every locale in which there is a court."

Mishnah-tractate Rosh Hashanah 4:1

Just as the Temple alone receives a sustained narrative hearing, as we shall see, so the Temple is the principal place in which history is taken into account in the portrait of the formation of the rules. Where we find a historical mode of thinking about the law and its formation, it is rare and ordinarily pertains to the cult and Temple.

B. COMPOSITE OF ONE-TIME EVENTS INTO A NARRATIVE

Where we find one-time events formed into a narrative of some sort, the cult defines the occasion. Where weighty, singular events matter, it is because of the impact upon the Temple or its cult. History then is absorbed into an ahistorical framework, being deprived of independent standing in the great scheme of things:

A.   When murderers became many, the rite of breaking the heifer's neck was cancelled.

B.   [This was] when Eleazar b. Dinai came along, and he was also called Tehinah b. Perishah. Then they called him, "Son of a murderer."

C.   When adulterers became many, the ordeal of the bitter water was cancelled.

D.   And Rabban Yohanan b. Zakkai cancelled it, since it is said, I will not punish your daughters when they commit whoredom, nor your daughters-in-law when they commit adultery, for they themselves go apart with whores (Hos. 4:14).

M. Sotah 9:9

A.   Yohanan, high priest, did away with the confession concerning tithe.

B.   Also: He cancelled the rite of the Awakeners and the Stunners,

C.   Until his time a hammer did strike in Jerusalem.

D.   And in his time no man had to ask concerning doubtfully tithed produce.

M. Sotah 9:10

A.   R. Simeon b. Eleazar says, "[When] purity [ceased], it took away the taste and scent; [when] tithes [ceased], they took away the fatness of corn."

B.   And sages say, "Fornication and witchcraft made an end to everything."

M. Sotah 9:13

A.   In the war against Vespasian they decreed against the wearing of wreaths by bridegrooms and against the wedding drum.

C.   In the war against Titus they decreed against the wearing of wreaths by brides,

D.   And [they decreed] that a man should not teach Greek to his son.

E.   In the last war [Bar Kokhba's] they decreed that a bride should not go out in a palanquin inside the town.

F.   But our rabbis [thereafter] permitted the bride to go out in a palanquin inside the town.

M. Sotah 9:13

Now these clear references to one-time events, treated as part of a coherent complex, do raise the possibility of a historical account of considerable proportions; these form not anecdotes but incidents in the presentation of a pattern, leading toward a conclusion. But, in due course, we shall see that they form not an exception to the rule that the first phase in the formation of the Rabbinic documents ignore the media of historical thinking, but proof of a different rule, namely, where sustained narrative does emerge in the Rabbinic literature in the initial phase of its unfolding, that narrative concerns only one topic, and that is, the Temple: the conduct of its cult, the history of its building. There we do find sustained narrative, and there we do find full utilization of the media of historical thinking; one-time events are formed into accounts that, if not linear, then at least show a sustained and cogent character.

C. THE RAW MATERIALS FOR BIOGRAPHY

Where we deal with named figures, not sages, we find nothing that would generate or sustain a biography. Rather, where those worthy of note are treated, they are turned into examples of virtue, on the one side, or the source of precedents, no different from sages, on the other. Here is a fine example of how a chapter in the life of a person is shaped by the requirements of finding, or fabricating, a useful precedent. Narrative of a specific person, other than a sage, in the setting of the fragment of a biography, is illustrated in the following:

A.   He who [while overseas] took a vow to be a Nazir for a long spell and completed his spell as a Nazir, and afterward came to the Land [of Israel]—

B.   the House of Shammai say, "He is a Nazir for thirty days."

C.   And the House of Hillel say, "He is a Nazir as from the very beginning."

D.   M'SH B: Helene the Queen—her son went off to war, and she said, "If my son comes home from war whole and in one piece, I shall be a Nazir for seven years." Indeed her son did come home from war, and she was a Nazir for seven years. Then at the end of the seven years she went up to the Land. The House of Hillel instructed her that she should be a Nazir for another seven years. Then at the end of the seven years she was made unclean. So she turned out to be a Nazir for twenty-one years.

E.   Said R. Judah, "She was a Nazir only fourteen years."

Mishnah-tractate Nazir 3:6

Not all named subjects of stories yield negative lessons. Here is a fine, if rare, instance of how an exemplary figure is recorded in a quite particular historical setting. But even here, we find nothing remotely resembling the raw materials of biography. The Jewish king of Adiabene supported the poor in time of trouble, even while using up his patrimony; the anecdote exemplifies the virtue of poverty, just as anecdotes may exemplify right practice of the law.

A.   M'SH B: Monobases the king [of Adiabene] went and gave [to the poor; all of his treasures during years of famine.

B.   His brothers sent [the following message] to him:

C.   "Your ancestors stored up treasures and increased the wealth [left for them by] their ancestors. But you went and gave away all of these treasures, both your own and those of your ancestors!"

D.   He replied to them, "My ancestors stored up treasures for this lower [world], but I [through giving charity, have stored up treasures for [the heavenly world] above, as it is stated [in Scripture], *Faithfulness will spring up from the ground below, and righteousness will look down from the sky* (Ps. 85:11).

E.   "My ancestors stored up treasures [for the material world], where the [human] hand can reach, but I have stored up treasures [for the non-material world], where the [human] hand cannot reach, as it is stated [in Scripture], *Righteousness and justice are the foundation of your throne, steadfast love and faithfulness go before you.* (Ps. 89:14)."

F.   "My ancestors stored up treasures [of a type] that produce no [real] benefits, but I have stored up treasures of the sort that do produce benefits, as it is stated [in Scripture], *Tell the righteous that it shall be well with them, for they shall reap the benefits.*

G.   "My ancestors stored up treasures of money, but I have stored up treasures of souls, as it is stated [in Scripture], *The fruit of the righteous is a tree of life, and a wise man saves the souls of the poor* (Prov. 11:30).

H.   "My ancestors stored up treasures [that eventually, after their deaths, would benefit only] others, but I have stored up treasures [that will benefit] myself [both in life and in death], as it is stated [in Scripture], *It shall be a righteousness to you before the Lord your God.*

I.   "My ancestors stored up treasures in this world, but I have stored up treasures for myself in the world-to-come, as it is stated [in Scripture] *Your righteousness shall go before you, and the glory of the Lord shall be your rear guard* (Isa. 58:8)."

Tosefta Peah 4:18

The treatment of individual lives conforms to the treatment of the historical setting of laws and the presentation of events in the form of stories. Two traits predominate. First of all, where we do have such stories, they are subordinated to the purpose of setting forth norms. Second, stories are told to portray what is not unique but what is exemplary.

D. LIVES OF SAGES

While we have noted a large variety of stories about sages, nothing in the documents considered here contributes to the formation of a sage's "life." What is noteworthy is that even the kinds of materials we find later on, for example, stories of sages' entry into Torah-study and their dignified deaths, makes an appearance in the first set of writings. Like narratives, where the first stage of writing admits named sages, it is for the narrow program of this stage; narratives then serve mainly the purpose of writing up precedents, biographical snippets likely are limited to an equally determinate and limited program.

iii. The Later Midrash-Compilations: Genesis Rabbah, Leviticus Rabbah, and Pesiqta deRab Kahana

A. ONE-TIME EVENTS

The second composite of documents changes the picture. We note a tendency to tell fairly substantial and well-articulated stories. The stories bear their own individual point, not merely a general point in a distinctive setting. Now we do find important presentations of one-time events, and these are set forth not for exemplary but for ad hoc purposes. A number of discrete, but well-composed, pictures of one-time events derives from the second set of documents. While we do not find anything approaching sustained narratives except for one item,[5] we still identify one-time events and more than routine pieces of biographical narrative, if not history, then more than exemplary anecdote and annotation. In the following we find the story of how the Romans permitted the Jews to rebuild the Temple, although nothing came of the project, due to Samaritan opposition:

Genesis Rabbah LXIV:X.

3.A.   In the time of R. Joshua b. Hananiah the government decreed that the house of the sanctuary should be rebuilt. Pappus and Lulianus set up money changing tables from Acco to Antioch

---

5.   Here we do note that in the two Talmuds, that one item, given presently, does find its counterparts.

to provide what was needed for those who came up from the Exile in Babylonia.

B.   The Samaritans went and reported to him, "Let it be known to the king that if this rebellious city is rebuilt and the walls are finished, they will not pay tribute (*mindah*), impost (*belo*) or toll (*halak*)" (Ezra 4:13).[6]

C.   He said to them, "What shall we do? For the decree has already been issued [for the rebuilding to go forward]."

D.   They said to him, "Send orders to them either to change its location or to add five cubits to it or to cut it down by five cubits, and they will give up the project on their own."

E.   The community was assembled on the plain of Beth Rimmon, when the royal orders arrived they began to weep. They had the mind to rebel against the government.

F.   They said, "Let one wise man go and calm the community." They said, "Let R. Joshua b. Hananiah do it, because he is a scholar of the Torah."

G.   He went up and expounded as follows: "A wild lion killed a beast and got a bone stuck in his throat. The lion said, 'To whoever will come and remove it I shall give a reward.' An Egyptian heron with a long beak came and removed the bone, then asked for his fee. The lion answered, 'Go. Now you can boast that you stuck your head into the lion's mouth whole and pulled it out whole.'

H.   "So it is enough for us that we entered into dealings with this nation whole and have come forth whole."

The story is told in its own terms; it may exemplify virtue, but its focus is upon the event itself. It does not take its place on a sustained narrative. It therefore does not suggest that a large-scale historical program animates the work of the compiler of the document, though the framer of the composition itself has certainly shown an interest in episodes that are not merely anecdotes.

Here is an account of an important, one-time event, bearing long-term consequences, in which the law does not figure, but in which politics in its

6. The words *mindah, belo,* and *halak,* respectively, mean land tax, poll tax, and a tax on crops (Freedman, p. 580, n. 2).

own terms intervenes. This story is important since it can have taken its place in a sustained narrative, and, in fact, it did. For a version of this story does yeoman service in Josephus's narrative history as well; but in the present context, it stands in no context and performs no service of a broader narrative character:

Genesis Rabbah XCI:III.

A. Three hundred Nazirites came up in the time of Simeon b. Shatah. For one hundred fifty of them he found grounds for the dissolution of their vows as Nazirites, and for one hundred and fifty he did not find grounds for the dissolution of their vows. He went over to King Yannai and asked him, "Three hundred Nazirites came up, and they require nine hundred offerings [to complete their purification rites]. You give half and I'll give half."

B. Yannai gave his half. Then the gossip circulated that Simeon b. Shatah had not give anything at all. Simeon heard the rumor and fled. After some time, Persian nobles came up and ate at a banquet of King Yannai. They said, "We remember that there was here a certain wise man, who said very profound things to us when we were here."

C. He said to his sister, "Send and bring him here."

D. She said to him, "Give your word, and he will come." He gave his word, and the other came and took his seat between the king and the queen.

E. He said to him, "What are you doing?"

F. He said to him, "For it is written in the book of Ben Sira, 'Esteem her so she shall exalt you and seat you between princes'."

G. He said to him, "Why did you cheat me?"

H. He said to him, "God forbid, I did not cheat you, but you gave what is yours to give, and I gave what is mine to give: *For wisdom is a defense even as money is a defense* (Qoh. 7:12)."

I. He said to him, "Then why did you not tell me?"

J. He said to him, "If I had told you, you would not have done your share."

K. He said to him, "Then why did you flee?"

L.   He said to him, "For it is written, *Hide yourself for a brief moment until the indignation is past* (Isa. 26:20)."

M.   He filled a cup of wine for him and said to him, "Recite the blessing for the food after the meal."

N.   He said, "Let us say a blessing for the food which Yannai and his friends have eaten."

O.   He said to him, "In my entire life I never heard this thing from you."

P.   He said to him, "What do you want me to say? 'Let us say a blessing for the food that I personally did not eat'?"

Q.   He ordered a cup of wine mixed for him a second time, and he said, "Let us say a blessing for the food which we have eaten."

The story itself is standard historical narrative, an incident that serves a larger narrative purpose; it forms an account of the relationships between sages and monarch. A history of Israel, sages, monarch, and nation as a whole, not only will have used the story to good purpose, but, in the case of Josephus, did. This is all the more reason to invoke the story as evidence of the presence of the skills needed for historical writing together with the absence of the medium of historical thought.

Even a chapter available for a biography of Diocletian turns out to serve an other-than-historical purpose; it is to teach the moral lesson that people should be careful in dealings with unimportant people; they may later on become very important indeed.

Genesis Rabbah LXIII:VIII.7

A.   Diocletian the king was originally a swineherd in Tiberias. When he came near a school, the children would go out and beat him up. After some time he was made king. He came and took up residence near Paneas and he sent letters to Tiberias just before the eve of the Sabbath, giving this command: "I command the rabbis of the Jews to appear before me on Sunday morning." He gave orders to the messenger, telling him not to give the command to them until the last light on Friday evening.

B.   R. Samuel bar Nahman went down to bathe. He saw Rabbi standing before his school, and his face was white. He said to him, "Why is your face white?"

C. He said to him, "Thus and so were the orders that were sent to me in letters from King Diocletian."

D. He said to him, "Go and bathe, for our creator will do miracles for you."

E. He went in to bath and a bath sprite came along, joking and dancing toward them. Rabbi wanted to rebuke him. Said to him R. Samuel bar Nahman, "Leave him alone, for there are times that they appear because of miracles."

F. He said to the sprite, "Your master is in distress, and you are laughing?"

G. He said to them, "Go, eat and celebrate a happy Sabbath, for your creator is doing miracles, and I will place you on Sunday morning where you wish to be."

H. At the end of the Sabbath, when the session ended, he went out and set them before the gates of Paneas. They went in and said to Diocletian, "Lo, they are standing before the gates."

I. He said to them, "Then close the gates."

J. He took them and set them on the rampart of the town.

K. They went in and told Diocletian. He said to them, "I order that you heat the baths for three days, then let them go in and bathe and come before me."

L. They went and heated the baths for three days, and the sprite went and cooled off the heat for them, so the rabbis went in, bathed, and appeared before him.

M. He said to them, "Because you people know that your God does miracles for you, you ridicule the king!"

N. They said to him, "True enough, we ridiculed Diocletian the swineherd, but to Diocletian the King we are loyal subjects."

O. He said to them, "Nonetheless, do not insult even an unimportant Roman or a soldier of the lowest rank."

Like the story about Yannai and the sages, the tale at hand shows how a singular event of a biographical order can have been composed; but such compositions prove not only rare but also episodic, never coalescing into biography in any conventional sense.

But stories of the character of the foregoing—specific, with individuals neatly distinguished by personal traits, so that names are not interchangeable—prove few and episodic, and much more common are those that provide a narrative setting for a picture of virtue. In contrast to the foregoing, a "one-time event" may also encapsulate a moral lesson in a historical framework. A single instance suffices to represent many. In the following narrative "the emperor" could have served as well as a named figure, and the lesson that is taught hardly requires the historical setting in which the tale is told. But as we have it, the emperor Hadrian honored an old man who planted trees, regarding foresight as valuable; the Jew who keeps the Torah is honored by the enemies of Israel:

Leviticus Rabbah XXV:V.2.

A.　　Hadrian (may his bones be ground up) was walking through the paths of Tiberias. He saw an old man standing and digging holes to plant trees. He said to him, "Old man, old man, if you got up early [to do the work, when you were young], you would not have stayed late [to plant in your old age]."

B.　　He said to him, "I got up early [and worked in my youth] and I stayed late [working in my old age], and whatever pleases the Master of heaven, let him do."

C.　　He said to him, "By your life, old man! How old are you today?"

D.　　He said to him, "I am a hundred years old."

E.　　He said to him, "Now you are a hundred years old, and you are standing and digging holes to plant trees! Do you honestly think that you're going to eat the fruit of those trees?"

F.　　He said to him, "If I have the merit, I shall eat it. But if not, well, just as my forefathers labored for me, so I labor for my children."

G.　　He said to him, "By your life! If you have the merit of eating of the fruit of these trees, be sure to let me know about it."

H.　　After some time the trees produced figs. The man said, "Lo, the time has come to tell the king."

I.　　What did he do? He filled a basket with figs and went up and stood at the gate of the palace.

J.　　[The guards] said to him, "What is your business here?"

K. He said, "To come before the king."

L. When he had gone in, he said to him, "What are you doing here?"

M. He said to him, "I am the old man you met. I was the one who was digging holes to plant trees, and you said to me, 'If you have the merit of eating the fruit of those trees, be sure to let me know.' Now I in fact did have the merit, and I ate of their fruit, and these figs here are the fruit of those trees."

N. Then said Hadrian, "I order you to bring a chair of gold for him to sit on.

O. "I order you to empty this basket of his and fill it with golden *denars*."

P. His servants said to him, "Are you going to pay so much respect to that old Jew?"

Q. He said to him, "His Creator honors him, and should I not honor him?"

R. The wife of the neighbor [of that man] was wicked. She said to her husband, "Son of darkness, see how the king loves figs and trades them for golden *denars*."

S. What did [the man] do? He filled a sack with figs and went and stood before the palace.

T. They said to him, "What is your business here?"

U. He said to them, "I heard that the king loves figs and trades them for golden *denars*."

V. They went and told the king, "There is an old man standing at the gate of the palace carrying a sackful of figs. When we asked him, 'What are you doing here,' he told us, 'I heard that the king loves figs and trades them for golden *denars*.'"

W. [The king] said, "I order you to set him up before the gate of the palace. Whoever goes in and out is to throw [a fig] in his face."

X. Toward evening they freed him and he went home. He said to his wife, "For all the honor [that I got], I owe you!"

Y. She said, "Go and boast to your mother that they were figs and not *etrogs*, that they were soft and not hard!"

Change the name of the king, and no detail of the story will shift; nothing depends on the specificity of the circumstances; and the goal of the narrative is clear.

B. COMPOSITE OF ONE-TIME EVENTS INTO A NARRATIVE

Nothing that would contribute to a sustained narrative comes to the fore in this layer of writing, so far as I am able to see.

C. THE RAW MATERIALS FOR BIOGRAPHY

As in the prior layer of writings, here again, named royal figures are presented as exemplars of virtue. They can have served as the focus of biography, and here is a chapter for such a document. A single example proves representative. The sons of King Ptolemy circumcised themselves and received divine protection on this account:

Genesis Rabbah XLVI:X.2

A.   There is the case of Monobases and Izates, sons of king Ptolemy, who were in session and studying the book of Genesis. When they came to this verse, *You shall be circumcised in the flesh of your foreskins [and it shall be a sign of the covenant between me and you]* (Gen. 17:11) this one turned his face to the wall and wept, and that one turned his face to the wall and wept.

B.   This one went and circumcised himself, and that one went and circumcised himself.

C.   After a while they were in session and studying the book of Genesis. When they came to the verse, "And you will circumcise...," one said to the other, "Woe is you, my brother" [thinking he was not circumcised]. The other said, "Woe is you, not me." Then each revealed the matter to the other.

D.   When their mother found out about the matter, she went and told their father, "As to your sons, a sore appeared on their flesh, and the doctor ordered that they be circumcised."

E.   He said, "Then let them be circumcised."

F.   How did the Holy One, blessed be he, pay him back?

G.   Said R. Phineas, "When he went out to battle, the enemy made for him in particular, but an angel came down and saved him."

D. LIVES OF SAGES

Here again, the raw materials of narrative are in hand, but in the end we are left with an anecdote, not a sherd of a continuous biography. The same is to be said of a sequence of stories about the patriarch. A life of Judah the Patriarch will include that he advised the emperor on the administration of the empire; one such story stands for them all:

Genesis Rabbah LXVII:VI.

2.A.   "... 'Behold, of the fat places of the earth shall your dwelling be" refers to the fat-pursed people of the earth.

B.   Antoninus sent to Our Master [Judah the Patriarch], saying to him, "Since our treasury lacks funds, what should we do to fill it up?"

C.   He took the messenger and brought him into his vegetable patch. He began to pull up big radishes and to plant little ones in their place.

D.   He said to him, "Give me the answer in writing."

E.   He said to him, "You do not need it."

F.   He went back and the king said to him, "Where is your answer?"

G.   He said to him, "He did not give me anything."

H.   "What did he say to you?"

I.   "He did not say anything to me, but he took me and brought me into his vegetable patch and began to pull up big radishes and to plant little ones in their place."

J.   He began to remove officers and bring in officers, until his treasury was filled [with the bribes people paid for high office].

The story sets forth a variety of lessons, and though they are particular to Judah's message, they also serve the exemplary purpose of defining rules of wise conduct; explaining how to formulate sage administrative procedures; and other worthwhile goals. An incident in Judah's life, the story makes only a marginal contribution to a biography; and a variety of such stories, such as we have, taken all together do not comprise a biography.

iv. The Latest Midrash-Compilations: Song of Songs Rabbah, Ruth Rabbah, Esther Rabbah I, and Lamentations Rabbah

A. ONE-TIME EVENTS

One-time incidents serve as the narrative framework for a philosophical polemic, as much as they present an occasion for recording law in the form of a case. In this instance, Hadrian and Joshua b. Hananiah conducted an argument which showed that the authority of Moses remained valid, while the authority of the emperor did not extend very far:

Ruth Rabbah XXI:i.10.

A. Hadrian—may his bones rot!—asked R. Joshua b. Hananiah, saying to him, "I am better off than your lord, Moses."

B. He said to him, "Why?"

C. "Because I am alive and he is died, and it is written, *For to him who is joined to all living there is hope; for a living dog is better than a dead lion* (Qoh. 9:4)."

D. He said to him, "Can you make a decree that no one kindle a fire for three days?"

E. He said to him, "Yes."

F. At evening the two of them went up to the roof of the palace. They saw smoke ascending from a distance.

G. He said to him, "What is this?"

H. He said to him, "It is a sick noble. The physician came to him and told him he will be healed only if he drinks hot water."

I. He said to him, "May your spirit go forth [drop dead]! While you are still alive, your decree is null.

J. "But from the time that our lord, Moses, made the decree for us, *You shall not burn a fire in your dwelling place on the Sabbath day* (Ex. 35:3), no Jew has ever kindled a flame on the Sabbath, and even to the present day, the decree has not been nullified."

K. "And you say you are better off than he is?"

Change Hadrian to Titus or Antoninus, Joshua to Eliezer or Judah the Patriarch, and the force of the story is in no way diminished. The incident serves as the setting for a great moral lesson, nothing more.

B. Composite of One-Time Events into a Narrative

One of the great, history-making moments, the war led by Bar Kokhba is represented in terms that qualify as fully-expressed narrative, a large and important chapter in a history of Israel. The following is the one important exception to the rule established in the items cited earlier. Here we do have the results of a sustained and coherent narrative, involving a variety of persons and incidents, not anecdotal or episodic but sustained and systematic. Writing of this kind points toward thinking of a historical character as defined by Scripture's indicators; it shows us what might have been, and underscores the negative results now on display. The documents before us contain little writing of the character of the following, and, where we find this kind of writing, it is in the second of the two Talmuds and the associated documents of Midrash-compilation:

Lamentations Rabbati LVIII:ii.5.

5.A.   When R. Aqiba saw Bar Koziba, he said, "This is the royal messiah."

B.   R. Yohanan b. Torta said to him, "Aqiba, grass will grow from your cheeks and he will still not have come."

6.A.   R. Yohanan interpreted the verse, *The voice is the voice of Jacob* (Gen. 27:22) in this way: "The voice is the voice of Caesar Hadrian, who killed eighty thousand myriads of people at Betar."

7.A.   Eighty thousand trumpeters besieged Betar. There Bar Koziba was encamped, with two hundred thousand men with an amputated finger.

B.   Sages sent word to him, saying, "How long are you going to produce blemished men in Israel?"

C.   He said to them, "And what shall I do to examine them [to see whether or not they are brave]?"

D.   They said to him, "Whoever cannot uproot a cedar of Lebanon do not enroll in your army."

E.   He had two hundred thousand men of each sort [half with an amputated finger, half proved by uprooting a cedar].

8.A.   When they went out to battle, he would say, "Lord of all ages, don't help us and don't hinder us!"

B.   That is in line with this verse: *Have you not, O God, cast us off? And do not go forth, O God, with our hosts* (Ps. 60:12).

9.A. What did Bar Koziba do?

B.   He could catch a missile from the enemy's catapult on one of his knees and throw it back, killing many of the enemy.

C.   That is why R. Aqiba said what he said [about Bar Koziba's being the royal messiah].

10.A. For three and a half years Hadrian besieged Betar.

B.   R. Eleazar the Modiite was sitting in sackcloth and ashes, praying, and saying, "Lord of all the ages, do not sit in judgment today, do not sit in judgment today."

C.   Since [Hadrian] could not conquer the place, he considered going home.

D.   There was with him a Samaritan, who said to him, "My lord, as long as that old cock wallows in ashes, you will not conquer the city.

E.   "But be patient, and I shall do something so you can conquer it today."

F.   He went into the gate of the city and found R. Eleazar standing in prayer.

G.   He pretended to whisper something into his ear, but the other paid no attention to him.

H.   People went and told Bar Koziba, "Your friend wants to betray the city."

I.   He sent and summoned the Samaritan and said to him, "What did you say to him?"

J.   He said to him, "If I say, Caesar will kill me, and if not, you will kill me. Best that I kill myself and not betray state secrets."

K.   Nonetheless, Bar Koziba reached the conclusion that he wanted to betray the city.

L.   When R. Eleazar had finished his prayer, he sent and summoned him, saying to him, "What did this one say to you?"

M.   He said to him, "I never saw that man."

N.   He kicked him and killed him.

O.   At that moment an echo proclaimed: "Woe to the worthless shepherd who leaves the flock, the sword shall be upon his arm and upon his right eye" (Zech. 11:17).

P.   Said the Holy One, blessed be He, "You have broken the right arm of Israel and blinded their right eye. Therefore your arm will wither and your eye grow dark."

Q.   Forthwith Betar was conquered and Ben Koziba was killed.

R.   They went, carrying his head to Hadrian. He said, "Who killed this one?"

S.   They said, "One of the Goths killed him," but he did not believe them.

T.   He said to them, "Go and bring me his body."

U.   They went to bring his body and found a snake around the neck.

V.   He said, "If the God of this one had not killed him, who could have vanquished him?"

W.   This illustrates the following verse of Scripture: *If their Rock had not given them over....* (Dt. 32:30).

11.A.   They killed the inhabitants of Betar until their horses waded in blood up to their nostrils, and blood rolled along in stones the size of forty-seah and flowed into the sea for a distance of four miles.

B.   And should you suppose that Betar was near the sea, it was four miles away.

14.A.   For fifty-two years Betar held out after the destruction of the house of the sanctuary.

B.   And why was it destroyed?

C.   Because they lit lamps on the occasion of the destruction of the house of the sanctuary.

19.A.   There were two brothers in Kefar Haruba, and no Roman could pass by there, for they killed him.

B.   They decided, "The whole point of the thing is that we must take the crown, put it on our head, and make ourselves kings."

C.   They heard that the Romans were coming to fight them.

D.   They went out to do battle, and an old man met them and said, "May the Creator be your help against them."

E.   They said, "Let him not help us nor hinder us!"

F.   Because of their sins, they went forth and were killed.

G.   They went, carrying his head to Hadrian. He said, "Who killed this one?"

H.   They said, "One of the Goths killed him," but he did not believe them.

I.   He said to them, "Go and bring me his body."

J.   They went to bring his body and found a snake around the neck.

K.   He said, "If the God of this one had not killed him, who could have vanquished him?"

L.   This illustrates the following verse of Scripture: *If their Rock had not given them over....* (Dt. 32:30).

The entire composite provides us with the one example of what, overall, the documents ought to have supplied, had they conformed to the rules of thought and exposition of a historical character that Scripture defined for us. This vast and sustained set of events, all of them portrayed as unique and singular, then formed into a large and coherent narrative, shows what might have been—and underlines, therefore, what we do have before us. Sustaining narratives of one-time events, set forth in the Rabbinic literature, are defined by the case at hand. Alas, it represents a series of one, as this survey has shown. The media of historical thinking prove entirely accessible to the author(s) of the compositions comprising this composite, and the capacity to formulate sustained historical narrative—a chapter in a history—certainly is realized here.

C. The Raw Materials for Biography

The one-time events given above may as well fit here; I see no firm distinction in context, except that the items catalogued earlier are formulated not to record the life and deeds of the named figures but to convey an event of other than personal consequence.

D. LIVES OF SAGES

The final set of documents contains some items of more than routine biographical interest, but no biography.

v. Does Rabbinic Literature Utilize the Media of Historical Thinking?

The testing of the null hypothesis yields a preponderance of evidence to characterize the Rabbinic writings—and therefore the Judaism that they portray—as profoundly different in conceptual and literary character from Scripture's Authorized History. If Scripture employs narrative to lay out a string of distinct and singular incidents, the Rabbinic literature knows no sustaining narrative of one-time events. In more than a single way, to be sure, the framers of this literature do derive meaning from events and do organize them in patterns they find sensible. But the patterns that encompass events differ from those of Scripture, as do the character of events.

The events themselves prove more often exemplary than specific, particular, and singular. When happenings are laid out, it is to illustrate or prove a point concerning a matter out of time, a proposition of an other-than-historical character, as shown by the contrast between then authentically-historical linkage of singular persons and events into a sustained narrative of Bar Kokhba, on the one side, and the ahistorical formulation of sequences of cases in the equally sustained sets of legal precedents or moral illustrations, on the other. The one certainly conforms to the indicators of historical thinking and shows us the utilization of the media of historical writing, as Scripture (in the opinion of all scholarship) defines those media. The other does not, ignoring these media in favor of others altogether.

The first of our tests of a null hypothesis—if history were the governing mode of thought and its media shaped the preferred media of expression, we should find elements of a narrative of one-time events—produces a mostly negative result. The preponderance of evidence stands against this hypothesis. The second test of a null hypothesis requires a test on a considerably less elaborate scale, as we shall now see.

CHAPTER IV

MISSING MESSAGES OF HISTORICAL THINKING:
THE PASTNESS OF THE PAST

... the entire Hebrew Bible revolves around that point in time, that historical moment when the life of the nation came to an end, when tragedy
struck in multiple blows at the kingdom, its ruling dynasty, and at the
sacred center of worship and service of their God. Such a decisive event
and its enveloping circumstances must have had a powerful effect and
pervasive influence over the literature as a whole, and most of what is written in the Bible reflects this unquestioned fact of Israel's (or Judah's) experience.

David Noel Freedman[1]

i. Temporal Order Does Not Apply to the Torah

We shall now see that, in the documents surveyed here, events are reversible; no fixed order governs. The logic of sequence—first this, then that,
therefore this caused that—plays no role. Under such conditions explaining
the world as it is by reference to the past is impossible because, in an exact
sense, it is unthinkable. That is to say, by means of thinking with principles
such as we shall now examine, history—a mode of accounting for the social
order by appeal to how things have been—in the simplest and most conventional definition then cannot be conceived.[2]

On what basis, then, shall I show that historical thinking simply cannot
be carried on, and in the main, was not carried on, among the framers of
the documents before us or among the authors of the compositions that the

1. Freedman, p. 6.

2. In fact, the Mishnah's portrayal of Israel's life ignores all considerations of time and
place (other than holy time and enchanted place) and sets forth a utopian Israel, ruling out
all considerations of historical time and circumstance. But for the present purpose, a survey
of how the past and present are treated as a single span of time is what is required.

framers assembled?[3] The single most important fact in the consideration of the unity of time past and time present is simple: considerations of temporal order simply do not apply. We need not infer that this view served as a premise, since it is stated in so many words that considerations of temporal order do not apply to the sequence of Scriptural stories. This is explicit and important in the exegesis of Scripture, but also in the interpretation of history:

Sifré to Numbers LXIV:I

I.A. *And the Lord spoke to Moses in the wilderness of Sinai in the first month of the second year after they had come out of the land of Egypt, saying, ["Let the people of Israel keep the passover at its appointed time. On the fourteenth day of this month, in the evening, you shall keep it at its appointed time; according to all its statutes and all its ordinances you shall keep it."]* (Num. 9:1-14):

B. Scripture here expresses the disgrace of Israel, for they had been camping before Mount Sinai for eleven months [and had not yet observed the Passover].

C. And Scripture further serves to teach you that considerations of temporal order do not apply to the sequence of scriptural stories.

D. For at the beginning of the present book Scripture states, *The Lord spoke to Moses in the wilderness of Sinai in the tent of meeting on the first day of the* second *month in the second year after they had come out of the land of Egypt* (Num. 1:1).

E. And here Scripture refers to "the *first* month,"

F. so serving to teach you that considerations of temporal order do not apply to the sequence of scriptural stories.

G. Rabbi says, "Such a proof is not required, for Scripture in any event says, *And the children of Israel ate mana for forty years, until they came to the border of the land* (Ex. 16:35).

H. "And at this point they had not eaten it? This statement thus service to teach you that considerations of temporal order do not apply to the sequence of scriptural stories."

---

3. For this distinction, see my *The Rules of Composition of the Talmud of Babylonia. The Cogency of the Bavli's Composite.* Atlanta, 1991: Scholars Press for South Florida Studies in the History of Judaism. It should be made explicit that my characterization here concerns not only the documents and their compilers, but the authors of the compositions that are assembled: the whole of Rabbinic Judaism as formulated by its authorities, the sages.

The several proofs make the same point. Scripture narrates events in an other-than-temporal sequence: this, then that, then the other thing, without regard to the order in which the things actually took place. Therefore, the framers of the passage maintain, the account of existence that Scripture portrays transcends considerations of temporal sequence altogether. It follows that, to begin with, sages reject history's conception of a linear and irreversible sequence of events, governed by the logic intrinsic in them: this cannot happen until that has happened, therefore this did not happen before that took place.

ii. General Considerations

A further, now familiar, premise of all historical thinking is that the past has come to closure and awaits description, analysis, and interpretation. All data are in hand, the story now awaits telling. Without a clear point of conclusion, marked by the present or the present's surrogate (e.g., a specific year at which the story is deemed to have come to fullness, even prior to the present), historical inquiry cannot identify its data and must suspend its work pending further information. Not only so, but if history cannot identify that dividing point between past and present, it also cannot project that linear sequence of events, singular and irreversible, that forms its second premise. For if past flows smoothly into present, then the reverse also commands plausibility, the present flowing into the past (as indeed we see in the paradigmatic mode of analyzing human events followed by our sages of blessed memory).

Hence the null-hypothesis that next requires testing is whether or not Rabbinic writings recognize the pastness of the past. If they do, we should find clear evidence, deriving from writings of both description and explanation, that the present is distinct from the past. The principal indicator of whether or not framers of documents view the past as distinct from, and prior to, their own day is simple to define: do we observe a sense of distance and difference between the writers and the events of Scripture that they consider?[4] We shall know the answer to this question, one way or the other, when we consider how events in the life of ancient Israel are portrayed. If

---

4. Anachronism by itself is not probative; we cannot expect our sages and their contemporaries to take account of considerations formulated only many centuries later. But people should be prepared to identify a gap in not only time but conception and conduct between themselves and their ancestors.

sages make the effort to project their formulation of such events into an age other than, and prior to, their own, then we may say that they see the past as a different age from the present.

We look for the direction of the continuity between past and present. Do sages treat the past as contemporary with their own time, bringing the past events into the language and framework of their situation? Or do they try to express their ideas in language calculated to conform to the character of the narrative of Scripture? In the former case, the past and present flow together, in the latter, the narrators intend to project themselves into the framework of the earlier age. An example of the latter mode of writing is the formulation of the book of Chronicles, which formulates its ideas in such a way as to persuade the reader the tale told in Samuel and Kings and that told in Chronicles were set forth at the same time. Then the much later writers of Chronicles meant to direct attention away from their own time and into times past. The first case given below shows the opposite flow of thought, the utter obliteration of the lines between past and present.

Now, as a matter of fact, we shall see the very opposite conceptions. Take the matter of language. Sages wrote a Hebrew different from that of Scripture, and they explicitly recognized the difference between the language of Scripture and the language of sages or of the Mishnah. Yet, when they invented conversations for Scriptural figures, it was in Mishnaic, not Scriptural Hebrew; there was no pretense at a pseudo-scriptural Hebrew or at replicating Scriptural morphology, syntax, or even word choice, when Scripture's own stories were taken up and retold in other terms altogether. This is striking evidence that the present was conceived to flow into the past, and that no distinction between present and past operated.

Scripture is rewritten to accord with contemporary convictions and conceptions; the present flows into the past, the past into the present, and at no point do we discern a trace of consciousness that the past is over and done with. These traits of the data before us cannot present any surprises, since, after all, until modern times, the West projected present onto past, representing the past, also, in the garments of today. So we shall not find it difficult to demonstrate that, for sages, the past and present formed a single plane of time—and consciousness. Accordingly, the survey of the data will remain appropriately brief.

*iii. The Mishnah, Tosefta, Abot, Sifra, Sifré to Numbers, and Sifré to
    Deuteronomy: The Present-Tense Past: Scripture Re-Presented in the
    Immediacy of the Moment*

It is the simple fact that Scripture was rewritten, its events recast to suit
the requirements of the authors of compositions. Innumerable examples of
the rewriting of Scripture fill the documents before us. Every one of them
exhibits the same traits: indifference to the criterion of evidence, oblivion
to the notion of testing allegations concerning the past against evidence
deriving from, or even pertinent to, the age, prior to the present one, that
is under discussion. Conversations are invented, events fabricated, the order
of Scriptural history recast, in complete indifference to all considerations of
historicity, evidence, and criticism. A single case suffices to show us how
events in Scripture were rewritten:

Sifré to Numbers LII:I

1.A.   *On the second day Nethanel the son of Zuar, the leader of Issachar,
       made an offering* (Num. 7:18):

B.   Why does Scripture provide this information?

C.   It is because the tribe of Reuben came and entered a complaint,
       saying, "It is enough that Judah came before me [the elder] in
       the order of the tribal journeys. Let me give an offering in the
       sequence of the birth of the tribal ancestors [hence, first]."

D.   Moses rebuked him, saying, "It is directly from the mouth of
       God that the instructions have come to me to present the offer-
       ings in accord with the order in which the tribes are arranged
       for the journeys."

E.   So it is said, "...Offer," and this word bears the sole meaning
       that the Holy One, blessed be he, instructed him for the tribes
       to make their offerings in accord with the order in which they
       are arranged for the journeys.

There are stories about events portrayed in Scripture, and, in a history
of Israel from the beginnings to the present, stories such as these will have
found a place along with the Scriptural narrative itself; in them, there is no
pretense at joining the present narrative into the language or thought-
patterns of Scripture.

Not only does the present flow into the past, the past is made to flow
into the present. To the contrary, in the type of narrative given here, Scrip-

ture is updated in every possible way; new speeches are written, and no one pretends these speeches were made long ago; new details are set forth without the slightest interest in formulating matters to conform to the style or discipline of Scripture:

Sifré to Numbers XCV:II

1.A. *So Moses went out and told the people [the words of the Lord, and he gathered seventy men of the elders of the people and placed them round about the tent.] Then the Lord came down in the cloud [and spoke to him, and took some of the spirit that was upon him and put it upon the seventy elders; and when the spirit rested upon them they prophesied, but they did so no more.] Now two men remained in the camp, [one named Eldad, and the other named Medad] (Num. 11:24-26):*

B. Some say that their names had remained in the lottery-box. For the Holy One, blessed be he, had said to Moses to choose seventy men for him. Moses replied, "How shall I do it? Lo, all of the tribes will get six representatives each except for two tribes, which will get only five. Which tribe will agree to have only five selected from its midst?"

C. Moses made an arrangement. He took seventy slips of paper and wrote on them the word "elder," and he took two further slips and left them blank and mixed them up and put them all into a lottery-box. He said to them, "Come and pick your slips."

D. To everyone who chose a slip on which was written, "elder," Moses said, "The Omnipresent has already sanctified you."

E. And to those who chose a slip on which was not written, "elder," Moses said, "It's from Heaven [and there is nothing I can do about it], so what can I do for you?"

Procedures attested in the Mishnah, e.g., for the division of the priestly sacrifices in Mishnah-tractate Tamid, are now retrojected into the remote past. No effort is invested into citing Scriptural evidence that the practice familiar from contemporary writings prevailed even long ago. This fact is simply taken for granted; past and present exist on the same plane. But more is at stake here than merely the atemporality of time. We shall now see how ancient times are fabricated out of contemporary materials.

iv. The Later Midrash-Compilations: Genesis Rabbah, Leviticus Rabbah, and Pesiqta deRab Kahana: The Present-Tense Past: Scripture Re-Presented in the Immediacy of the Moment

Not only do scriptural stories undergo an up-dating and are made to accept a reformulation in acutely contemporary terms, but sages invent chapters for the life of biblical figures, e.g., Abraham. Once more we find no interest in joining the story to Scripture's account; it is told entirely in its own terms, in the manner of a Rabbinic polemic-narrative. A single case suffices to make the point that, just as in the first set of documents, events are invented or totally recast, so in the second as much as in the first, considerations of the pastness of the past do not prevent fabrication of whole chapters in lives of saints. The premise once more is that the present is part of the past, and vice versa.

I have chosen for my illustrative case the matter of David. When David is reworked into the model of the sages, the conception that the conditions of David's life, as portrayed in Scripture, and those of Torah study that rabbis recognized from day to day, were treated as uniform; here is a fine example of what I mean by obliterating the sense of the pastness of the past, while, at the very same time, insisting on the presence of the past in the time of the sages as well. No lines distinguished one age from the other, even while the account of Scripture, read in its own terms, is scarcely acknowledged as exhibiting points of contrast:

Pesiqta deRab Kahana II:I.1

A.   *O Lord, how many are my foes! Many are rising against me; many are saying of me, there is no help for him in God. Sela* (Ps. 3:2-3):

B.   R. Samuel bar Immi and Rabbis:

C.   R. Samuel bar Immi interpreted the verse to speak of Doeg and Ahitophel:

D.   "'...many are saying of me' refers to Doeg and Ahitophel. Why does he refer to them as 'many'?

E.   "For they formed a majority in Torah-study.

F.   "'...many are saying of me'—They say to David, 'A man who has seized a ewe-lamb, killed the shepherd, and made Israelites fall by the sword—will he have salvation? There is no help for him in God.'

G. "Said David, 'And you, O Lord, have concurred with them, writing in your Torah, saying, *The adulterer and the adulteress will surely die* (Lev. 20:10).

H. "*But you, O Lord, are a shield about me* (Ps. 3:4): For you have formed a protection for me through the merit attained by my ancestors.

I. "*My glory* (Ps. 3:4): For your restored me to the throne.

J. "*And the lifter of my head* (Ps. 3:4): While I was liable to you to have my head removed, you raised my head through the prophet, Nathan, when he said to me, *Also the Lord has removed your sin and you will not die* (2 Sam. 12:13).'"

The point hardly requires elaboration. David is now turned into something that Scripture's account does not adumbrate, a disciple of sages, and the politics of his court followed those of the academy. The flow from present to past is unimpeded.

v. The Latest Midrash-Compilations: Song of Songs Rabbah, Ruth Rabbah, Esther Rabbah I, and Lamentations Rabbah: The Present-Tense Past: Scripture Re-Presented in the Immediacy of the Moment

A still more striking revision of times past into the framework of the rabbis' own times involves the rewriting of the story of Hezekiah and the Babylonians. Now the past forms a palpable component of the present. What is important in this example is the provision of an elaborate, sustained narrative, in which history is invented through a process of invention of anecdotes or events; not a single indicator of the presence of a historical mentality can be located in this historical narrative:

Song of Songs Rabbah XXXVIII:ii

34.A. [*At that time Merodach Baladan, the son of Baladan, sent* (Isa. 39:1)— Spelling out the story to which allusion has just now been made:] he was a sun-worshipper, and he would ordinarily eat at the sixth hour and sleep to the ninth hour.

B. But, in the time of Hezekiah, king of Judah, when the sun reversed its course, he slept through it and woke up and found it was dawn.

C.   He wanted to kill his guards. He accused them, "You let me sleep all day and all night long."

D.   They said to him, "It was the day that returned [the sun having reversed its course]."

E.   He said to them, "And what god reversed it?"

F.   They said to him, "It was the God of Hezekiah who reversed it."

G.   He said to them, "Then is there a god greater than mine?"

H.   They said to him, "The God of Hezekiah is greater than yours."

I.   Forthwith he sent letters and a present to Hezekiah: *At that time Merodach-baladan, son of Baladan, king of Babylonia, sent letters and a present to Hezekiah [for he had heard that he had been sick and recovered]* (Isa. 39:1).

J.   And what was written in them?

K.   He wrote him, "Peace to King Hezekiah, peace to the city of Jerusalem, peace to the Great God!"

L.   But when the letters had been sent, his mind was at ease, and he said, "I did not do it right, for I greeted Hezekiah before his God."

M.   Forthwith he arose and took three steps and retrieved the letter and wrote another instead, in which he said, "Peace to the great God, peace to the city of Jerusalem, peace to King Hezekiah."

N.   Said the Holy One, blessed be He, "You have risen from your throne and taken three steps in order to pay honor to me. By your life, I shall raise up from you three cosmopolitan kings, who will rule from one end of the world to the other."

O.   And who are they? Nebuchadnezzar, Evil-Merodach, and Belshazzar.

P.   But when they went and blasphemed, the Holy One, blessed be He, crushed their eggs out of the world and set up others in their place.

The story is made up, beginning to end; Scripture's event is recast in a process of imagination and retrojection, and we discern not the slightest interest in harmonizing the story with Scripture's data. The process of writing history in the model of the present, obliterating all lines of differentiation between past and the present age, may be illustrated by one final case. In the following the prophet is given a reprise from death.

Here, the story-teller retrojects the destruction of the second Temple into the events of the first, or, more to the point, finds no point in distinguishing one from the other.

Lamentations Rabbati CXIII.i.1.

A. "This was for the sins of her prophets and the iniquities of her priests, who shed in the midst of her the blood of the righteous:"

B. R. Yudan asked R. Aha, "Where did the Israelites kill Zechariah? Was it in the courtyard of women or in the courtyard of the Israelites?"

C. He said to him, "It was neither in the women's courtyard nor in the Israelites' courtyard, but in the priests' courtyard.

D. "But they did not dispose of his blood like the blood of a hind or a ram: *He shall pour out the blood thereof and cover it with dust* (Lev. 17:13).

E. "But here: *For the blood she shed is still in her; she set it upon a bare rock; she did not pour it out on the ground to cover it with earth* (Ezek. 24:7).

F. "*She set her blood upon the bare rock, so that it was not covered, so that it may stir up my fury to take vengeance* (Ezek. 24:8)."

2.A. Seven transgressions did the Israelites commit on that day: they murdered [1] a priest, [2] prophet, [3] judge, [4] they spilled innocent blood, [5] they blasphemed the divine name, [6] they imparted uncleanness to the courtyard, and it was, furthermore, [7] a Day of Atonement that coincided with the Sabbath.

B. When Nebuzaradan came in, he saw the blood of Zechariah begin to drip. He said to them, "What sort of blood is this dripping blood?"

C. They said to him, "It is the blood of oxen, rams, and sheep that we offered on the altar."

D. He forthwith sent and brought oxen, rams, and sheep and slaughtered them in his presence, but the blood continued to drip.

E. He said to them, "If you tell the truth, well and good, but if not, I shall comb your flesh with iron combs."

F.   They said to him, "What shall we tell you? He was a prophet who rebuked us. We conspired against him and killed him. And lo, years have passed, but his blood has not stopped seething."

G.   He said to them, "I shall appease it."

H.   He brought before him the great sanhedrin and the lesser sanhedrin and killed them, [until their blood mingled with that of Zechariah: *Oaths are imposed and broken, they kill and rob, there is nothing but adultery and licence, one deed of blood after another* (Hos. 4:2)].

I.   Still the blood seethed. He brought boys and girls and killed them by the blood, but it did not stop seething.

J.   He brought youngsters from the schoolhouse and killed them over it, but it did not stop seething.

K.   Forthwith he took eighty thousand young priests and killed them on his account, until the blood lapped the grave of Zechariah. But the blood did not stop seething.

L.   He said, "Zechariah, Zechariah, All the best of them I have destroyed. Do you want me to exterminate them all?"

M.   When he said this, the blood forthwith came to rest.

N.   Then he considered repenting, saying, "Now if one soul matters are thus, as to that man who has killed all these souls, how much the more so!"

O.   On the spot the Holy One, blessed be He, was filled with mercy and made a gesture to the blood, which was swallowed up in place.

P.   To that Scripture refers when it says, "This was for the sins of her prophets and the iniquities of her priests, who shed in the midst of her the blood of the righteous."

A final instance allows us to follow the sages' bold recasting of the scriptural narrative, inventing dialogue, action, and motive, without the slightest interest in inserting any detail into the framework of the Scripture's picture. The following is invented out of whole cloth, no consideration is given to distinguishing the time of Moses from the time of the narrator; we detect not the slightest interest in identifying the sources of the story, e.g., in remote antiquity:

The Fathers According to Rabbi Nathan XXXIII:V.1

A.   When our fathers stood at the sea, Moses said to them, "Get up and pass through."

B.   They said to him, "We are not going to pass through until the sea is turned into passages." Moses took his staff and hit the sea, and the sea was turned into passages, as it is said, *You have hit through with rods, the head of his rulers* (Hab. 3:14).

C.   Moses said to them, "Get up and pass through."

D.   They said to him, "We are not going to pass through until the sea is turned a valley before us." Moses took his staff and hit the sea, and the sea was turned into a valley before them, as it is said, *He made a valley of the sea and caused them to pass through* (Ps. 78:13), and it is said, *As the cattle that go down into the valley, so did you lead your people* (Isa. 63:14).

E.   Moses said to them, "Get up and pass through."

F.   They said to him, "We are not going to pass through until the sea is cut into two parts before us." Moses took his staff and hit the sea, and the sea was cut into two parts before them, as it is said, *To him who divided the Red Sea into two parts* (Ps. 136:13).

G.   Moses said to them, "Get up and pass through."

H.   They said to him, "We are not going to pass through until the sea is turned to clay for us." Moses took his staff and hit the sea, and the sea was turned into clay, as it is said, *You have trodden on the sea with your horses, through the clay of mighty waters* (Hab. 3:15).

I.   Moses said to them, "Get up and pass through."

J.   They said to him, "We are not going to pass through until the sea is turned into a wilderness before us." Moses took his staff and hit the sea, and the sea was turned into a wilderness, as it is said, *And he led them through the deep as through a wilderness* (Ps. 106:9).

K.   Moses said to them, "Get up and pass through."

L.   They said to him, "We are not going to pass through until the sea is turned into pieces before us." Moses took his staff and hit the sea, and the sea was turned into pieces, as it is said, *You broke the sea in pieces by your strength* (Ps. 74:13).

M. Moses said to them, "Get up and pass through."

N. They said to him, "We are not going to pass through until the sea is turned rocks before us." Moses took his staff and hit the sea, and the sea was turned into rocks, as it is said, *You shattered the heads of the sea monsters* (Ps. 74:13).

O. Moses said to them, "Get up and pass through."

P. They said to him, "We are not going to pass through until the sea is turned into dry land before us." Moses took his staff and hit the sea, and the sea was turned into dry land, as it is said, *He turned the sea into dry land* (Ps. 66:6), and further, *But the children of Israel walked on dry land in the midst of the sea* (Ex. 14:29).'

Q. Moses said to them, "Get up and pass through."

R. They said to him, "We are not going to pass through until the sea is turned into walls before us." Moses took his staff and hit the sea, and the sea was turned into walls, as it is said, *And the waters were a wall for them on their right hand and on their left* (Ex. 14:29).

S. Moses said to them, "Get up and pass through."

T. They said to him, "We are not going to pass through until the sea [stands up and is] turned into the shape of a bottle before us." Moses took his staff and hit the sea, and the sea was turned into the shape of a bottle, as it is said, *The water stood up right like a bottle containing liquid* (Ex. 15:8).

U. Fire came down and licked up the water between the parts, as it is said, *When fire caused that which melts to disappear, and the fire lapped up the water, to make your name known to your adversaries* (Isa. 64:1).

V. And the bottles let out oil and honey into the mouths of infants, and they sucked from them, as it is said, *And he made them suck honey out of the rock* (Dt. 32:13).

W. And some say, "They produced fresh water from the sea and they drank it in the paths,

X. "(for sea water is salty),

Y. "as it is said, *Flowing streams* (Dt. 32:13), and *flowing streams* refers only to sweet water, as it is said, *A well of living water and flowing streams from Lebanon* (Song 4:15)."

The examples just now set forth can be duplicated many times over. They embody the fundamental attitudes toward historical time that characterize Rabbinic literature throughout its formative age (and beyond). To the past is imputed no autonomy; between past and present is conceived no dividing line of any kind; vastly transcending the mere flaws of anachronism, the conception that time past and time present flow together yields the principle that events may be ordered in accord with a logic quite autonomous of temporal order. The point at which we started forms a fitting conclusion to this brief experiment in the testing of a null-hypothesis. Not only do we find not a trace of historical thinking, as that mode of thought is defined in the Hebrew Scriptures. We find expressions of a quite different mode of thought altogether.

Among the several quite viable definitions of history reviewed in Chapter One, one suffices to frame the question before us, that of Jan Huizinga: "History is the intellectual form in which a civilization renders account to itself of its past."[5] We have now to ask ourselves, if history does not define the intellectual form in which Rabbinic Judaism explains to itself its own past, then precisely how does it render account to itself of its experience and existence? What alternative to historical thinking comes to full exposure? The next chapter answers this question, and the two that follow, corresponding to the last chapter and this one, then show the alternative to historical thinking when we raise precisely the questions answered, also, by history.

5. Cited by John van Seters, p. 1.

Part Three

THE PRESENCE OF THE PAST,
THE PASTNESS OF THE PRESENT

CHAPTER V

THE ENDURING PARADIGM

> We live only in the present, but this present has several dimensions: the present of past things, the present of present things, and the present of future things...
>
> Augustine, cited by LeGoff[1]

> Your years are like a single day...and this today does not give way to a tomorrow, any more than it follows a yesterday. Your today is Eternity...
>
> Augustine, *Confessions* 10:13[2]

i. *Making Connections and Drawing Conclusions in Paradigmatic Thinking*

For our sages of blessed memory, the Torah, the written part of the Torah in particular, defined a set of paradigms that served without regard to circumstance, context, or, for that matter, dimension and scale of happening. A very small number of models emerged from Scripture, captured in the sets [1] Eden and Adam, [2] Sinai and the Torah, [3] the land and Israel, and [4] the Temple and its building, destruction, and rebuilding. These paradigms served severally and jointly, e.g., Eden and Adam on its own but also superimposed upon the Land and Israel; Sinai and the Torah on its own but also superimposed upon the Land and Israel, and, of course, the Temple, embodying natural creation and its intersection with national and social history, could stand entirely on its own or be superimposed upon any or all of the other paradigms. In many ways, then, we have the symbolic equivalent of a set of two-, three-, or even four-dimensional grids. A given pattern forms a grid on its own, one set of lines being set forth in terms of, e.g., Eden, timeless perfection, in contrast against the other set of lines, Adam, temporal disobedience; but upon this grid, a comparable grid can be superimposed,

---

1. Jacques LeGoff, *History and Memory*, p. 3.
2. Cited by LeGoff, p. 13.

the Land and Israel being an obvious one; and upon the two, yet a third and fourth, Sinai and Torah, Temple and the confluence of nature and history.

By reference to these grids, the critical issues of existence, whether historical, whether contemporary, played themselves out in the system and structure of Rabbinic Judaism. In particular, I identify four models by which, out of happenings of various sorts, consequential or meaningful events would be selected, and by reference to which these selected events would be shown connected ("meaningful") and explicable in terms of that available logic of paradigm that governed both the making of connections and the drawing of conclusions. These issues pertain to the following questions, systematically developed in this chapter:

> *The Paradigm of Israel's Past, Present, and Future (= "History" in the Counterpart Structure of Historical Thinking)*: how shall we organize happenings into events? On the largest scale the question concerns the division into periods of not sequences but mere sets of happenings. Periodization involves explanation, of course, since even in a paradigmatic structure, once matters are set forth as periods, then an element of sequence is admitted into the processes of description and therefore analysis and explanation.

> *Israel and the Nations*: moving from large aggregates, bordering on abstraction, we turn to the very concrete question of how Israel relates to the rest of the world. This involves explaining not what happened this morning in particular, but what always happens, that is, defining the structure of Israel's life in the politics of this world, explaining the order of things in both the social, political structure of the world and also the sequence of actions that may occur and recur over time (the difference, paradigmatically, hardly matters).

> *Explaining the Pattern of Events: Making Connections, Drawing Conclusions*: paradigmatic thinking, no less than historical, explains matters; but the explanation derives from the character of the pattern, rather than the order of events, which governs historical explanation. Connections then drawn between one thing and something else serve to define a paradigm, rather than to convey a temporal explanation based on sequences, first this, then that, therefore this explains why that happened. The paradigm bears a different explanation altogether, one that derives from its principle of selection, and therefore the kinds of explanations paradig-

matic thinking sets forth, expressed through its principles of selection in making connections and drawing conclusions, will demand rich instantiation.

The Future History of Israel: just as studying the past is supposed to explain the present and point to the future—surely the rationale for historical thinking and writing, as Chapter One's account of principles of history in the Hebrew Scriptures showed us—so paradigmatic thinking bears the same responsibility. This concerns not so much explaining the present as permitting informed speculation about what will happen in the future. And this speculation will appeal to those principles of order, structure, and explanation that the paradigm to begin with sets forth. So future history in historical thinking and writing projects out of past and present a trajectory over time to come, and future history in paradigmatic thinking forms projects along other lines altogether.

I limit my presentation to an acutely-abbreviated exemplary repertoire, covering only the main points of a rich and complex literature of models, their definition and application. The important point throughout is that these paradigms serve to form and inform events large and small, now and then, here and there, without regard to dimensions or considerations of past, present, or future. Whatever happens that bears consequence and demands explanation is accommodated within these patterns, which serve equally well for past and present, public and private, small and large occasions. To refer once more to the analogy drawn from mathematics, fractal thinking, paradigmatic thinking in place of the historical kind finds sameness without regard to scale, from small to large and so makes possible the quest for a few specific patterns, which, controlling for chaos by claiming only a proportionate order, isolate points of regularity or recurrence and describe, analyze, and permit us to interpret them.

ii. *The Mishnah, Tosefta, Abot, Sifra, Sifré to Numbers, and Sifré to Deuteronomy*

A. THE PARADIGM OF ISRAEL'S HISTORY

Here is how the entire history of Israel, beginning to end, is to be portrayed in a systematic narrative of an other-than-historical character. The exegesis of "remember the days of yore" leads us to a review of God's relationship with the world through Israel. "Remember" here does not precipitate a review of times perceived as past—not at all. Memory is an act that is contemporary, calling up the past as a player in the acutely-present tense of today's world. Not only so, but the climax focuses not on the past but on the future. The catalogue is complete, the message clear. The past is now invoked as a model for the messianic future, which is to be anticipated. I abbreviate the passage to highlight the structure of the paradigm that takes the place of history in the description of the existence of Israel.

Sifré to Deuteronomy CCCXIII:I

1.A. [*He found him in a desert region, in an empty howling waste. He engirded him, watched over him, guarded him as the pupil of his eye. Like an eagle who rouses his nestlings, gliding down to his young, so did he spread his wings and take him, bear him along on his pinions; the Lord alone did guide him, no alien god at his side* (Dt. 32:10-12).]

B. "He found him in a desert region:"

C. This refers to Abraham.

2.A. "...He engirded him:"

B. In line with this verse: *The Lord said to Abram, "Go from your land"* (Gen. 12:1).

3.A. "...watched over him:"

B. Before Abraham came into the world, it was as if the Holy One, blessed be he, was king only over heaven alone, as it is said, *The Lord, God of heaven, who has taken me...* (Gen. 24:7).

C. But when Abraham our father came into the world, he made him king over heaven and also over earth, as it is said, *I impose an oath upon you, by the Lord, God of heaven and God of earth* (Gen. 24:2).

4.A. "...guarded him as the pupil of his eye:"

B. Even if the Holy One, blessed be he, had asked from our father Abraham the pupil of his eye, he would have given it to him, and not only the pupil of his eye, but even his soul, which was the most precious to him of all things.

C. For it is said, *Take your son, your only son, Isaac* (Gen. 22:2).

D. Now was it not perfectly self-evident to him that it was his son, his only son.

E.   But this refers to the soul, which is called "only," as it is said, *Deliver my soul from the sword, my only one from the power of the dog* (Ps. 22:21).

Sifré to Deuteronomy CCCXIII:II

1.A. Another teaching concerning, "He found him in a desert region:"

B.   This refers to Israel, as it is said, *I found Israel like grapes in a desert* (Hos. 9:10).

2.A. "...in an empty howling waste:"

B.   It was in a difficult situation, a place in which were marauding bands and thugs.

3.A. "He engirded him:"

B.   Before Mount Sinai, as it is said, *And you shall set a boundary for the people round about* (Ex. 19:12).

4.A. "...watched over him:"

B.   Through the Ten Commandments.

C.   This teaches that when the act of speech went forth from the mouth of the Holy One, blessed be he, the Israelites saw it and understood it and knew how much amplification was contained therein, how much law was contained therein, how many possibilities for lenient rules, for strict rulings, how many analogies were contained therein.

5.A. "...guarded him as the pupil of his eye:"

B.   They would fall back twelve mils and go forward twelve mils at the sound of each and every act of speech,

C.   yet they did not take fright on account of the thunder and lightning.

Sifré to Deuteronomy CCCXIII:IV

1.A. Another teaching concerning, "He found him in a desert region:"

B.   This refers to the age to come.

C.   So Scripture says, *Therefore behold, I will seduce her and bring her into the wilderness and speak tenderly to her* (Hos. 2:16).

2.A. "...in an empty howling waste:"

B. This refers to the four kingdoms, as it is said, *Who led your through the great and dreadful wilderness* (Dt. 8:15).

3.A. "He engirded him:"

B. with elders.

4.A. "...watched over him:"

B. With prophets.

5.A. "...guarded him as the pupil of his eye:"

B. He guarded them from demons, that they not injure them, in line with this verse: *Surely one who touches you touches the apple of his eye* (Zech. 2:12).

The paradigm then covers Abraham, Israel, and the world to come—person, community, age. It is not a historical paradigm, since it does not organize and classify sequential periods of the same character. What is set into relationship are three modes of being: Abraham, the model; Israel, to conform to the model; the world to come, to mark the fruition of the model.

B. ISRAEL AND THE NATIONS

The urgent question confronted by this Judaic system (among others before and since) takes up the relationship of Israel and the nations. How is Israel's place in world affairs to be accounted for? Elected by God, Israel's this-worldly fate contradicted its supernatural standing. Now this question is readily framed in this-worldly, historical terms, and a variety of conventional historical writing did just that. What makes the following important is its demonstration of the way in which paradigmatic thinking takes over historical events. The paradigm defines that which counts, among the variety of events at hand: defines, but then explains:

Sifré to Deuteronomy to Eqeb XLIII:III

7.A. Rabban Gamaliel, R. Joshua, R. Eleazar b. Azariah, and R. Aqiba were going toward Rome. They heard the sound of the city's traffic from as far away as Puteoli, a hundred and twenty *mil* away. They began to cry, while R. Aqiba laughed.

B. They said to him, "Aqiba, why are we crying while you are laughing?"

C. He said to them, "Why are you crying?"

D. They said to him, "Should we not cry, since gentiles, idolators, sacrifice to their idols and bow down to icons, but dwell securely in prosperity, serenely, while the house of the footstool of our God has been put to the torch and left a lair for beasts of the field?"

E. He said to them, "That is precisely why I was laughing. If this is how he has rewarded those who anger him, all the more so [will he reward] those who do his will."

8.A. Another time they went up to Jerusalem to Mount Scopus. They tore their garments.

B. They came to the mountain of the house [of the temple] and saw a fox go forth from the house of the Holy of Holies. They began to cry, while R. Aqiba laughed.

C. They said to him, "You are always giving surprises. We are crying while you laugh!"

D. He said to them, "But why are you crying?"

E. They said to him, "Should we not cry over the place concerning which it is written, *And the common person who draws near shall be put to death* (Num. 1:51)? Now lo, a fox comes out of it.

F. "In our connection the following verse of Scripture has been carried out: *For this our heart is faint, for these things our eyes are dim, for the mountain of Zion which is desolate, the foxes walk upon it* (Lam. 5:17-18)."

G. He said to them, "That is the very reason I have laughed. For lo, it is written, *And I will take for me faithful witnesses to record, Uriah the priest and Zechariah the son of Jeberechiah* (Isa. 8:2).

H. "And what has Uriah got to do with Zechariah? What is it that Uriah said? *Zion shall be plowed as a field and Jerusalem shall become heaps and the mountain of the Lord's house as the high places of a forest* (Jer. 26:18).

I. "What is it that Zechariah said? *Thus says the Lord of hosts, "Old men and women shall yet sit in the broad places of Jerusalem"* (Zech. 8:4).

J.   "Said the Omnipresent, 'Lo, I have these two witnesses. If the words of Uriah have been carried out, then the words of Zechariah will be carried out. If the words of Uriah are nullified, then the words of Zechariah will be nullified.

K.   "'Therefore I was happy that the words of Uriah have been carried out, so that in the end the words of Zechariah will come about.'"

L.   In this language they replied to him: "Aqiba, you have given us comfort."

Here the paradigm that Aqiba finds in Scripture tells him which data require attention, and which do not. The prosperity of the idolators matters only because the paradigm explains why to begin with we may take account of their situation. The destruction of the Temple matters also because it conforms to an intelligible paradigm. In both cases, we both select and also understand events by appeal to the pattern as defined by the working of God's will. The data at hand then yield inferences of a particular order— the prosperity of idolators, the disgrace of Israel in its very cult. We notice both facts because they both complement one another and illustrate the workings of the model: validating prophecy, interpreting experience in light of its message.

C. Explaining the Pattern of Events

The social world of Israel, subject to the historians' description and explanation, requires a more nuanced pattern than one focused solely on the Temple. There is good in the world: how to account for it? And what paradigm explains evil as well? Here is a theory of the rhythm and direction of events in this world:

Tosefta Sotah 10:1

A.   When righteous people come into the world, good comes into the world and retribution departs from the world.

B.   And when they take their leave from the world, retribution comes into the world, and goodness departs from the world.

10:2 A. When bad people come into the world, retribution comes into the world, and goodness departs from the world.

B.   And when they depart from the world, goodness comes back into the world, and retribution departs from the world.

C.   How do we know that, when righteous people come into the world, goodness comes into the world, and retribution departs from the world? Since it is said, *And he called him Noah, saying, This one will comfort us in our work and in the toil of our hands* (Gen. 5:29)....

Here is a distinct paradigm, in which the periods into which spans of natural time may be divided are set aside, and time is classified in terms of "fire anger" or retribution as against goodness.

D. THE FUTURE HISTORY OF ISRAEL

Paradigmatic thinking, finding no interest in divisions of time into past, present, and future, nonetheless possesses in the paradigm a sure guide to what will be. This we have already noted in the colloquy between Aqiba and sages concerning the prosperity of Rome and the disgrace of the Temple. The working of the paradigm at one point provides assurance that it will work equally well at some other point, and considerations of future or past time play no role at all.

iii. The Later Midrash-Compilations: Genesis Rabbah, Leviticus Rabbah, and Pesiqta deRab Kahana

A. THE PARADIGM OF ISRAEL'S HISTORY

I claimed that the paradigm does its work on all data, without regard to scale or context or circumstance. Any paradigmatic case—personality, event, idea—imposes structure and order on all data; and the structure will be the same for the small and the large, the now and the then. By this criterion of paradigmatic structuring of "history," we should be able to tell the story of Israel's past, present, and future, by appeal to any identified model, and what we need not predict is which model will yield what pattern, for the patterns are always the same, whatever the choice of the model. In the following, for a striking example, we are able to define the paradigm of Israel's history out of the lives of the founders of the Israelite tribes. This is not a matter of mere generalities. The tribal progenitors moreover correspond to the kingdoms that will rule over Israel, so there is a correspondence of opposites:

Genesis Rabbah XCIX:II.

I.A. *For the Lord God will do nothing unless he reveals his secret to his servants the prophets* (Amos 3:7).

B. Jacob linked two of his sons, corresponding to two of the monarchies, and Moses linked two of the tribes, corresponding to two of the monarchies.

C. Judah corresponds to the kingdom of Babylonia, for this is compared to a lion and that is compared to a lion. This is compared to a lion: *Judah is a lion's whelp* (Gen. 49:9), and so too Babylonia: *The first was like a lion* (Dan. 7:4).

D. Then by the hand of which of the tribes will the kingdom of Babylonia fall? It will be by the hand of Daniel, who comes from the tribe of Judah.

E. Benjamin corresponds to the kingdom of Media, for this is compared to a wolf and that is compared to a wolf. This is compared to a wolf: *Benjamin is a ravenous wolf, [in the morning devouring the prey, and at even dividing the spoil]* (Gen. 49:27). And that is compared to a wolf: *And behold, another beast, a second, like a wolf* (Dan. 7:5).

F. Then by the hand of which of the tribes will the kingdom of Media fall? It will be by the hand of Mordecai, who comes from the tribe of Benjamin.

G. Levi corresponds to the kingdom of Greece. This is the third tribe in order, and that is the third kingdom in order. This is written with a word that is made up of three letters, and that is written with a word which consists of three letters. This one sounds the horn and that one sounds the horn; this one wears turbans and that one wears helmets; this one wears pants and that one wears knee-cuts.

H. To be sure, this one is very populous, while that one is few in numbers. But the many came and fell into the hands of the few.

I. On account of merit deriving from what source did this take place? It is on account of the blessing that Moses bestowed: *Smite through the loins of them that rise up against him* (Dt. 33:11).

J.   Then by the hand of which of the tribes will the kingdom of Greece fall? It will be by the hand of sons of the Hasmoneans, who come from the tribe of Levi.

K.   Joseph corresponds to the kingdom of Edom [Rome], for this one has horns and that one has horns. This one has horns: *His firstling bullock, majesty is his, and his horns are the horns of the wild ox* (Dt. 33:17). And that one has horns: *And concerning the ten horns that were on its head* (Dan. 7:20). This one kept away from fornication while that one cleaved to fornication. This one paid respect for the honor owing to his father, while that one despised the honor owing to his father. Concerning this one it is written, *For I fear God* (Gen. 42:18), while in regard to that one it is written, *And he did not fear God* (Dt. 25:18).

L.   Then by the hand of which of the tribes will the kingdom of Edom fall? It will be by the hand of the anointed for war, who comes from the tribe of Joseph.

The same mode of thought, seeking correspondences, comparisons and contrasts, yields the scheme of the "history" of Israel in a variety of formulations.

In the following, which I regard as the best formulation of paradigmatic thinking in the present set of documents, Israel's history is taken over into the structure of Israel's life of sanctification, and all that happens to Israel forms part of the structure of holiness built around cult, Torah, synagogue, sages, Zion, and the like; I give only a small part:

Genesis Rabbah LXX:VIII.

2.A.   "As he looked, he saw a well in the field:"

B.   R. Hama bar Hanina interpreted the verse in six ways:

C.   "'As he looked, he saw a well in the field:' this refers to the well [of water in the wilderness, Num. 21:17].

D.   "'...and lo, three flocks of sheep lying beside it:' specifically, Moses, Aaron, and Miriam.

E.   "'...for out of that well the flocks were watered:' from there each one drew water for his standard, tribe, and family."

F.   "And the stone upon the well's mouth was great:"

G.   Said R. Hanina, "It was only the size of a little sieve."

H.   "'…and put the stone back in its place upon the mouth of the well:' for the coming journeys.[3]

3.A.   "'As he looked, he saw a well in the field:' refers to Zion.

B.   "'…and lo, three flocks of sheep lying beside it:' refers to the three festivals.

C.   "'….for out of that well the flocks were watered:' from there they drank of the holy spirit.

D.   "'…The stone on the well's mouth was large:' this refers to the rejoicing of the house of the water-drawing."

E.   Said R. Hoshaiah, "Why is it called 'the house of the water drawing'? Because from there they drink of the Holy Spirit."

F.   "'…and when all the flocks were gathered there:' coming from *the entrance of Hamath to the brook of Egypt* (1 Kgs. 8:66).

G.   "'…the shepherds would roll the stone from the mouth of the well and water the sheep:' for from there they would drink of the Holy Spirit.

H.   "'…and put the stone back in its place upon the mouth of the well:' leaving it in place until the coming festival.[4]

5.A.   "'As he looked, he saw a well in the field:' this refers to Zion.

B.   "'…and lo, three flocks of sheep lying beside it:' this refers to the first three kingdoms.[5]

C.   "'…for out of that well the flocks were watered:' for they enriched the treasures that were laid up in the chambers of the Temple.

D.   "'…The stone on the well's mouth was large:' this refers to the merit attained by the patriarchs.

E.   "'…and when all the flocks were gathered there:' this refers to the wicked kingdom, which collects troops through levies over all the nations of the world.

---

3.   Thus the first interpretation applies the passage at hand to the life of Israel in the wilderness.

4.   Thus the second interpretation reads the verse in light of the Temple celebration of the Festival of Tabernacles.

5.   Babylonia, Media, Greece.

F. "'...the shepherds would roll the stone from the mouth of the well and water the sheep:' for they enriched the treasures that were laid up in the chambers of the Temple.

G. "'...and put the stone back in its place upon the mouth of the well:' in the age to come the merit attained by the patriarchs will stand [in defense of Israel].[6]

7.A. "'As he looked, he saw a well in the field:' this refers to the synagogue.

B. "'...and lo, three flocks of sheep lying beside it:' this refers to the three who are called to the reading of the Torah on weekdays.

C. "'...for out of that well the flocks were watered:' for from there they hear the reading of the Torah.

D. "'...the stone on the well's mouth was large:' this refers to the impulse to do evil.

E. "'...and when all the flocks were gathered there:' this refers to the congregation.

F. "'...the shepherds would roll the stone from the mouth of the well and water the sheep:' for from there they hear the reading of the Torah.

G. "'...and put the stone back in its place upon the mouth of the well:' for once they go forth [from the hearing of the reading of the Torah] the impulse to do evil reverts to its place."[7]

So much for the correlation of the structures of the social and cosmic order with the condition of Israel. In the passage just reviewed, paradigms take over the organization of events. Time is no longer sequential and linear. What endures are the structures of cosmos and society: prophets, Zion, sanhedrin, holy seasons, and on and on. Clearly, the one thing that plays no role whatsoever in this tableau and frieze is Israel's linear history; past and future take place in an eternal present.

---

6. So the fourth interpretation interweaves the themes of the Temple cult and the domination of the four monarchies.

7. The sixth and last interpretation turns to the twin themes of the reading of the Torah in the synagogue and the evil impulse, temporarily driven off through the hearing of the Torah.

This formulation, however, cannot complete the picture, since Israel's experience encompasses the nations, on the one side, Rome, on the other. Any claim to classify spells of time has to take account of the worldly political experience of Israel; this, after all, is what sets the agenda of thought to begin with. The periodization of history can be worked out in terms of Rome's rule now, Israel's dominance in the age to come. The comparability of the two is expressed in various ways, e.g.:

Genesis Rabbah LXIII:VII.

2.A.   *Two nations are in your womb, [and two peoples, born of you, shall be divided; the one shall be stronger than the other, and the elder shall serve the younger]* (Gen. 25:23):

B.   There are two proud nations in your womb, this one takes pride in his world, and that one takes pride in his world.

C.   This one takes pride in his monarchy, and that one takes pride in his monarchy.

D.   There are two proud nations in your womb.

E.   Hadrian represents the nations, Solomon, Israel.

F.   There are two who are hated by the nations in your womb. All the nations hate Esau, and all the nations hate Israel.

G.   The one whom your creator hates is in your womb: *And Esau I hated* (Mal. 1:3).

Thus far, paradigmatic thinking has come to expression in the transformation of actions or traits of the patriarchs into markers of time, modes of the characterization of what history treats as historical. But any conception that thinking about social experience by appeal to patterns or models, rather than sequences in teleological order, requires attention to data of a narrowly historical character, e.g., persons or events paradigmatized, misconstrues the character of the mode of thinking that is before us. We may indeed make sense of Israel's social world by appeal to the deeds or traits of the patriarchs or tribal progenitors. But other statements of the Torah serve equally well as sources for paradigmatic interpretation: models of how things are to be organized and made sensible, against which how things actually are is to be measured.

B. Israel and the Nations

The foregoing takes over Israel's institutions; in what follows, we see a similar transformation of its history among the nations. Paradigmatic thinking by definition treats events of the past not as privileged but as comparable to ahistorical data. History is subordinated to the model or pattern, and the paradigm takes into itself data in no way historical in category alongside events of a world-historical order. No better example of paradigmatic thinking and its outcome in Rabbinic Judaism can be presented than the one at hand. Here, the history of Israel among the nations is foreseen by prophecy and conveyed by apocalyptic. The nations at hand are Babylonia, Media, Greece, and Rome, time and again differentiated from the first three. The matter unfolds rather majestically, introducing first one theme—the nations' role in the history of Israel, their hostile treatment of Israel—and then the next—the food taboos—finally bringing the two themes together.

We can identify each of the successive kingdoms with the four explicitly tabooed animals of Lev. 11:1-8: camel, rock badger, hare, and pig. Then, as we see, the reasons for the taboo assigned to each of them are worked out, in a triple sequence of plays on words, with special reference to the secondary possibilities presented by the words for "chew the cud," "bring up GRH." So while the first impression is that a diverse set of materials has been strung together, upon a closer glance we see quite the opposite: a purposive and careful arrangement of distinct propositions, each leading to, and intensifying the force of, the next. This is why at the climax comes the messianic reference to Israel's ultimate inheritance of the power and dominion of Rome. The following statement best represents paradigmatic thinking: encompassing, balanced, proportionate, pertinent to all the dimensions of human existence, taking account of time past, present, and future within a single, homogenizing structure. Once more, I abbreviate and give only a few of the systematic demonstrations of the same proposition:

Leviticus Rabbah XIII:V

1.A.   Said R. Ishmael b. R. Nehemiah, "All the prophets foresaw what the pagan kingdoms would do [to Israel]....

7.A.   (=Gen. R. 42:2:) Abraham foresaw what the evil kingdoms would do [to Israel].

   B.   *[As the sun was going down,] a deep sleep fell on Abraham; [and lo, a dread and great darkness fell upon him]* (Gen. 15:12).

C.   "Dread" (YMH) refers to Babylonia, on account of the statement, *Then Nebuchadnezzar was full of fury* (HMH) (Dan. 3:19).

D.   "Darkness" refers to Media, which brought darkness to Israel
through its decrees: *to destroy, to slay, and to wipe out all the Jews*
(Est. 7:4).

E.   "Great" refers to Greece.

F.   "Fell on him" (Gen. 15:12).

G.   This refers to Edom, on account of the following verse: *The earth
quakes at the noise of their [Edom's] fall* (Jer. 49:21).

8.A.   Daniel foresaw what the evil kingdoms would do [to Israel].

B.   [Daniel said], I saw in my vision by night, and behold, the four
winds of heaven were stirring up the great sea. And four great
beasts came up out of the sea, [different from one another. The
first was like a lion and had eagles' wings. Then as I looked, its
wings were plucked off...And behold, another beast, a second
one, like a bear...After this I looked, and lo, another, like a leopard...After this I saw in the night visions, and behold, a fourth
beast, terrible and dreadful and exceedingly strong; and it had
great iron teeth] (Dan. 7:3-7).

C.   If you enjoy sufficient merit, it will emerge from the sea, but if
not, it will come out of the forest.

D.   The animal that comes up from the sea is not violent, but the
one that comes up out of the forest is violent.

E.   "The first was like a lion [and had eagles' wings]" (Dan. 7:4).

F.   This refers to Babylonia.

G.   Jeremiah saw [Babylonia] as a lion. Then he went and saw it as
an eagle.

H.   He saw it as a lion: *A lion has come up from his thicket* (Jer. 4:7).

I.   And [as an eagle:] *Behold, he shall come up and swoop down as the
eagle* (Jer. 49:22).

J.   [People] said to Daniel, "What do you see?"

K.   He said to them, "I see a face like that of a lion and wings like
those of an eagle: The first was like a lion and had eagles' wings.
Then, as I looked, its wings were plucked off, and it was lifted

up from the ground [and made to stand upon two feet like a man and the heart of a man was given to it]" (Dan. 7:4).

L.   "And behold, another beast, a second one, like a bear. [It was raised up one side; it had three ribs in its mouth between its teeth, and it was told, Arise, devour much flesh]" (Dan. 7:5).

M.   This refers to Media.

N.   Said R. Yohanan, "It is like a bear."

O.   It is written, "Similar to a wolf" (DB); thus, "And a wolf was there."

P.   This is in accord with the view of R. Yohanan, for R. Yohanan said, "'Therefore a lion out of the forest [slays them] [Jer. 5:6]— this refers to Babylonia.

Q.   "'A wolf of the deserts spoils them' [Jer. 5:6] refers to Media.

R.   "'A leopard watches over their cities' [Jer. 5:6] refers to Greece.

S.   "'Whoever goes out from them will be savaged' [Jer. 5:6] refers to Edom.

T.   "Why so? *Because their transgressions are many, and their back-slidings still more* (Jer. 5:6).

U.   "After this, I looked, and lo, another, like a leopard [with four wings of a bird on its back; and the beast had four heads; and dominion was given to it]" (Dan. 7:6).

V.   This [leopard (NMR)] refers to Greece, which persisted (MNMRT) impudently in making harsh decrees, saying to Israel, "Write on the horn of an ox that you have no share in the God of Israel."

W.   "After this I saw in the night visions, and behold, a fourth beast, terrible and dreadful and exceedingly strong; [and it had great iron teeth; it devoured and broke in pieces and stamped the residue with its feet. It was different from all the beasts that were before it; and it had ten horns]" (Dan. 7:7).

X.   This refers to Edom [Rome].

9.A.   Moses foresaw what the evil kingdoms would do [to Israel].

B.   *The camel, rock badger, and hare* (Dt. 14:7).

C. The camel (GML) refers to Babylonia, [in line with the following verse of Scripture: *O daughter of Babylonia, you who are to be devastated!*] *Happy will be he who requites* (GML) *you, with what you have done to us* (Ps. 147:8).

D. "The rock badger" (Dt. 14:7)—this refers to Media.

E. Rabbis and R. Judah b. R. Simon.

F. Rabbis say, "Just as the rock badger exhibits traits of uncleanness and traits of cleanness, so the kingdom of Media produced both a righteous man and a wicked one."

G. Said R. Judah b. R. Simon, "The last Darius was Esther's son. He was clean on his mother's side and unclean on his father's side."

H. "The hare" (Dt. 14:7)—this refers to Greece. The mother of King Ptolemy was named "Hare" [in Greek: *lagos*].

I. "The pig" (Dt. 14:7)—this refers to Edom [Rome].

It would not be possible to identify a more ample statement of paradigmatic thinking about matters dealt with, also, by history. Here we transform events into patterns, patterns into encompassing structures, capable of accommodating all of the experience of humanity that the community addressed by the paradigm chooses to take into account. The basic outline set forth here governs in numerous other passages in the documents of the present group and the next set as well. One of the traits of paradigmatic thinking—by definition—is its repetitive character. Just as, in historical thinking, events are set forth because they are singular and proceed one to the next, so in paradigmatic thinking, events are set forth because they are exemplary and conform to no single linear pattern at all.

C. EXPLAINING THE PATTERN OF EVENTS

The passages just now reviewed leave no doubt about the character of the explanations of the paradigms of Israel's experience. Explanation will derive from whether or not Israel obeys the Torah, whether or not Israel studies the Torah, the character of Israel's moral condition, Israel's separating itself from the ways of the gentiles, and the like. None of these explanations will have surprised or even much puzzled the framers of the Authorized History. A single case suffices to show the character of paradigmatic explanation. Here we have quite a remarkable statement, that the great men and the nation are punished for their sins in such a way that the punishment derives from them themselves; we move along a rather strange line of people who sinned through their arrogance: Adam, Esau, Sennacherib, Hiram, Nebuchadnezzar, then: Israel. But the part of Israel under discussion is the part punished through the affliction, through natural, internal causes, of leprosy or flux. This then yields a comprehensive theory of Israel's history:[8]

Leviticus Rabbah XVIII:II.1

A. *Dread and terrible are they; their justice and dignity proceed from themselves* (Hab. 1:7).

B. "Dread and terrible" refers to the first Man.

C. *Their justice and dignity proceed from themselves* (Hab. 1:7).

D. This refers to Eve.

E. This is in line with the following verse of Scripture: *The woman whom you gave to be with me is the one who gave me of the tree, and I ate* (Gen. 3:2).

2.A. Another interpretation: "Dread and terrible" refers to Esau.

B. This is in line with the following verse of Scripture: *And Rebecca took the most coveted garments of Esau, her elder son* (Gen. 27:15).

C. *Their justice and dignity proceed from themselves* (Hab. 1:7).

D. This refers to [the prophet] Obadiah.

E. Said R. Isaac, "Obadiah was a proselyte of Edomite origin, and he gave a prophecy concerning Edom, *And there shall not be any remnant of the house of Esau for the mouth of the Lord has spoken it* (Ob. 1:18)."

3.A. Another interpretation: "Dread and terrible" refers to Sennacherib.

B. *Who among all the gods of the lands has saved their country from my hand?* (Isa. 36:20).

C. *Their justice and dignity proceed from themselves* (Hab. 1:7).

D. This refers to his sons: *And it came to pass, as Sennacherib was worshipping in the house of Nisroch, his god, [that Adrammelech and Sarezer, his sons, smote him with the sword]* (2 Kgs. 19:37).

---

8. I have abbreviated the passage as much as possible.

Once more, we notice that the appeal to one paradigm obliterates lines of structure and order that we should have anticipated, e.g., differentiation between the personal and the public, or the social and the natural. As much as lines of differentiation among spells of time (past, present, future) are obscured, so all other indicators of classification are set aside by the ones that are in play here. Indeed, the power of paradigmatic thinking is not only to order what should be classified, but also to treat as lacking all differentiation which does not require classification, yielding a reordering of all of the lines of existence, nature's and humanity's, as much as an obliteration of conventional points of differentiation, e.g., of time or space.

D. THE FUTURE HISTORY OF ISRAEL

The purpose of paradigmatic thinking, as much as historical, points toward the future. History is important to explain the present, also to help peer into the future; paradigms serve precisely the same purpose. The choice between the one model and the other, then, rests upon which appeals to the more authentic data. In that competition Scripture, treated as paradigm, met no competition in linear history, and it was paradigmatic, not historical, thinking that proved compelling for a thousand years or more. The future history of Israel is written in Scripture, and what happened in the beginning is what is going to happen at the end of time. This sense of order and balance prevailed. It comes to expression in a variety of passages:

Genesis Rabbah XLII:II.

2.A.   Said R. Abin, "Just as [Israel's history] began with the encounter with four kingdoms, so [Israel's history] will conclude with the encounter with the four kingdoms.

B.   *"Chedorlaomer, king of Elam, Tidal, king of Goiim, Amraphel, king of Shinar, and Arioch, king of Ellasar, four kings against five* (Gen. 14:9).

C.   "So [Israel's history] will conclude with the encounter with the four kingdoms: the kingdom of Babylonia, the kingdom of Medea, the kingdom of Greece, and the kingdom of Edom."

Another pattern serves as well, resting as it does on the foundations of the former. It is the familiar one that appeals to the deeds of the founders. The lives of the patriarchs stand for the history of Israel; the deeds of the patriarchs cover the future historical periods in Israel's destiny.

A single formulation of matters suffices to show how the entire history of Israel was foreseen at the outset:

Pesiqta deRab Kahana XXI:V

1.A.   R. Hiyya taught on Tannaite authority, "At the beginning of the creation of the world the Holy One, blessed be He, foresaw that the Temple would be built, destroyed, and rebuilt.

   B.   "*In the beginning God created the heaven and the earth* (Gen. 1:1) [refers to the Temple] when it was built, in line with the following verse: *That I may plant the heavens and lay the foundations of the earth and say to Zion, You are my people* (Is. 51:16).

   C.   "*And the earth was unformed* – lo, this refers to the destruction, in line with this verse: *I saw the earth, and lo, it was unformed* (Jer. 4:23).

   D.   "*And God said, Let there be light*–lo, it was built and well constructed in the age to come."

A single specific example of the foregoing proposition suffices. It is drawn from this same mode of paradigmatic thinking that imposes the model of the beginning upon the end. In the present case the yield is consequential: we know what God is going to do to Rome. What God did to the Egyptians foreshadows what God will do to the Romans at the end of time. What we have here is the opposite of cyclical history; here history conforms to a pattern, end-time recapitulated creation's events and complementing them. The following passages are a good example of how paradigmatic thinking addresses the possibility of cyclicality and insists instead upon closure:

Pesiqta deRab Kahana VII:XI.3

   A.   R. Levi in the name of R. Hama bar Hanina: "He who exacted vengeance from the former [oppressor] will exact vengeance from the latter.

   B.   "Just as, in Egypt, it was with blood, so with Edom it will be the same: *I will show wonders in the heavens and in the earth, blood, and fire, and pillars of smoke* (Job 3:3).

   C.   "Just as, in Egypt, it was with frogs, so with Edom it will be the same: *The sound of an uproar from the city, an uproar because of the palace, an uproar of the Lord who renders recompense to his enemies* (Is. 66:6).

D.   "Just as, in Egypt, it was with lice, so with Edom it will be the same: *The streams of Bosrah will be turned into pitch, and the dust thereof into brimstone, and the land thereof shall become burning pitch* (Isa. 34:9). *Smite the dust of the earth that it may become lice* (Ex. 8:12).

E.   "Just as, in Egypt, it was with swarms of wild beasts, so with Edom it will be the same: *The pelican and the bittern shall possess it* (Isa. 34:11).

F.   "Just as, in Egypt, it was with pestilence, so with Edom it will be the same: *I will plead against Gog with pestilence and with blood* (Ezek. 38:22).

G.   "Just as, in Egypt, it was with boils, so with Edom it will be the same: *This shall be the plague wherewith the Lord will smite all the peoples that have warred against Jerusalem: their flesh shall consume away while they stand upon their feet* (Zech. 14:12).

H.   "Just as, in Egypt, it was with great stones, so with Edom it will be the same: *I will cause to rain upon Gog...an overflowing shower and great hailstones* (Ezek. 38:22).

I.   "Just as, in Egypt, it was with locusts, so with Edom it will be the same: *And you, son of man, thus says the Lord God: Speak to birds of every sort...the flesh of the mighty shall you eat...blood shall you drink...you shall eat fat until you are full and drink blood until you are drunk* (Ezek. 39:17-19).

J.   "Just as, in Egypt, it was with darkness, so with Edom it will be the same: *He shall stretch over Edom the line of chaos and the plummet of emptiness* (Isa. 34:11).

K.   "Just as, in Egypt, he took out their greatest figure and killed him, so with Edom it will be the same: *A great slaughter in the land of Edom, among them to come down shall be the wild oxen* (Isa. 34:6-7).

The exposition of matters through the small sample given here leaves no doubt as to precisely how paradigmatic thinking recast Israel's recorded experience ("history") into a set of models that pertained everywhere and all the time. The picture does not change in the final set of documents, which we shall survey only cursorily.

*iv. The Latest Midrash-Compilations: Song of Songs Rabbah, Ruth Rabbah,
Esther Rabbah I, and Lamentations Rabbah*

A. THE PARADIGM OF ISRAEL'S HISTORY

The history of Israel in Egypt, at the Sea, at Sinai, and subjugated by the
gentile kingdoms, ends when the redemption will come. The entire message
of history is contained within these theological statements:

Song of Songs Rabbah XVIII.i

4.A. Another explanation of the phrase, "I am a rose of Sharon":

B. Said the Community of Israel, "I am the one, and I am beloved.

C. "I am the one who was hidden in the shadow of Egypt, but in
a brief moment the Holy One, blessed be He, brought me
together to Raamses, and I blossomed forth in good deeds like
a rose, and I said before him this song: *You shall have a song as in
the night when a feast is sanctified* (Isa. 30:29)."

5.A. Another explanation of the phrase, "I am a rose of Sharon":

B. Said the Community of Israel, "I am the one, and I am beloved.

C. "I am the one who was hidden in the shadow of the sea, but in
a brief moment I blossomed forth in good deeds like a rose, and
I pointed to him with the finger (opposite to me): *This is my
God and I will glorify him* (Ex. 15:2)."

6.A. Another explanation of the phrase, "I am a rose of Sharon":

B. Said the Community of Israel, "I am the one, and I am beloved.

C. "I am the one who was hidden in the shadow of Mount Sinai,
but in a brief moment I blossomed forth in good deeds like a
lily in hand and in heart, and I said before him, *All that the Lord
has said we will do and obey* (Ex. 24:7)."

7.A. Another explanation of the phrase, "I am a rose of Sharon":

B. Said the Community of Israel, "I am the one, and I am beloved.

C. "I am the one who was hidden and downtrodden in the shadow
of the kingdoms. But tomorrow, when the Holy One, blessed
be He, redeems me from the shadow of the kingdoms, I shall
blossom forth like a lily and say before him a new song: *Sing to
the Lord a new song, for he has done marvelous things, his right hand
and his holy arm have wrought salvation for him* (Ps. 98:1)."

In this final set of documents, a single statement serves to bring to a climax
and conclusion a pattern of reading Scripture that proves uniform, beginning
to end. Here is a summary statement of matters. The merit of the fathers
sustains the children for generations to come; what Abraham did provoked
an exact correspondence in God's dealing with the Israelites in Egypt; Israel's
history spins out the effects of the ancestors' merits:

The Fathers According to Rabbi Nathan XXXIII:III.1

A.   In response to the ten trials inflicted upon Abraham, our father,
      from all of which he emerged whole, the Holy One, blessed be
      he, performed ten miracles for his children in Egypt.

B.   And corresponding to them also, the Holy One, blessed be he,
      brought ten plagues on the Egyptians in Egypt.

C.   And corresponding to them also, ten miracles were done for the
      Israelites at the sea.

D.   And corresponding to them also, he brought ten plagues on the
      Egyptians at the sea.

B. ISRAEL AND THE NATIONS

Just as the paradigm transforms history, so paradigmatic thinking takes
over the natural symbols of Scripture and makes those symbols into further
statements of the same model that prevails elsewhere. Here the pattern is a
simple one. God surrounds Israel with enemies, but in the end, when the
last empire collapses, God will save Israel. This pattern comes to expression
not in a paradigmatization of historical events, but in an equivalent treatment
of poetic formulations of a different order altogether:

Song of Songs Rabbah XIX:i

9.A. R. Abihu interpreted the cited verse to speak of the coming
      redemption:

B.   "['As a lily among brambles':] when the lily is among the bram-
      bles, it is hard for the farmer to pick it, so what does he do? He
      burns the thorns around it and plucks it.

C.   "So: *The Lord has commanded concerning Jacob that those who are
      around him should be his enemies* (Lam. 1:17),

D.   "for example, Halamo [which is gentile, is enemy] to Naveh [which is Israelite], Susita to Tiberias, Qastra to Haifa, Jericho to Nauran, Lud to Ono.

E.   "This is in line with the following verse of Scripture: *This is Jerusalem. I have set her in the midst of the gentiles* (Ezek. 5:5).

F.   "Tomorrow, when redemption comes to Israel, what will the Holy One, blessed be He, do to them? He will bring a flame and burn the area around Israel.

G.   "This is in line with this verse: *And the peoples will be as burnings of lime, as thorns cut down that are burned in fire* (Isa. 33:12).

H.   "And in the same connection: *The Lord alone shall lead him* (Dt. 32:12)."

10.A.   R. Abun said, "Just as a lily wilts so long as the hot spell persists, but when the dew falls on it, the lily thrives again,

B.   "so Israel, so long as the shadow of Esau falls across the world, Israel wilts,

C.   "but when the shadow of Esau passes from the world, Israel will once more thrive:

D.   "*I shall be like the dew for Israel. It will blossom as the lily* (Hos. 14:6)."

We see that not only historical events are made to serve the purposes of the paradigm; all of Scripture is taken over and reworked for that one purpose.

C. Explaining the Pattern of Events

The history of Israel and humanity is written in terms of sin, specifically, impulses to do evil. Whatever happens forms a response of God to Israel's behavior, and nothing takes place that violates that pattern and rule:

The Fathers According to Rabbi Nathan XXXVIII:VI.1

A.   Exile comes into the world because of those who worship idols, because of fornication, and because of bloodshed, and because of the neglect of the release of the Land [in the year of release].

B.   On account of idolatry, as it is said: *And I will destroy your high places...and I will scatter you among the nations* (Lev. 26:30,33).

C.   Said the Holy One, blessed be he, to Israel, "Since you lust after idolatry, so I shall send you into exile to a place in which there is idolatry.

D.   Therefore it is said, *And I will destroy your high places...and I will scatter you among the nations.*

The rest is predictable. We once more are struck by the uniformity and simplicity of the paradigm, alongside the elaborate and detailed manner in which it is elaborated.

D. The Future History of Israel

The Exodus and conquest, the return to Zion, and the ultimate salvation then form the entire corpus for which the language of the Song serves as metaphor. The Messiah's coming, drawing to a close the gentiles' rule, will be marked by this-worldly historical events, spelled out in the following:

Song of Songs Rabbah XXX:iv

2.A.   "Arise, my love, my fair one, and come away, for lo, the winter is past":

B.   Said R. Azariah, "'...for lo, the winter is past': this refers to the kingdom of the Cutheans [Samaritans], which deceives the world and misleads it through its lies: *If your brother, son of your mother ̄oentices you* (Dt. 13:7)."

3.A.   "...the rain is over and gone":

B.   this refers to the subjugation.

4.A.   "The flowers appear on the earth":

B.   the conquerors appear on the earth.

C.   Who are they?

D.   R. Berekhiah in the name of R. Isaac: "It is written, *And the Lord showed me four craftsmen* (Zech. 2:3),

E.   "and who are they? Elijah, the royal Messiah, the Melchizedek, and the military Messiah."

We need hardly tarry over a passage such as this, which mixes the historical and the cultic, the social and the natural.

v. Paradigmatic Thinking about "History"

This survey of the way in which paradigmatic thinking comes to expression now permits a more general statement of matters. As a medium of organizing and accounting for experience, history—the linear narrative of singular events intended to explain how things got to their present state and therefore why—does not enjoy the status of a given. Nor does historical thinking concerning the social order self-evidently lay claim on plausibility. It is one possibility among many. For reasons proposed in the opening chapter, historical thinking—sequential narrative of one-time events—presupposes order, linearity, distinction between time past and time present, and teleology, among data that do not self-evidently sustain such presuppositions. Questions of chaos intervene; the very possibility of historical narrative meets a challenge in the diversity of story-lines, the complexity of events, the bias of the principle of selection of what is eventful, of historical interest, among a broad choice of happenings. Narrative history first posits a gap between past and present, but then bridges the gap; why not entertain the possibility that to begin with there is none? These and similar considerations invite a different way of thinking about how things have been and now are, a different tense structure altogether.

A way of thinking about the experience of humanity, whether past or contemporary, that makes other distinctions than the historical ones between past and present and that eschews linear narrative and so takes account of the chaos that ultimately prevails, now competes with historical thinking. Paradigmatic thinking, a different medium for organizing and explaining things that happen, deals with the same data that occupy historical thinking, and this is why when we refer to paradigmatic thinking, the word "history" gains its quotation marks: it is not a datum of thought, merely a choice; contradicting to its core the character of paradigmatic thinking, the category then joins its opposite, paradigm, only by forming the oxymoron before us: paradigmatic thinking about "history."

The category, "history," as conventionally defined and as further realized in the Authorized History of Scripture, Genesis through Kings, therefore forms merely one way of addressing the past in order to find sense and meaning therein. Clearly, with its emphasis on linear, irreversible events and the division between past and present, history's is not the way taken by Rabbinic Judaism in organizing Israel's experience. The very opposite traits predominate. Rabbinic literature contains no sustained historical or biographical narrative, only anecdotes, makes no distinction between past and present but melds them. But this writing, resting as it does on the Hebrew Scriptures, then presents a paradox. A set of writings of a one-sidedly historical character, the Hebrew Scripture deriving from ancient Israel finds itself expounded in an utterly ahistorical way by its heirs, both Judaic and Christian.

For, it is clear, the records represented as recording events of the past—the written Torah, the Old Testament—form a massive presence in Judaism and Christianity respectively. So history in the conventional sense formed a principal mode of thinking in the documents that educated the framers of the dual Torah of Judaism and the Bible of Christianity. It must follow, both of those religions defined as an important component of God's revelation to humanity documents that by all accounts constituted systematic statements of the past: history-books above all else. But, we shall now see, these accounts of the past, received into the entire Torah, oral and written, of Judaism, and into the Bible, Old and New Testaments, of Christianity, received a reading that I define as one of a paradigmatic character. Given the fundamentally historical character of the Hebrew Scriptures transformed into written Torah and Old Testament, respectively, we must identify the basis for the rereading imposed thereon by the heirs.

That is to say, what Scripture ("written Torah," "Old Testament") yields for Rabbinic Judaism is not one-time events, arranged in sequence to dictate meaning, but models or patterns of conduct and consequence. These models are defined by the written Torah or the Old Testament (read in light of the perspective of the Oral Torah or the New Testament). No component of the paradigm we shall consider emerges from other than the selected experience set forth by Scripture. But the paradigms are at the same time pertinent without regard to considerations of scale and formulated without interest in matters of singular context. Forthrightly selective—this matters, that is ignored—the principle of selection is not framed in terms of sequence; order of a different sort is found.

The models or paradigms that are so discerned then pertain not to one time alone—past time—but to all times equally—past, present and future. Then "time" no longer forms an organizing category of understanding and interpretation. The spells marked out by moon and sun and fixed stars bear meaning, to be sure. But this meaning has no bearing upon the designation of one year as past, another as present. The meaning imputed to the lunar and solar marking of time derives from the cult, on the one side, and the calendar of holy time, on the other: seven solar days, a Sabbath; a lunar cycle, a new month to be celebrated, the first new moon after the vernal equinox, the Passover, and after the autumnal, Tabernacles. Rabbinic Judaism tells time the way nature does and only in this way; events in Rabbinic Judaism deemed worth recording in time take place the way events in nature do. What accounts for the difference, between history's time and paradigmatic time as set forth here is a conception of time quite different from the definition of historical time that operates in Scripture: the confluence of the nature's time and history's way of telling time: two distinct chrono-graphies brought together, the human one then imposed upon the natural one.

In Rabbinic Judaism (and not there alone), the natural way of telling time precipitated celebration of nature. True, those same events were associated with moments of Israel's experience as well: the exodus above all. The language of prayer, e.g., the Sabbath's classification as a memorial to creation and also a remembrance of the exodus from Egypt, leaves no doubt on the dual character of the annotation of time. But the exodus, memorialized hither and yon through the solar seasons and the Sabbath alike, constituted no more a specific, never-to-be-repeated, one-time historical event, part of a sustained narrative of such events, than any other moment in Israel's time, inclusive of the building and the destruction of the Temple. Quite to the contrary, linking creation and exodus classified both in a single category; the character of that category—historical or paradigmatic—is not difficult to define; the exodus is treated as consubstantial with creation, a paradigm, not a one-time event.

It follows that this Judaism's Israel kept time in two ways, and the one particular to Israel (in the way in which the natural calendar was not particular to Israel) through its formulation as a model instead of a singular event was made to accord with the natural calendar, not vice versa. That is to say, just as the natural calendar recorded time that was the opposite of historical, because it was not linear and singular and teleological but reversible and repetitive, so Israel kept time with reference to events, whether past or present, that also were not singular, linear, or teleological. These were, rather, reconstitutive in the forever of here and now—not a return to a perfect time but a recapitulation of a model forever present. Israel could treat as comparable the creation of the world and the exodus from Egypt (as the liturgy commonly does, e.g., in connection with the Sabbath) because Israel's paradigm (not "history") and nature's time corresponded in character, were consubstantial and not mutually contradictory, in the terms introduced in Chapters One and Two.

And this consubstantiality explains why paradigm and natural time work so well together. Now, "time" bears a different signification. It is here one not limited to the definition assigned by nature—yet also not imposed upon natural time but treated as congruent and complementary with nature's time. How so? Events—things that happen that are deemed consequential—are eventful, meaningful, by a criterion of selection congruent in character with nature's own. To understand why I think so, we must recall the character of the Torah's paradigms:

> [1] Scripture set forth certain patterns which, applied to the chaos of the moment, selected out of a broad range of candidates some things and omitted reference to others.

> [2] The selected things then are given their structure and order by appeal to the paradigm, or described without regard to scale by the fractal, indifference to scale forming the counterpart to the paradigm's indifference to context, time, circumstance.

> [3] This explains how some events narrated by Scripture emerged as patterns, imposing their lines of order and structure upon happenings of other times.

And this yields the basis for the claim of consubstantiality:

> [4] Scripture's paradigms—Eden, the Land—appealed to nature in another form.

The result, then, I state with heavy emphasis: *the rhythms of the sun and moon are celebrated in the very forum in which the Land, Israel's Eden, yields its celebration to the Creator.* The rhythmic quality of the paradigm then compares with the rhythmic quality of natural time: not cyclical, but also not linear. Nature's way of telling time and the Torah's way meet in the Temple: its events are nature's, its story a tale of nature too. Past and present flow together and join in future time too because, as in nature, what is past is what is now and what will be. The paradigms, specified in a moment, form counterparts to the significations of nature's time.

These events of Israel's life (we cannot now refer to Israel's "history")—or, rather, the models or patterns that they yielded—served as the criteria for selection, among happenings of any time, past, present, or future, of the things that mattered out of the things that did not matter: a way of keeping track, a mode of marking time. The model or paradigm that set forth the measure of meaning then applied whether to events of vast consequence or to the trivialities of everyday concern alone. Sense was where sense was found by the measure of the paradigm; everything else lost consequence. Connections were then to be made between this and that, and the other thing did not count. Conclusions then were to be drawn between the connection of this and that, and no consequences were to be imputed into the thing that did not count.

This is not an ideal way of discovering or positing order amid chaos; much was left, if not unaccounted for, then not counted to begin with. We cannot take for granted that the range of events chosen for paradigms struck everyone concerned as urgent or even deserving of high priority, and we also must assume that other Israelites, besides those responsible for writing and preserving the books surveyed here, will have identified other paradigms altogether. But—for those who accorded to these books authority and self-evidence—the paradigm encompassing the things that did conform to the pattern and did replicate its structure excluded what it did not explain. So it left the sense that while chaos characterized the realm beyond consciousness, the things of which people took cognizance also made sense—a self-fulfilling system of enormously compelling logic. For the system could explain what it regarded as important, and also dismiss what it regarded as inconsequential or meaningless, therefore defining the data that fit and dismissing those that did not.

When religion takes into account the failure of linear logic with its premise of order, it does so through the formation of paradigms or models of order, which, as I said, in Chapter One, describe how things are, whether large or small, whether here or there, whether today or in a distant past or an unimaginable future. Not all things are orderly, but some things are. Fractal thinking (in mathematics) and paradigmatic thinking (in religion) makes possible the quest for a few specific patterns, which isolate points of regularity or recurrence and describe, analyze, and even in the face of chaos and disorder, permit us to interpret them. Proportionality as much as context gives way; the cosmic and the humble conform to the same paradigm (much as is the case *mutatis mutandis* in fractal mathematics).

This is the reward of paradigmatic thinking in place of historical; but it also represents a considerable charge. Why was it worthwhile? At stake in the paradigm is discerning order and regularity not everywhere—in the setting of these books, "everywhere" defied imagining—but in some few sets of happenings. The scale revised both upward and downward the range of concern: these are not all happenings, but they are the ones that matter—and they matter very much. Realizing or replicating the paradigm, they uniquely constitute events, and, this is why by definition, these are the only events that matter. Paradigmatic thinking about past, present, and future ignores issues of linear order and temporal sequence because it recognizes another logic all together, besides the one of priority and posteriority and causation formulated in historical terms.

This mode of thinking, as its name states, appeals to the logic of models or patterns that serve without regard to time and circumstance, on the one side, or scale, on the other. The sense for order unfolds, first of all, through that logic of selection that dictates what matters and what does not. And, out of the things that matter, this same logic defines the connections of things, so forming a system of description, analysis, and explanation that consists in the making of connections between this and that, but not the other thing, and the drawing of conclusions from those ineluctable, self-evident connections. At stake now is the definition of self-evidence: how did our sages know the difference between event and mere happening?

Part Four

FROM HISTORY TO PARADIGM

CHAPTER VI

NARRATIVE: THE CONDUCT OF THE CULT AND THE STORY OF THE TEMPLE

In the intense struggle to relate to the tradition, Israel encounters again through the medium of her memory the God of the past. Her attention no longer focuses on specific historical events, but on the divine reality who imprinted her history…To remember is to grasp after, to meditate upon, indeed, to pray to God.

Brevard S. Childs[1]

i. The Paradigmatic Counterpart to Continuous Narrative

History enjoys no monopoly on narrative, since seeking in the past explanations for the present condition of things does not alone provoke telling the tale of another time, or this time, or all times. Paradigmatic thinking also yields narrative, including stories about events and persons. But while historical thinking produces its sustaining narrative of one-time events and biography, paradigmatic thinking utilizes a different way of organizing narrative to tells its story and invoke the lives of named individuals as well. History's insistence on the linear sequence and singular character of events accounts for the kind of writing it requires. Paradigmatic thinking, predictably, assigns no consequence to the linearity of events and does not see value in long sequences of events either. Persons as such, with lives with beginnings, middles, and ends, enjoy no privilege in the realm of writing. But paradigmatic thinking in part utilizes the form of narrative to set forth its paradigms.

The writing expresses the structure of the thinking. The paradigm takes the place, in the expression of the sense and order of things, of the notion that events relate to one another. What captures such order as unpredictable affairs produce is the paradigmatic event, and this stands in no sequence with other such patterns or models of how things are.

The result, for writing, must be the exemplary story, meant to convey the model on its own, and not in relationship, linear or otherwise, with other

---

1. Brevard S. Childs, *Memory and Tradition in Israel* (London, 1962: SCM Press), pp. 64-65.

such exemplary moments. The character of the writing corresponds to the quality of the thinking, and paradigmatic thinking calls forth the writing down of exemplary cases. The location of those cases—not in sustained narratives but in other contexts altogether—will then be dictated also by the requirements of this same mode of thought. The realization of the paradigm, without regard to time or context, then is conveyed through the story standing on its own: the moment viewed alone. The linear sequences of events that sustaining narrative sets forth serve no purpose and they elicit a deep sense of not so much improbability as irrelevance: how many events must be strung together to state the paradigm anyhow? Linear logic dismissed, the world of fractal shapes (in mathematics) or models (in religion) is comprised by one-time, all-time episodes, and this accounts for the anecdotal character of story-telling in the Rabbinic writings.

The following is an example of the kind of writing of narrative we find in the account of the history of the cult, exemplifying the manner in which these narratives are taken over into the law. The collection of grain for the sheaf of new grain that is waved on the fifteenth of Nisan as an indication that the new crop of grain may be utilized is formulated in the same narrative style; here is how history—how things "used" to be done—shades over into paradigm—how things are to be done:

Mishnah-tractate Menahot 10:3

A.   How did they do it?

B.   Agents of the court go forth on the eve of [the afternoon before] the festival [of Passover].

C.   And they make it into sheaves while it is still attached to the ground, so that it will be easy to reap.

D.   And all the villagers nearby gather together there [on the night after the first day of Passover], so that it will be reaped with great pomp.

E.   Once it gets dark [on the night of the sixteenth of Nisan], he says to them, "Has the sun set?"

F.   They say, "Yes."

G.   "Has the sun set?"

H.   They say, "Yes."

I.   "[With] this sickle?"

J. They say, "Yes."

K. "[With] this sickle?"

L. They say, "Yes."

M. "[With] this basket?"

N. They say, "Yes."

O. "[With] this basket?"

P. They say, "Yes."

Q. On the Sabbath, he says to them, "[Shall I reap on] this Sabbath?"

R. They say, "Yes."

S. "[Shall I reap on] this Sabbath?"

T. They say, "Yes."

U. "Shall I reap?"

V. They say, "Reap."

W. "Shall I reap?"

X. They say, "Reap"—

Y. three times for each and every matter.

Z. And they say to him, "Yes, yes, yes."

AA. All of this [pomp] for what purpose?

BB. Because of the Boethusians, for they maintain, "The reaping of the [barley for] the *omer* is not [done] at the conclusion of the festival."

Mishnah-tractate Menahot 10:4

A. They reaped it,

B. and they put it into baskets.

C. They brought it to the court [of the Temple].

D. "They did parch it in fire, so as to carry out the requirement that it be parched with fire [Lev. 2:14]," the words of R. Meir.

E. And sages say, "With reeds and with stems of plants do they [first] beat it [to thresh it] so that it not be crushed.

F. "And they put it into a tube.

G. "And the tube was perforated, so that the fire affect all of it."

H.   They spread it out in the court, and the breeze blows over it.

I.   They put it into a grist mill and took out therefrom a tenth *ephah*,

J.   which is sifted through thirteen sieves [M. 6:7].

K.   And the residue is redeemed and eaten by anyone. And it is liable for the dough offering, but exempt from tithes.

L.   R. Aqiba declares it liable for both dough offering and tithes.

M.   He came [on the sixteenth of Nisan] to the tenth [*ephah* of flour], and put in its oil and frankincense [M. 6:3].

N.   He poured in [oil] and mingled it and waved it.

O.   And he brought it near [M. 5:6] and took out the handful and offered it up.

P.   And the residue is eaten by the priests.

This protracted narrative shows that our sages had the capacity to tell long stories. But here do we have a one-time story, to be included in some larger sustained narrative? The language portrays how things were done, which also is how things are done. But how is the passage situated? It is in the account not of the annual cycle of rites of the Temple, e.g., a sustained narrative from beginning to end, but rather the tractate of the law on grain-offerings, of which the waving of the sheaf of new grain (the *omer*) is an important instance. So the narrative is subordinated to a topical program, preserving an episode or anecdote only in language that conveys the exemplarity of the anecdote. Here is paradigmatic thinking's counterpart to a historical story, and here is how this same thinking uses narrative style to re-present an element of its large model. Since the generative paradigm concerns the social counterpart to nature's order, namely, the Temple and its cult, it is not surprising that the narrative style utilized in the case before us characterizes accounts of the cult, for the Mishnah, and the Temple's course through time ("history"), for the exegetical compilations.

It is in this context that the matter of narrative in the Rabbinic writings has to be taken up. What we should now expect to find is what we do in fact identify: narratives of the cult and of the Temple. In the earlier phase of the documents, the former predominates, in the later, the latter. So far as stories concern history, it is the history of the Temple. So far as anecdotes portray events, they are events in the actual cult. Between these two matters, which are one, we account for nearly the entire corpus of narratives before us.

ii. The Mishnah, Tosefta, Abot, Sifra, Sifré to Numbers, and Sifré to Deuteronomy

A. THE CONDUCT OF THE CULT

A survey of the Mishnah and closely related documents yields a striking result. Most, though not all, of the narratives of these writings concern the conduct of the Temple cult. By collecting all of the narratives on the cult that the Mishnah sets forth, moreover, we are able to reconstruct an orderly and quite encompassing account of how the cult is carried on. The language of the narrative appeals to continuous action: this is how things are done ordinarily, always, regularly; here is the pattern of action. The character of the narrative—episodic, always dictated by the context of the story, never by the relationship of one story to another—corresponds to the requirement of paradigmatic thought. The negative requirement is already clear. We do not conceive of the world in linear sequences of events, so we also do not present the model of cult event and action in linear sequences either. But how are we supposed to set out the exemplary tales? The answer is in the larger context of the law's presentation of the details of the model in all their splendor. What establishes the context of narrative, for the paradigm, is the larger setting of the exposition of the paradigm; to this exposition, narrative is useful, not constitutive. This is why the narrative of the cult is not continuous and sustained but episodic. But it does exhibit traits of coherence, in this one episode preserves the stylistic character of the next, and all of the episodes, put together, do portray a single cogent cultic program.

To show the character of the narrative, I lay out severely-abbreviated parts of the various abstracts, in the order, in the Mishnah, in which they occur. The form is the historical present tense, expressed in brief declarative sentences, and very commonly, with the use of dialogue. This form is different from the ordinarily formal character of the Mishnah, on the one side, and it is utilized, in the Mishnah, only for the exposition of episodes in the enduring, sustaining life of the cult. Our first episode involves a historical account of the annual sequence of events connected with the maintenance of the Temple house and its public offerings:

Mishnah-tractate Sheqalim 1:1, 3

A.   On the first day of Adar they make public announcement concerning [payment of] sheqel dues and concerning the sowing of mixed seeds [Lev. 19:19, Dt. 22:9].

B.   On the fifteenth day of that month they read the Megillah [Scroll of Esther] in walled cities.

C.   And they repair the paths, roads, and immersion pools.

1:3 A.   On the fifteenth of that same month [Adar] they set up money changers' tables in the provinces.

B.   On the twenty-fifth [of Adar] they set them up in the Temple.

C.   Once they were set up in the Temple, they began to exact pledges [from those who had not paid the tax in specie].

Mishnah-tractate Sheqalim 3:4

A.   He took up [heave offering] the first time and covered [the residue] with coverings.

B.   [He took up the heave offering] a second time and covered [the residue] with covers.

C.   But the third time he did not cover [it up].

D.   [He covered the first two times], lest he forget and take up heave offering from those sheqels from which heave offering already had been taken.

E.   He took up the heave offering the first time on behalf of the Land of Israel, the second time on behalf of cities surrounding it, and the third time on behalf of Babylonia, Media, and the more distant communities.

The same tractate presents a broad range of information on the organization and management of the temple. Most of it is framed in "historical" terms, meaning, specific offices and the names of specific persons who occupied those offices; continuous-present tense descriptions of how things were and what procedures were followed.

The following entries serve as a narrative of the conduct of the Temple rite of the Day of Atonement; they form the basis for a historical account of how things were done on that occasion:

Mishnah-tractate Yoma 1:1

A.   Seven days before the Day of Atonement they set apart the high priest from his house to the councillors' chamber.

B.   And they [also] appoint another priest as his substitute,

C.   lest some cause of invalidation should overtake him.

Mishnah-tractate Yoma 1:2

A. All seven days he tosses the blood, offers up the incense, trims the lamp, and offers up the head and hind leg [of the daily whole offering],

B. But on all other days, if he wanted to offer it up he offers it up.

Mishnah-tractate Yoma 1:3

A. They handed over to him elders belonging to the court, and they read for him the prescribed rite of the Day [of Atonement].

B. And they say to him, "My lord, high priest, you read it with your own lips,

C. "lest you have forgotten—or never [even] learned it to begin with."

D. On the eve of the Day of Atonement at dawn they set him up at the eastern gate and bring before him bullocks, rams, and sheep,

E. so that he will be informed and familiar with the service.

Mishnah-tractate Yoma 1:4

A. All seven days they did not hold back food or drink from him.

B. [But] on the eve of the Day of Atonement at dusk they did not let him eat much,

C. for food brings on sleep.

Mishnah-tractate Yoma 1:5

A. The elders of the court handed him over to the elders of the priesthood,

B. who brought him up to the upper chamber of Abtinas.

C. And they imposed an oath on him and took their leave and went along.

D. [This is what] they said to him, "My lord, high priest: We are agents of the court, and you are our agent and agent of the court.

E. "We abjure you by Him who caused His name to rest upon this house, that you will not vary in any way from all which we have instructed you."

F.   He turns aside and weeps.

G.   And they turn aside and weep.

What we have in this continuous present-tense story is, of course, an account of how things are done in general, not a specific, "historical" event. But the intrusions of the more characteristic Mishnah-style—abstract, general formulation of a rule in legal terms, with equivalently-framed contrary opinion—show us the true character of what is before us, which is narrative as a mode of presenting the law. The paradigmatic account of time and explanation of Israel's world finds legal and narrative modes of writing equally suitable; but when it comes to the cult, it is narrative that takes over. Let us continue our survey with the picture of how the rite is carried forward:

Mishnah-tractate Yoma 3:1

A.   The supervisor said to them, "Go and see whether the time for slaughtering the sacrifice has come."

B.   If it has come, he who sees it says, "It is daylight!"

C.   Mattithiah b. Samuel says, "[He says], 'Has the whole east gotten light?'

D.   "'To Hebron?'

E.   "And he says, 'Yes.'"

Mishnah-tractate Yoma 3:4

3:4 A.   They spread out a linen sheet between him and the crowd.

B.   He took off his clothes, went down, immersed, came up, and dried off.

C.   They brought him golden garments, and he put them on, and he sanctified his hands and feet.

D.   They brought him the daily whole offering.

E.   He cut [the windpipe and gullet], and another priest completed the slaughtering on his behalf.

F.   He received the blood and tossed it.

G.   He went in to offer up the incense offering of the morning, to trim the lamps, and to offer up the head and limbs, baked cakes, and wine.

Mishnah-tractate Yoma 3:6

A.   They brought him to the Parvah chamber, and it was in the sanctuary.

B.   They spread out a linen sheet between him and the crowd.

C.   He sanctified his hands and feet and took off his clothes.

D.   R. Meir says, "He took off his clothes, sanctified his hands and feet."

E.   He went down, immersed, came up, and dried off.

F.   They brought him white clothes.

G.   He put them on and sanctified his hands and feet.

Nearly the whole of the tractate's presentation of the rite of the Day of Atonement follows the same story-telling mode. The tractate forms the counterpart to Leviticus 16 (indeed, it is incomprehensible without a line-by-line reading in the context of that chapter). But while Leviticus 16 says what Aaron should do—"with this shall he come to the sanctuary...," "and he shall do such and so..."—the Mishnah-chapter's authorship prefers to use the descriptive past tense or the continuous present tense, interchangeably; the jussive (or its counterpart) never occurs. The stylistic preference stems from a more profound theory of how paradigms form the organizing, enduring principle of reality: this is how things were or are done, and out of the narrative we derive an account of how they are always to be replicated.

Along these same lines, Mishnah-tractate Tamid presents a sustained narrative of the conduct of the cult in the presentation of the daily whole offering:

Mishnah-tractate Tamid 1:1

A.   In three places do the priests keep watch in the sanctuary: in the room of Abtinas, in the room of the flame, and in the room of the hearth.

B.   The room of Abtinas and the room of the flame were upper rooms.

C.   And youngsters keep watch there.

D.   The room of the hearth is vaulted.

E.   And it was a large room surrounded by a raised pavement of stone.

F.   And the mature members of the [priestly] household [of the day] sleep there [on the raised pavement],

G.   with the keys to the courtyard in their charge,

H.   and [there sleep] the fledgling priests, each with his mattress on the ground.

I.   They [the priests] did not sleep in the consecrated garments.

J.   But they spread them out, double them over, lay them down under their heads, and cover themselves with their own clothes.

K.   [If] one of them should have a nocturnal emission of semen, he goes out, proceeding along the passage that leads below the building

L.   and lamps flicker on this side and on that

M.   until he reaches the immersion room.

N.   And there was a fire there,

O.   and a privy in good taste.

P.   And this was its good taste: [if] he found it locked, he knows that someone is there; [if he found it] open, he knows that no one is there.

Q.   He went down and immersed, came up and dried off, and warmed himself by the fire.

R.   He came and sat himself down with his brothers, the priests [in the house of the hearth],

S.   until the gates were opened.

T.   He goes out, proceeding on his way [home].

Nearly the whole of the tractate unfolds in the same narrative style. Not only rites involving the community, but those concerning individuals are presented in the same way. Here is the presentation of the trial of the wife accused of adultery:

Mishnah-tractate Sotah 1:4

A.   They would bring her up to the high court which is in Jerusalem and admonish her as they admonish witnesses in a capital crime.

B.   They say to her, "My daughter, much is done by wine, much is done by joking around, much is done by kidding, much is done by bad friends. For the sake of the great Name which is written in holiness, do it so that it will not be blotted out by water [Num. 5:23]."

C.   And they tell her things which neither she nor the family of her father's house should be hearing.

Mishnah-tractate Sotah 1:5

A.   [Now] if she said, "I am unclean," she gives a quittance for her marriage contract [which is not paid over to her], and goes forth [with a writ of divorce].

B.   And if she said, "I am clean," they bring her up to the eastern gate, which is at the entrance of Nicanor's Gate.

C.   There it is that they force accused wives to drink the bitter water,

D.   and they purify women after childbirth and purify lepers.

E.   And a priest grabs her clothes—if they tear, they tear, and if they are ripped up, they are ripped up—until he bares her breast.

F.   And he tears her hair apart [Num. 5:18].

G.   R. Judah says, "If she had pretty breasts, he did not let them show. And if she had pretty hair, he did not pull it apart."

Another cultic rite concerned the preparation of purification-water in line with the requirements of Numbers Chapter Nineteen. The presentation of the theme follows the usual legal style. But when it comes to the account of the rite itself, the tractate's framers turned to the narrative style and set forth an exemplary account of an episode:

Mishnah-tractate Parah 3:1

A.   Seven days before the burning of the cow, they separate the priest who burns the cow from his house, [bringing him] to the chamber which faces the northeast corner of the Temple building, and it was called the stone house.

B.   And they sprinkle on him all seven days [with a mixture] from all the purification [waters] which were there.

Mishnah-tractate Parah 3:2

A. There were courtyards in Jerusalem, built on rock, and under them was a hollow, [which served as a protection] against a grave in the depths.

B. And they bring pregnant women, who give birth there, and who raise their sons there.

C. And they bring oxen, and on them are doors, and the youngsters sit on top of them, with cups of stone in their hands.

D. [When] they reached the Siloam, they descended and filled them, and mounted and sat on top of them.

Mishnah-tractate Parah 3:3

A. They came to the Temple mount and dismounted.

(B. The Temple mount and the courtyards—under them is a hollow against a grave in the depth.)

C. And at the door of the courtyard was set up a flask of [ashes of] purification [rites done in the past].

D. And they bring a male sheep, and tie a string between its horns, and they tie a stick or a bushy twig on the head of the rope, and one throws it into the flask.

E. And one hits the male, and it starts backward.

F. And one takes [the ashes spilled onto the stick] and mixes as much of it as could be visible on the surface of the water.

G. R. Yosé says, "Do not give the Sadducees an opportunity to cavil. But he takes it and mixes it."

Mishnah-tractate Parah 3:7

A. And the elders of Israel would precede [them] on foot to the Mount of Olives.

B. And a house for immersion was there.

C. And they would render the priest who burns the cow unclean, because of the Sadducees,

D. so that they should not say, "It is done by one on whom the sun has set."

Mishnah-tractate Parah 3:8

A.   They placed their hands on him, and they say to him, "My lord, High Priest, immerse one time."

B.   He descended and immersed, emerged and dried off.

Another purification rite involved the leper. The presentation of the cultic rite at the same time ignores Leviticus Chapter Fourteen and also replicates its facts, in Mishnah-style and language:

Mishnah-tractate Negaim 14:1

A.   How do they purify the leper?

B.   He would bring a new flask of clay, and put in it a quarter-log of living water, and bring two undomesticated birds.

C.   He slaughtered one of them over the clay utensil and over the living water.

D.   He dug [a hole] and buried it before him [the leper].

E.   He took cedar-wood, hyssop, and scarlet wool and bound them together with the ends of the strip [of wool] and brought near to them the tips of the wings and the tip of the tail of the second [bird].

F.   He dipped [them in the blood of the slaughtered bird] and sprinkled [the blood] seven times on the back of the hand of the leper.

G.   There are some who say, "On his forehead."

H.   And thus did he sprinkle on the lintel of the house on the outside.

These cases represent a considerably large corpus of narratives in the Mishnah. Nearly all of the narratives of this document portray either the conduct of the cult or incidents in connection with the Temple cult.

B. THE STORY OF THE TEMPLE

For paradigmatic thinking to yield a sustained picture of time, counterpart to history's, however, it will not suffice to tell us only about the cult. We need a picture of events spread over time, to help us organize not only the here and now of incidents in conformity to models, but the sustained sequence of months, seasons, and solar years. These too require presentation in a large-scale framework, or paradigmatic thinking will not accomplish all of the systemic goals that historical thinking, for its part, carries out. The

Mishnah presents the story of the Temple, not only the narrative of its rites. The larger documents then expand on this story, leaving to the legal writings the exposition of the details of the cult. Here is a general, large-scale theory of the decline of the times, which could have guided the writing of history in a conventional sense: and this, predictably, involves the cult and the Temple as the key to everything else:

Mishnah-tractate Sotah 9:15

R. Pinhas b. Yair says, "When the Temple was destroyed, associates became ashamed and so did free men, and they covered their heads. And wonder workers became feeble. And violent men and big talkers grew strong. And none expounds and none seeks [learning] and none asks. Upon whom shall we depend? Upon our Father in heaven."

R. Eliezer the Great says, "From the day on which the Temple was destroyed, sages began to be like scribes, and scribes like ministers, and ministers like ordinary folk. And the ordinary folk have become feeble. And none seeks. Upon whom shall we depend? Upon our Father in heaven. With the footprints of the Messiah: presumption increases. The vine gives its fruit and wine at great cost. And the government turns to heresy. There is no reproof, and dearth increases. The gathering place will be for prostitution. And Galilee will be laid waste. And the Gablan will be made desolate. And the men of the frontier will go about from town to town, and none will take pity on them. And the wisdom of scribes will putrefy. And those who fear sin will be rejected. And the truth will be locked away. Children will shame elders, and elders will stand up before children. For the son dishonors the father and the daughter rises up against her mother, the daughter-in-law against her mother-in law; a man's enemies are the men of his own house (Mic. 7:6). The face of the generation in the face of a dog. A son is not ashamed before his father. Upon whom shall we depend? Upon our Father in heaven."

Not only the cult, but the Temple, therefore, is situated in time; but we note that, when it is, the story-telling gives way to a different mode of expression altogether; we find no dialogue, and specific incidents no longer occur. Here is a way of thinking about time that is at once systematic and also other than episodic.

In the setting of the history of the Temple, the Mishnah and related writings include specific events, not only general accounts of the conduct of the cult in narrative form. These specific events deal with named persons and they speak of one-time anecdotes. But when the Mishnah records particular persons and incidents, these commonly concern Temple rules and rites, as in the following cases:

Mishnah-tractate Yoma 2:2

A.   M'SH S: There were two who got there at the same time, running up the ramp.

B.   And one shoved his fellow.

C.   And he [the other] fell and broke his foot.

D.   When the court saw that the matter was dangerous, they ordained that the right of clearing off the ashes from the altar should be apportioned only by lot.

The treatment of the above story in the Tosefta shows how a received ("historical") incident will be expanded, dialogue invented, the narrative reshaped to make its point in a more dramatic way. A single example suffices to show how sages amplified received incidents and recast them in dramatic form:

Tosefta Yoma 1:12

A.   There was this incident: *There were two who got there at the same time, running up the ramp. One shoved the other* [M. Yoma 2:2A-B], within four cubits [of the altar]. The other then took out a knife and stabbed him in the heart.

B.   R. Sadoq came and stood on the steps of the porch and said,

C.   "Hear me, O brethren of the house of Israel! Lo, Scripture says, *If in the land which the Lord your God gives you to possess, any one is found slain, lying in the open country, and it is not known who killed him, then your elders and your judges shall come forth, and they shall measure the distance to the cities which are around him who is slain* (Dt. 21:1-2).

D.   "Come, let us measure to find out for what area it is appropriate to bring the calf, for the sanctuary, or for the courts!"

E.   All of them moaned after his speech.

F.   And afterward the father of the youngster came to them, saying,
      "O brethren of ours! May I be your atonement. His [my] son
      is still writhing, so the knife has not yet been made unclean."

G.   This teaches you that the uncleanness of a knife is more grievous
      to Israelites than murder. And so it says, *Moreover Manasseh shed
      very much innocent blood, till he had filled Jerusalem from one end to
      the other* (2 Kgs. 21:16).

H.   On this basis they have said, "Because of the sin of murder the
      Presence of God was raised up, and the sanctuary was made
      unclean."

The picture then is clear: narrative concerned the cult in particular, the
Temple in general. The paradigmatic mode of thought dealt in its own way
with the past, treating it as not subject to distinction from the present at all.
This same mode of thought, in the case of this Judaism, identified as the
source and focus of its model the Temple in particular. In due course we
shall ask why Rabbinic Judaism should mark time by appeal to this paramount topic.

*iii. The Later Midrash-Compilations: Genesis Rabbah, Leviticus Rabbah, and
      Pesiqta deRab Kahana*

A. THE CONDUCT OF THE CULT

The Midrash compilations contain narratives of a historical character,
e.g., events, and, for the cult, they provide narratives of a historical character
about the one source of story that matters, which is, the Temple, hence,
episodes in the Temple's paradigmatic existence. This collection of documents yields no stories about the conduct of the cult. But it provides something still more indicative: the history of the Temple.

B. THE STORY OF THE TEMPLE

The second and third sets of documents tell the story of the Temple,
rather than the cult, but principally in one chapter of its history alone, the
destruction. This one event defines the task of narrative, and, while as we
have already noted in prior chapters, we find in these compilations a variety
of narratives, e.g., concerning Bar Kokhba and the like, it is the destruction
of the Temple, in 586 and again in 70, that takes up most of the narrative
energies of the authors of compositions that are collected in these compos-

ites. Only a few examples are necessary to portray the character of narrative. Here is the story of Titus's conquest of Jerusalem:

Leviticus Rabbah XXII:III.2.

A. Titus, the wicked, entered the house of the Holy of Holies, with his sword drawn in his hand. He pierced the two veils.

B. He took two whores and spread out a scroll of the Torah under them and had intercourse with them on the altar.

C. And his "sword" came out covered with blood.

D. There are some who say that it was covered with the blood of the holy things.

E. And there are some who say it was covered with the blood of the goat of the Day of Atonement.

F. He began to curse and blaspheme toward Heaven, saying, "The one who makes war with a king in the desert and conquers him is not the same as the one who makes war with the king in his own palace and conquers him!"

G. What did he do? He collected all the utensils of the House of the Sanctuary and put them into a single net and lowered them into a boat. When he had embarked, a powerful storm broke over the sea.

H. He said, "It appears to me that the power of the god of this nation rules only in water.

I. "The generation of Enosh was punished only by water, the generation of the Flood was punished only by water, the generation of the Dispersion was punished only by water, Pharaoh and his entire army were punished only by water. So as to me, when I was in his house and in his domain, he could not stand against me. Now he has gotten here before me."

J. Said to him the Holy One, blessed be he, "By your life! By the least of all the creatures that I created in the six days of Creation I shall exact punishment of that wicked man."

K. Forthwith the Holy One, blessed be he, signaled to the sea and it ceased from its fury.

L. When [Titus] reached Rome, the citizens of Rome came out and celebrated him: "Victor over the barbarians!"

M.	Then they heated the bath for him and he went in and bathed. When he came out, they mixed for him a double shot of a drink for after the bath.

N.	The Holy One, blessed be he, prepared a gnat for him, and it flew into his nose. It just kept eating its way in until it reached his brain. It began to bore into his brain.

O.	He said, "Call the physicians to split open that wicked man's [my] skull, so that I may know how the god of that nation exacted vengeance from that wicked man [me]."

P.	Forthwith they called the physicians, who split open his skull, and they found in it something like a young pigeon, weighing two litres.

Q.	Said R. Eleazar b. R. Yosé, "I was there, and they put the pigeon on one side and two litre weights on the other side, and each one weighed exactly what the other did."

R.	They took it and put it into a bowl. Just as this one [the pigeon] changed, so that one changed.

S.	When the gnat flew off, the soul of the wicked Titus flew off.

Here is a single example of the kind of sustained narrative that, in the second set of documents, is devoted to the destruction of the Temple. Not fixed into a larger story of Israel's history in the manner of the framers of the Authorized History, Genesis through Kings, the account at hand can certainly have formed a larger chapter in such a sustained history. But it is situated in an exegetical setting instead, serving to make a point in the presentation of a paradigm, even though the point is expressed through a sequence of one-time, and not-exemplary, actions.

iv. The Latest Midrash-Compilations: Song of Songs Rabbah, Ruth Rabbah, Esther Rabbah I, and Lamentations Rabbah

A. THE CONDUCT OF THE CULT

This collection of documents yields no stories about the conduct of the cult.

B. THE STORY OF THE TEMPLE

What we observe in the foregoing set of exegetical compilations recurs here. Once more, a few examples suffice to show how matters are set forth. First, we account for the tragic events that led to the destruction, and this we do in the style of historians, by telling about a one-time event in explaining the condition of the world today. In the following the destruction of Jerusalem was caused by a particular incident:

Lamentations Rabbati Parashah CII:i

4.A.   There was the case of a man who was in Jerusalem and made a banquet. He said to his messenger, "Go and bring my friend, Qamsa."

B.   He went and brought to him his enemy, Bar Qamsa.

C.   The latter came in and sat himself among the invited guests.

D.   He said to him, "How is it that you are my enemy and you sit in my house? Get out of here."

E.   He said to him, "Since I have come, don't humiliate me. I'll pay you back for the cost of whatever I eat."

F.   He said to him, "You are not to recline at this banquet."

G.   He said to him, "Get out of here."

H.   R. Zechariah b. Eucolus, who was there, could have stopped it, but he did not intervene.

I.   Bar Qamsa then left. He said to himself, "Since these are feasting in luxury, I am going to go and inform against them at court."

J.   What did he do? He went to the ruler and said to him, "These sacrifices that you contribute [to the temple] they eat, and they offer others in their place [which are inferior]."

K.   He put him off [rejecting the charge].

L.   He went back to him again and said, "These sacrifices that you contribute [to the temple] they eat, and they offer others in their place [which are inferior]. If you don't believe me, send a hyparch and some animals for sacrifice back with me, and you will know that I am not a liar."

M.   He sent with him a third-grown calf.

N.   While they were on the way, the hyparch dozed off, and the other got up by night and secretly blemished the beasts [so that they could not be offered on the altar and had to be replaced].

O.   When the priest saw it, he substituted others for them.

P.   The king's agent said to him, "Why don't you offer the animals I brought?"

Q.   He said to him, "I'll do it tomorrow."

R.   He came on the third day, but the priest had not offered them up.

S.   He sent word to the king, "That matter involving the Jews is true."

T.   The king immediately came forth against the temple and destroyed it.

U.   This is the source of the saying, "Because of the difference between Qamsa and Bar Qamsa, the temple was destroyed."

V.   R. Yosé said, "It was the self-effacing character of Zechariah b. Eucolus that burned the temple."

Events of course serve a paradigm when they illustrate a rule not bound by time or location. The fall of Betar is similarly accounted for by appeal to the moral failures of the generation. The past yields rules, and the rules govern without regard to occasion or time. The reason that the past is present, the present cast backward as well, is that rules apply under all circumstances; the paradigm takes over and obliterates considerations of time, because it provides a still more compelling explanation than that of history. Here is a restatement of precisely the point given above:

Lamentations Rabbati Parashah CXVIII:i.2.

A.   For fifty-two years Betar held out after the destruction of the house of the sanctuary.

B.   And why was it destroyed?

C.   Because they lit lamps on the occasion of the destruction of the house of the sanctuary.

3.A.   They say that there was a place in which the councillors of Jerusalem would go into session, in the center of the city.

B.   Someone from Betar would go up for prayer, and they would say, "Do you want to become a councillor?"

C.   He would say, "No."

D.   Someone would say to him, "Would you like to become a city magistrate?"

E.   He would say, "No."

F.   Some would say to him, "I heard you have an estate for sale. Will you sell it to me?"

G.   He would say, "I never thought of it."

H.   The Jerusalemite would write out and send a deed of possession to the steward of the man from Betar, bearing the message, "If so-and-so [the owner] comes, do not let him enter the property, for he has sold it to me."

I.   The man would exclaim, "Would that my leg had been broken, so that I could not have gone up to that corner."

J.   This illustrates the verse of Scripture: *Our steps were checked, [we could not walk in our squares. Our doom is near, our days are done, alas, our doom has come]* (Lam. 4:18).

We see that, had our sages wished to write continuous history, they certainly had the capacity to frame suitable chapters for their history-book. But this was not their purpose. The "narrative" of the destruction of the Temple served paradigmatic, not historical purposes—like all other data, without regard to its character as historical, political, cultic, or personal.

This brief survey of narratives in the several sets of compilations shows how the history of the Temple, with special attention to its destruction, supplied the occasion for narrative.[2] A survey of the same documents will turn up no other event than the story of the Temple, in particular, its destruction, to which sustained and systematic attention is devoted, just as the law of the Mishnah will produce no other topic, besides the cult of the Temple, for which narrative style is the selected medium for the presentation of the law. We have now to explain why paradigmatic writing in narrative

2.   To save space, I have not reproduced the enormous tales of Yohanan ben Zakkai that occur, respectively, in Lamentations Rabbati Parashah XXXIX:ii.1 and The Fathers According to Rabbi Nathan IV:VI.1. These provide excellent instances of how the latest Midrash-compilations portray, in a protracted and sustained narrative, the destruction of the Temple. But they do not change the picture supplied by what I have cited.

form, e.g., stories of actions of a certain classification or of events of a particular venue, past or present, selects as its principal topic the story of the cult
and the Temple.

v. Paradigmatic Literature: Nature's Time Instead of History's: Episode in Place of Continuous Narrative

The presentation of the narratives is not sustained and sequential, as are
the narratives of Scripture—the Authorized History of Genesis through
Kings forming one of the great, sustained histories in world literature.
Rather, what we have are brief chapters, narratives with a beginning,
middle, and end, which can be located where needed, without regard to
the inner order and sequence of groups of chapters. The topic and formulation of these narrative units present no surprises; dialogue commonly bears
the burden of the tale; a simple and unadorned style does the rest. But their
placement requires notice. As is clear, no effort is invested into joining one
chapter to another. Rather, the narratives are situated in the setting of, for
the legal documents, legal topics, for the exegetical ones, exegesis. Episodes
remain anecdotal, not joined into sustained narratives, for instance,
complete documents like the documents of law and exegesis, for an obvious
reason. A mode of thought that does not conceive of sustained, linear,
connected narratives also is not going to choose as a medium of expression
the documentary formulation of narrative.

Rabbinic literature does not contain history books because its conception of time does not make provision for sustained history; rabbinic literature
treats stories as exemplary because its fundamental mode of thought
comprises rules that demand only exemplary cases, paradigms to be replicated, but not tales to be told by way of explanation of how things are. Once
people do not think historically, they do not write history; and when they
think paradigmatically, they produce the counterpart of the paradigm,
which is, on the one side, law and realizations in narrative of law; and, on
the other side, cases that serve in the exegesis of the permanent, enduring,
constantly replicated, received text. Law and exegesis of Scripture serve as
two media for the re-presentation of paradigms. Then stories, subordinated
to law and exegesis, do their service too.

The simple character of the paradigm defines the use of narrative in paradigmatic formulation and expression. First, the topic of the narrative is
readily predicted, when we recall the way in which our sages of blessed
memory contemplate time. To recapitulate: history's time imposes its own

divisions, or taxic indicators as to the measurement and character of spans of time indicated by nature, upon nature's time. History's insistence on the singularity of events and their logical, orderly and irreversible sequence takes over nature's patterned moments, replaceable and reversible in character. Now, paradigmatic thinking formulates its conception of time by counting time in line with nature. Time is divided into nature's sequences—lunar, solar alike. But then, paradigmatic time attaches to nature's sequences the components of its own order: Eden/Adam = Land of Israel/Land, to take a principal one. Then how shall we tell time? It must be in that correlation between nature and the generative and exemplary moment's of Israel's life that culminated in the place and program realized in the Temple, whence lines of structure and order emanate through space and time alike. For that is where nature is celebrated and, at the same time, the orderly structure of Israel's life is also commemorated.

The rites are organized to respond to natural time: new moons, seasons, the day, the seven-day week, and the like. The offerings signify the day ("daily whole offering"), week (Sabbath and additional offerings), month (New Moon offerings), and seasons (Passover-Pentecost, then Tabernacles in particular, for spring and fall. The personnel of the Temple are organized in linear relationship with the social order of Israel (as imagined by the priests, at any rate), with the orderly hierarchy of society culminating in the priesthood itself. The place and the actions being permanent ("eternal"), moreover, the eternity of nature finds its counterpart in the eternity of the celebration of nature in Jerusalem: the highest place in natural geography set aside to return to God the products of the holy land in age succeeding age. One axis of the paradigm runs from nature represented by Eden and Adam, through the Temple, represented by the Land of Israel and Israel's priesthood. The other runs from Sinai, represented by the Torah, through the sage. If narrative, sequential and linear history is subsumed under and replaced by continuous nature, then narrative, linear biography gives way to nature's counterpart, the Torah, with episodic lives focused upon the embodiment of the virtues of the Torah or the negotiation of its issues, as we shall now see.

CHAPTER VII

BIOGRAPHY: EXEMPLARY PATTERN
IN PLACE OF THE LIVES OF SAGES

i. The Paradigmatic Counterpart to Biography

Paradigmatic episodes in place of distinctive and individual biography yielded the model of the life framed by the Torah: a life lived within the rules of nature, but facing outward toward supernature, a life transcending the natural world, measured by moments of transcendence: advent into the Torah, the active and complex realm of negotiation within the Torah, virtue measured by the Torah and responding to the special vices that the Torah can nurture, and death in the supernatural setting that overcomes nature: not dirt to dirt, but soul to Heaven, along with the Torah. To make this statement, narrative yielding an account of the realization of nature in the cult cannot have served; only anecdotes about persons convey the message of how Israel through the Torah transcends nature. The question asked at Eden for Adam, restated in the Land of Israel for Israel, finds its answer in the Torah, and its resolution in the person of the sage. Exemplary pattern was the only way to say so.

Linear and sustained narrative of the events of the social entity ("nation," in general, "Israel" in particular) corresponds to biography, in the present context, lives of sages. Just as the historical mode of thought generates the composition of sustained narratives, so practitioners of history also will write lives of persons, e.g., Moses, or at least continuous tales of a biographical character, with some sort of connected narrative, real or contrived, to give the impression of personal history. Practitioners of the historical sciences—Josephus for instance—give us not only biography but autobiography, just as much as philosophers or theologians of history, Augustine being the best example, will supply a biographical counterpart to a history. It obviously follows that where history leads, biography follows close behind.[1]

---

1. This chapter does not provide a significant sample of biographical stories, but selects only a few to make with special force the points that pertain. For a complete repertoire, I

Exemplary anecdotes, the counterpart to singular events, are also the counterpart to biography. Yet paradigmatic thinking about the social order yields not only anecdotes instead of continuous history. It also attends to the representation of persons, but solely for paradigmatic purposes and in a manner calculated to yield not continuous narrative but that which is here deemed of definitive consequence: a restatement, in individual terms, of the paradigm. And this is to be expected. For once time loses its quality of continuity and sequentiality, marking time calls upon other indicators of order and division than those demanded by the interplay of nature's telling time and humanity's interposing its rhythms. Lives of persons, beginning to end, need not be told; indeed, cannot be told, for the same reason that sequential, continuous narrative also cannot be constructed.

The paradigm, formed out of the congruence of humanity's and nature's time, rather than their incongruity, will identify, out of the moments presented by a human life, those that gain importance by appeal to the paradigm itself. The natural course of a human life, from death to birth, bears no more meaning in the amplification of the paradigm than the passage of empires, viewed as singular, or the story of a reign or a dynasty, viewed in its own terms. These matter, for paradigmatic thinking, when the pattern or model determines; otherwise, they do not register at all. Of the many empires of antiquity, four counted to the paradigm of Rabbinic Judaism, Babylonia, Media, Greece, and Rome. What of Parthians, what of Sassanian, certainly weighty as Greece and Rome and for long centuries quite able to hold their own (with their huge Jewish populations) against Greece and Rome? They did not count and so were not counted.

We know, of course, why they did not matter: they never intersected with the natural life of the holy people, Israel, in the holy land, the Land of Israel; they never threatened Jerusalem, in the way in which Babylonia, Greece (in Seleucid times), and Rome did. This principal part of the paradigm points to one main principle of selection in the range of events. Working back from events to the principle of selection that operates within the model governing Rabbinic Judaism's disposition of time, we are able to define out of what is selected the operative criterion: the congruence of the

---

refer the reader to my *From Text to Historical Context in Rabbinic Judaism: Historical Facts in Systemic Documents*. Because the stories are readily in hand, I am able to introduce only a few of the most important and representative ones to portray the character and uses of stories about named persons ("biography") in the documents surveyed here.

selected model to nature's time. Then what is to be said about the paradigm's points of interest in human lives? Since the paradigm will not elicit interest in a continuous life and so will not produce biography let alone autobiography, at what points will the model encompass episodes in human lives? To state the question more simply: where, when, and why, will individual persons make a difference, so as to warrant the writing down of details of personal lives?

Asked in this way, the question produces a ready answer, in three parts, two of which take but a moment for their exposition. First, does the paradigm before us take an interest in the lives of persons? We shall see that it does. Second, if it does, then at what point in a human life will anecdotes preserve the model for exemplary conduct, defining, then, the principle of selection, out of a human life as much as out of the happenings of the social world, of what counts? The principle of selection, at each point, somehow relates to the Torah. And, third, how does the paradigm emerge, having received a richer and more nuanced definition, out of the encounter with individual lives?

The answer is that the model that governs the formation of the Rabbinic writings examined here certainly does narrate episodes in personal lives, not only events in the social order. Second, the points of special interest are [1] how an individual studies the Torah; [2] remarkable deeds of virtue in the individual's life; [3] how the individual dies. Learning, virtue, and a dignified death—these form the paradigmatic points of interest.

ii. *The Mishnah, Tosefta, Abot, Sifra, Sifré to Numbers, and Sifré to Deuteronomy*

A. BIRTH. FIRST PUBLIC APPEARANCE

These documents contain no reference to the birth or beginnings of sages; rarely is reference made to private life, outside of the setting of the Torah. Individuals on their own terms bear nothing of interest to the paradigm. This explains why birth-stories, accounts of up-bringing, early signs of distinction, and other conventions of standard historical biography play slight if any role in the documents overall, and none in the first group of them.

People matter for two reasons. First, they represent the exemplary study and realization of the Torah. Second, they stand for the concrete realization of virtue. The first point at which an individual will emerge, therefore, will be when he presents himself as a master of the Torah, a principal authority, endowed with powerful reason or compelling tradition. This explains why we do find attention to the first public moment in the lives of principal figures.

In the first compilation of writings, one account of the first appearance of a principal player is set forth: Hillel's confrontation, in the Temple, with an opposition group. Just as paradigmatic history takes its sights on the conduct of the cult and the history of the Temple, so interest in individuals ("biography" being no more appropriate a word in this setting than "history") begins with their initial self-manifestation in the Temple and in connection with the cult. The self-manifestation-story involves Hillel, telling how the combination of reasoning and mastery of traditions elevated him to the position of patriarch. (To highlight what is to be learned in the example at hand, I have italicized the words that for my argument are operative):

Tosefta Pisha 4:13

A. One time the fourteenth of Nisan coincided with the Sabbath.

B. *They asked Hillel the Elder, "As to the Passover-sacrifice, does it override [the prohibitions of] the Sabbath?"*

C. He said to them, "Now do we have only a single Passover-sacrifice in the course of the year which overrides [the prohibitions] of the Sabbath? We have many more than three hundred Passover-sacrifices in the year, and they all override [the prohibitions of] the Sabbath."

D. All the people in the courtyard ganged up on him.

E. He said to them, "The daily whole-offering is a public offering, and the Passover-sacrifice is a public offering. Just as the daily whole-offering is a public offering and overrides [the prohibitions of] the Sabbath, so the Passover-sacrifice is a public offering [and] overrides [the prohibition of] the Sabbath."...

F. *"And furthermore: I have received a tradition from my masters* that the Passover-sacrifice overrides [the prohibitions of the Sabbath]— and not [solely] the first Passover but the second Passover-sacrifice, and not [solely] the Passover-sacrifice of the community but the Passover sacrifice of an individual."

G. *They said to him, "What will happen with the people who did not bring knives and Passover-lambs to the sanctuary?"*

H. *He said to them, "Do not worry about them. The holy spirit rests upon them. If they are not prophets, they are disciples of prophets."*

I. What did the Israelites do in that hour?

J. He whose animal for the Passover-sacrifice was a lamb had hid it [the knife] in its wool.

K. He whose animal for the Passover-sacrifice was a goat had tied it between its horns.

L. So they had [in any event] brought both their knives and their Passover-sacrifices to the sanctuary.

M. And they sacrificed their Passover-sacrifices.

N. *On that very day they appointed Hillel to be patriarch, and he taught them laws of Passover.*

Only the italicized passages are particular to the named authority; everything else is impersonal, and the anecdote does little more than provide a dramatic setting for the presentation of logical arguments. Without most of the details, the passage could have been phrased in a completely impersonal way with: named sages + he said to him...he said to him.

What is important for our study should not be missed. It is, first, that the story has no interest in any personal traits of Hillel; he is not characterized in any way. What he says or does is cited, but any other name will have served equally well. What individuates Hillel is his election to the patriarchate, but what accounts for this election is not his personal traits but his mastery of the skills of argument, on the one side, and his knowledge of traditions from acknowledged authorities, on the other. What we learn from this story is not biography but an anecdote concerning the social order; a named sage matters when he is not individual but exemplary.

B. TORAH

The "Torah" defines not an inert taxon, that is, something that one studies, that which is acted upon; nor even a uniform one, that is, something that, when mastered, produces predictable results, that which acts but in one way only, not as a source of differentiation, in context, individuation. The use of "Torah" as a taxon in the presentation of persons for the purposes of the governing paradigm, is as a point of differentiation—the one active and uncertain, therefore individuating component of the corpus of personal stories. Stories in which Torah-study and its consequences figure in the present part of the documents yield a variety of particular points. This fact is reinforced by the clear allegation that studying the Torah does not guarantee virtue and may not even hold a sage within the fold. The Torah locates arenas for negotiation, areas where nothing is certain, though everything is of worth.

The first exemplary story indicates that studying the Torah produces supernatural consequences, not only those affecting virtue or public order:

Tosefta Hagigah 2:1

2:1 A. M'SH B: Rabban Yohanan b. Zakkai was riding on an ass, and R. Eleazar b. Arakh was driving the ass from behind.

B. He [Eleazar] said to him, "Rabbi, repeat for me a chapter of the works of the Chariot."

C. He said to him, "Have I not ruled for you to begin with that they do not repeat [the tradition] concerning the Chariot for an individual, unless he was a sage and understands of his own knowledge"

D. He said to him, "Now may I lay matters out before you?"

E. He said to him, "Say on."

F. R. Eleazar b. Arakh commenced and expounded concerning the works of the Chariot.

G. Rabban Yohanan b. Zakkai got off his ass, wrapped himself in his cloak, and the two of them sat down on a rock under an olive tree, and [Eleazar] laid matters out before him.

H. [Yohanan] got up and kissed him on his head and said to him "Blessed be the Lord, God of Israel, who gave to Abraham, our father, a son who knows how to understand and expound upon the glory of his father who is in heaven.

I. "Some preach nicely but do not practice nicely, or practice nicely but do not preach nicely.

J. "Eleazar b. Arakh preaches nicely and practices nicely.

K. "Happy are you, O Abraham, our father, for Eleazar b. Arakh has gone forth from your loins,

L. "who knows how to understand and expound upon the glory of his Father who is in heaven."

Here we really do find a matter of individuation; Eleazar b. Arakh is distinguished by his exposition, so that Heaven itself responds to what he says. Not only so, but what is exemplified here is the power of the Torah within, and over, the natural world. Mastery of the Torah affords, and also signifies, natural power, not only social virtue. The Torah then stands for the union of nature and society, forming the bridge from one to the other. It is here that this natural union of nature's time and Israel's time comes to fruition; it is in the person of the sage that the union takes place. In our context, the one thing that an exposition of the Torah yields is a supernatural event, vastly transcending the limits of the Torah. Nothing in the conception of an inert Torah, that which is to be studied, prepares us for the conception of the Torah as an active verb, yielding results for nature as much as society and personality.

This claim, represented in behalf of the governing paradigm in the anecdote ("life") of the sage but not in the presentation of the story ("history") of the social order of Israel, does not stand by itself. To the contrary, the union of nature and society in the Torah's principal embodiment, the sage, produces unpredictable results:

Tosefta Hagigah 2:3

A. Four entered the garden [Paradise]: Ben Azzai, Ben Zoma, the Other [Elisha ben Abbuya], and Aqiba.

B. One gazed and perished, one gazed and was smitten, one gazed and cut down sprouts, and one went up whole and came down whole.

C. Ben Azzai gazed and perished.

D. Concerning him Scripture says, *Precious in the sight of the Lord is the death of his saints* (Ps. 116:15).

E. Ben Zoma gazed and was smitten.

F. Concerning him Scripture says, *If you have found honey, eat only enough for you, lest you be sated with it and vomit it* (Prov. 25:16).

G. Elisha gazed and cut down sprouts.

H. Concerning him Scripture says, *Let not your mouth lead you into sin* (Qoh. 5:5).

2:4 A. R. Aqiba went up whole and came down whole.

B. Concerning him Scripture says, *Draw me after you, let us make haste. The king has brought me into his chambers* (Song of Songs 1:4).

We cannot take for granted, then, that mastery of the Torah by itself secures for the sage the status of exemplar. The same passage completes its account with the explanation of the fate of one master:

Tosefta Hagigah 2:6

A. M'SH B: R. Joshua was walking in a piazza, and Ben Zoma was coming toward him.

B. When he reached him, he did not greet him.

C. He said to him, "From whence and whither, Ben Zoma?"

D. He said to him, "I was concentrating upon the works of Creation, and there is not even a handbreadth [of distance] between the upper waters and the nether waters,

E. "for it says, *The spirit of God was moving over the face of the waters* (Gen. 1:2).

F. "And it says, *Like an eagle that stirs up its nest [that flutters over its young, spreading out its wings, catching them, bearing them on its pinions, so the Lord alone did lead him]* (Dt. 32:12).

G. "Just as this eagle flutters above its nest, touching and not touching, so there is no more space between the upper waters and the nether waters than a handbreadth."

H. Said R. Joshua to his disciples, "Ben Zoma already is on the outside [among the sectarians]."

I. The days were only a few before Ben Zoma disappeared.

When, at various points, the Mishnah and its successor-documents allege that the study of the Torah is the principal action, when they say that man was created to study the Torah, and when they tell numerous stories about how Torah-study secures one in this world and opens the door to the world to come, they scarcely prepare us for the delineation of the concrete power of Torah-study in individual lives. In the present instance, the role of personality (once again, biographical anecdote) serves to make concrete and individual what is set forth in the legal sources in general and impersonal terms. But in the process of concretization and individuation, the Torah and its study serve a more formidable purpose than merely exemplification of the character and consequence of Torah-study. They form a bridge between the two components of the paradigm: nature and Israel. It is only through attention to specific personalities—personal names—that the writers attend to the paradigm's own requirement, to specify how the private person enters into the paradigmatic framework. The answer, while always aimed at defining a model, proves remarkable for its attention to a much more specific matter, the relationship between nature and Israel via the Torah. Here again, the paradigm utilizes the Torah to raise the issue of uncertainty: just because one has studied the Torah, this does not mean the result is sure; learning in the Torah may destroy, not build.

C. VIRTUE

Social virtue meant bringing the social order into conformity with the natural order, and personal virtue, according with the requirements of the nature of things, the nature of being. The individual could attain virtue, therefore, only by obscuring traits of individuality and exemplifying those of the Torah, which, in social terms, conveyed the same structure that, in natural ones, the order of nature set forth. What this entailed in concrete terms proved as various as the results of mastery of the Torah—as various and as unpredictable. On the negative side, it meant excluding even the valid teaching of a heretic or schismatic. Jacob of Kefar Sama and Eliezer b. Hyrcanus both figure in stories that make this point. In its own way, the present story is as astonishing as the one that blames a sage's disappearance upon his mastery of the Torah:

Tosefta to Hullin (Shehitat Hullin) 2:22

2:24 A. M'SH B: R. Eliezer was arrested on account of *minut* [heresy, schism; suspicion of Christianity]. They brought him to court for judgment.

   B. That *hegemon* said to him, "Should an elder of your standing get involved in such things?"

   C. He said to him, "The Judge is reliable in my view."

   D. That *hegemon* supposed that he referred only to him, but he referred only to his Father in heaven.

   E. He [the *hegemon*] said to him, "Since you have deemed me reliable for yourself, so thus I have ruled: Is it possible that these grey hairs should err in such matters? [Obviously not, therefore.] [You are] Dimissus [pardoned]. Lo, you are free of liability."

F. And when he left court, he was distressed to have been arrested on account of matters of *minut.*

G. His disciples came to comfort him, but he did not accept their words of comfort.

H. R. Aqiba came and said to him, "Rabbi, may I say something to you so that you will not be distressed?"

I. He said to him, "Go ahead."

J. He said to him, "Perhaps some one of the *minim* told you something of *minut* which pleased you."

K. He said to him, "By Heaven! You remind me. Once I was strolling in the camp of Sepphoris. I bumped into Jacob of Kefar Sikhnin, and he told me a teaching of *minut* in the name of Jesus ben Pantiri, and it pleased me.

L. "So I was arrested on account of matters of *minut,* for I transgressed the teachings of Torah: *Keep your way far from her and do not go near the door of her house* ... [Prov. 5:8]."

Avoiding actions that were not virtuous by the standard of the Torah included not accepting valid teachings from an invalid source—a paradox that makes a point critical to the system as a whole. It is not the appearance of a teaching in the Torah (inclusive of oral tradition) that validates the teaching. It is the validity of the source of the teaching that accounts for its inclusion in the Torah. Or, to state matters in more familiar terms, context, not only contents, dictate what is virtuous.

A further formulation of virtue, among many candidates, tells us that within the group of sages a hierarchy governs, so that obedience to the master—in the following story, the patriarch, but in others, the sage's authority—takes precedence over the facts of the case. The following story forms a counterpart to the one concerning Jacob and Eliezer in relationship to the perfectly valid teaching of the Torah that Jesus had put forth. Just as the source of Torah-teaching takes priority over the validity of the teaching, so acknowledging the authority of Torah-tradition takes priority over the facts of the case, on the one side, or even the validity of compelling reason (as in Hillel's rise to the patriarchate), on the other:

Mishnah-tractate Rosh Hashanah 2:8

A. A picture of the shapes of the moon did Rabban Gamaliel have on a tablet and on the wall of his upper room, which he would show ordinary folk, saying, "Did you see it like this or like that?"

B. M'SH S: Two witnesses came and said, "We saw it at dawn [on the morning of the twenty-ninth] in the east and at eve in the west."

C. Said R. Yohanan b. Nuri, "They are false witnesses."

D. Now when they came to Yabneh, Rabban Gamaliel accepted their testimony [assuming they erred at dawn].

E. And furthermore two came along and said, "We saw it at its proper time, but on the night of the added day it did not appear [to the court]."

F. Then Rabban Gamaliel accepted their testimony.

G. Said R. Dosa b. Harkinas, "They are false witnesses.

H. "How can they testify that a woman has given birth, when, on the very next day, her stomach is still up there between her teeth [for there was no new moon!]?"

I. Said to him R. Joshua, "I can see your position."

2:9 A. Said to him Rabban Gamaliel, "I decree that you come to me with your staff and purse on the Day of Atonement which is determined in accord with your reckoning."

B. R. Aqiba went and found him troubled.

C. He said to him, "I can provide grounds for showing that everything that Rabban Gamaliel has done is validly done, since it says, *These are the set feasts of the Lord, even holy convocations, which you shall proclaim* (Lev. 23:4). Whether they are in their proper time or not in their proper time, I have no set feasts but these [which you shall proclaim] [vs. M. 2:7D]."

D. He came along to R. Dosa b. Harkinas.

E. He [Dosa] said to him, "Now if we're going to take issue with the court of Rabban Gamaliel, we have to take issue with every single court which has come into being from the time of Moses to the present day,

F.   "since it says, *Then went up Moses and Aaron, Nadab and Abihu, and seventy of the elders of Israel* (Ex. 24:9).

G.   "Now why have the names of the elders not been given? To teach that every group of three [elders] who came into being as a court of Israel—lo, they are equivalent to the court of Moses himself."

H.   [Joshua] took his staff with his purse in his hand and went along to Yabneh, to Rabban Gamaliel, on the Day of Atonement which is determined in accord with his [Gamaliel's] reckoning.

I.   Rabban Gamaliel stood up and kissed him on his head and said to him, "Come in peace, my master and my disciple—my master in wisdom, and my disciple in accepting my rulings."

The exemplary character of the story hardly presents a surprise. Joshua's submission to authority, to the continuity of authority, is of course a virtue. What is noteworthy, rather, is the congruity of this story to the earlier ones; in all instances, the Torah's truth proves relative to questions of context, whether the source of the Torah-teaching, on the one side, or the status of the teacher, on the other. The Torah's truth then is subject to negotiation; is stipulatory, conditional, relative. These then conform to the natural order of things: right source, in proper hierarchy. Facts of the Torah or of nature for that matter by themselves, like logical arguments, prove interesting but not decisive. Considerations of that inner structure and logic of being represented by the Torah properly set forth in tradition by an authorized master of tradition override all considerations of mere fact.

The anecdote finds its setting rarely in a sequence of stories about a named person, important in himself, but ordinarily on its own. It stands by itself, not continuous with other stories of its classification, for the same reason that, when it comes to writing the counterpart of history, events stand on their own and are not made to form a sequence leading from somewhere to some other, determinate point defined by teleology. Our anecdotes are entirely ahistorical, considerations of time and circumstance playing no role. A literature that to begin with treats the past as very present, but the present as undifferentiated from the past, has no reason to introduce points of differentiation, in describing a story about a person, that underscore the pastness of the past. Exemplarity on its own may be expressed in times past as much as in times present; the exclusion of such considerations here is not by reason of the intention to exemplify virtue. It is because divisions of time into past and present are simply irrelevant to the story, which takes place—as most events portrayed in these writings take place—in a timeless world that is neither present nor past.

So much for what is general. What is particular here is the profound reflection on the interplay of what is true, what is compelling by reason of powerful reason, what is traditional, what is in the Torah, and what is revealed by nature. Nature of course figures not at all; stories about named persons are unlikely to provide a suitable setting for speculation on the interplay of nature and the Torah. But the analysis, through anecdote, of the limits of the Torah's truth—the social, hierarchical and contextual limits in particular—is well served here. Truth is not true because it is valid by the standards of the Torah alone; for a truth to be true, the source must cohere with the Torah; the authority of the Torah's hierarchy must be affirmed; and tradition must consent.

The social order sustains the Torah: the community of sages, its members, its authorities, its traditions. Moving from outward to within, then, we explore the question of the relationship between nature and the Torah. This we do by asking a question familiar in more abstract language, subject to generalization, from philosophical tradition: is something true because the Torah says it, or does the Torah say it because it is true? Does truth enjoy autonomous standing, which the Torah then confirms? The answer sidesteps the question. And to all of these matters, it goes without saying, biography is monumentally irrelevant, though the lives of sages prove critical.

D. DEATH

Human life and natural life converge at death, when the dust that made up the person returns to the dust of the earth. While tales of birth and early precocity, e.g., in Torah-study, prove rare, death-stories do occur. These are of two kinds. First, reference to changes in the order of society or nature when a sage died make the point that the sage marks the confluence of the natural and social order, which are not distinguished from one another in his person. The death of various authorities marked the decline of the age and of the generations:

Tosefta Sotah 15:3

A.   When R. Eliezer died, the glory of the Torah ceased.

B.   When R. Joshua died, men of counsel ceased, and reflection ended in Israel [cf. M. Sot 9:15D].

C. When R. Aqiba died, the arms of Torah were taken away, and the springs of wisdom ceased [cf. M. Sot. 9:15G].

The Tosefta's version stresses the correspondence between the sages' deaths and the character of the social order, the Mishnah's adds the decline in the natural order. The point is the same.

A second, and separate type of presentation of the closing chapter in human life underscores the matter of martyrdom. In each group of stories of a personal ("biographical") character we find important statements concerning how and why people give their lives for the faith, with the Torah always the critical embodiment thereof. What renders the general paradigm particular to Rabbinic Judaism is the center of things, which is, burning the sage along with the Torah-scroll. Here the paradigm, to be replicated without regard to circumstance or temporal context, makes its most particular and characteristic statement:

Sifré to Deuteronomy CCCVII:IV

1.A. Another comment concerning the verse, "The Rock—his deeds are perfect. [Yes, all his ways are just; a faithful God, never false, true and upright is he:]".

B. When they arrested R. Haninah b. Teradion, a decree against him was issued that he be executed by burning, along with his scroll.

C. They told him, "A decree against you has been issued, that you be executed by burning, along with your scroll."

D. He recited this verse: "The Rock—his deeds are perfect."

E. They informed his wife, "A decree against your husband has been issued, that he be executed by burning, along with his scroll, and against you that you be put to death," and she recited this verse: *a faithful God, never false, true and upright is he.*

F. They told his daughter, "A decree against your father has been issued, that he be executed by burning, along with his scroll, and against your mother, that she be executed, and against you, that you 'do work'," and she recited this verse: *Great in counsel and mighty in work, whose eyes are open* (Jer. 32:19).

G. Said Rabbi, "What great righteous people are these, for in their hour of trouble they called forth three verses which justify God's decree in a way that none of the rest of the verses of Scripture do.

H.   "All three of them formed the exact intention in such a way as to justify the judgment of God concerning them."

2.A.   A philosopher went to the ruler and said to him, "My lord, do not boast that you have burned the Torah, for to the place [heaven] from which it has come forth, it now returns, namely, to the house of its father."

B.   He said to him, "Tomorrow you will be judged in the same way as these [and be put to death]."

C.   He said to him, "You give me very good news, that tomorrow my share will be with theirs in the world to come."

In the context of a body of writings that proposes to join nature to the social order through the instrumentality of the Torah, the martyr-story presents a special message. As the body returns to nature, so the Torah returns to heaven. What the martyr earns is that same trip to heaven that the Torah is going to take. None of this bears political consequence; the entire matter is represented in terms that are personal, on the one side, natural, on the other.

iii. The Later Midrash-Compilations: Genesis Rabbah, Leviticus Rabbah, and Pesiqta deRab Kahana

A. BIRTH. FIRST PUBLIC APPEARANCE

The story about Eliezer's entry into Torah-study and his first public appearance has Eliezer break with his father and enter into a supernatural family, indicated by the disinheritance, but then find acceptance from the father and family by reason of his achievement in Torah-exposition.

Genesis Rabbah XLII:I.

1.A.   *It came to pass in the days of Amraphel, [king of Shinar, Arioch, king of Ellasar, Chedorlaomer, king of Elam, and Tidal, king of Goiim]* (Gen. 14:1):

B.   R. Joshua in the name of R. Levi opened discourse [by citing the following verse]: *The wicked have drawn out the sword* (Ps. 37:15).

C.   The illustrative case concerns R. Eliezer. His brothers were ploughing on level ground, and he was ploughing on hilly ground. His cow fell and broke its leg. But it was to his advantage that his cow had broken its leg. [For] he fled and went to R. Yohanan b. Zakkai.

D.   He was eating clods of dirt [having no money to buy food] until his mouth produced a bad odor. They went and told Rabban Yohanan b. Zakkai, "R. Eliezer's breath stinks."

E.   He said to him, "Just as the odor of your mouth stank on account of your studying the Torah, so may the fragrance of your learning pervade the world from one end to the other."

F.   After some days his father came up to disinherit him from his property, and he found him sitting and expounding a lesson with the great figures of the realm in session before him, namely, Ben Sisit Hakkeset, Nicodemus son of Gurion, and Ben Kalba Shabua.

G.   He was giving an exposition of this verse, as follows: "'The wicked have drawn out the sword and have bent the bow' (Ps. 37:14) refers to Amraphael and his allies.

H.   "'To cast down the poor and needy' (Ps. 37:14) refers to Lot.

I.   "'To slay such as are upright in the way' (Ps. 37:14) refers to Abraham.

J.   "'Their sword shall enter into their own heart' (Ps. 37:15) in line with this verse: *And he divided his forces against them by night, he and his servants, and routed them* (Gen. 14:15)."

K.   His father said to him, "My son, I came up here only to disinherit you from my property. Now, lo, all of my property is handed over to you as a gift."

L.   He said to him, "So far as I am concerned, the property falls into the category of *herem* [and is forbidden to me]. Rather, divide them equally among my brothers."

This story underscores the conception that study of the Torah imposes a new set of relationships upon the family, removing the disciple from the authority of the father and placing him under that of the master. This is, of course, by reason of the supernatural character of what is learned—and the consequently enchanted nature of the relationship to the master, from whom it is learned.

B. Discipleship and Study of the Torah

Study of the Torah encompassed knowledge of nature, and, further, the proper tending of one's health and hygiene. But none of the illustrative anecdotes warrants presentation here.

C. Virtue

The virtue that the Torah is supposed to inculcate is humility, certainly as rare a virtue as the attitude of forbearance, conciliation, and forgiveness. This second virtue, which concludes our very brief survey of the matter, corresponds to the first, once more translating into biographical terms the virtue defined also for social relationships between Israel and the nations:

Leviticus Rabbah IX:IX.7

A. R. Meir would sit and expound [the Torah] on Sabbath nights. A certain woman would attend regularly. [Once] when his exposition ran on, she remained until he was finished. When she got home, she found that the lamp had gone out. Her husband said to her, "Where were you?"

B. She said to him, "I was in the session and listening to the exposition."

C. He said to her, "You will not come in here until you go and spit in the face of the expositor."

D. She stayed away [from home] one week, then a second, then a third. Her neighbors said to her, "Are you people still mad at one another? Let us go with you to the expositor."

E. When R. Meir saw them, he understood through the Holy Spirit [what was going on]. He said to the women, "Among you is there a woman who is knowledgeable about whispering over [treating] a sore eye?"

F. Her neighbors said to her, "If you go and spit in his face, you will be permitted to go back to your husband."

G. But when the woman sat down before him, she became afraid of him. She said to him, "My lord, I am not really an expert at whispering over a sore eye."

H. He said to her, "Spit in my face seven times, and I'll get better."

I. She spit in his face seven times. He said to her, "Go and tell your husband, 'You said to do it once, but I did it seven times.'"

J. His disciples said to him, "My lord, is this the way people should abuse the Torah? Could you not have told one of us to whisper [over your eye] for you?"

K. He said to them, "Is it not sufficient [honor] for Meir to be merely equal to his Creator?

L. "For R. Ishmael has taught, 'The greatness of peace is shown in that the great name [of God], which is written in a state of sanctification, did the Holy One, blessed be he, instruct to have blotted out in water, if only to bring peace between a man and his wife.'"

The purpose in examining these stories should not be missed. It is not to survey ideas of virtue in Rabbinic literature; it is to identify the occasions on which stories about what named persons did ("biographical stories") are introduced. We wanted to know how the framers of the documents utilized episodes involving named persons to accomplish their purposes. The answer is, to make that same statement, in terms of individuals, that the documents make through stories. We note that the latter never are set into relationship with sustained and continuous narratives; doing so would not accomplish the purposes of telling stories about events.

Now we see the comparable quality: stories about individuals are not situated in the setting of a life or biography. Sustained narrative and lives formed media for the presentation of history and biography, because the conception of time that history, including biography, as defined by Scripture proposed to set forth required just that. And the conception of paradigm, in place of historical time, required just the opposite: a sustained narrative or a life would not serve the paradigmatic purpose, constituted a medium found not useless but misleading and wrong. This is why I invoke to account for the character of Rabbinic Judaism the conception of a paradigm, meaning, a model that finds and describes sameness without regard to scale, from small to large, one that makes possible the quest for a few specific patterns, which will serve this and that, hither and yon. Noting the congruity of biographical episodes with historical narratives—the one says in the setting of private life what the other conveys in the context of national politics—shows what is at stake. Sages' writings yield no narrative because they find narrative useless; they tell episodic stories set into a different context all together because this is the form and the context they find congruent to their view of time, their expectation of where and how order and sense are conveyed.

D. DEATH

The primary focus of stories about death remained martyrdom. The martyrs show perfect loyalty to God, even in the smallest things, and do everything they can to appease their creator, even at the loss of their life. Life in Eden is the reward. The following presents no surprises:

Genesis Rabbah LXV:XXII.4

A. "See the smell of my son is as the smell of a field which the Lord has blessed:"

B. For example, Joseph Meshitha and Yaqim of Serorot.

C. As to Yosé, when the time came that the enemies wanted to enter the mountain of the house [of the sanctuary], they said, "Let one of them go in first."

D. They said to Yosé, "Go in. Whatever you take out will belong to you."

E. He went in and took out the golden candelabrum.

F. They said to him, "It is not proper for an ordinary person to make use of such a thing, so go in a second time, and what you take out will belong to you."

G. But he did not agree to do so.

H. Said R. Phineas, "They offered him the taxes for three years, but he did not agree to go in."

I. He said, "It is not enough for you that I have made my God angry once, should I now outrage him yet a second time?"

J. What did they do to him? They put him on a carpenter's vice and they sawed him in two, and he cried out, "Woe, woe that I angered my creator!"

K. Yaqim of Serurot was the son of the sister of R. Yosé b. Yoezer of Seridah. He was riding on his horse. He passed before the beam on which [Yosé] was to be hanged. He said to him, "Look at the horse on which my master has set me riding and look at the horse on which your master has set you riding!"

L.   He said to him, "If this is what he does for those who spite him, how much the more will he do for those who do his will!"

M.   He said to him, "And has anyone done his will more than you have?"

N.   He said to him, "And if this is what happens to those who do his will [that they are tortured to death], all the more so will he do for those who spite him."

O.   This statement penetrated into his heart like the venom of a snake, and he went and applied to himself the four modes of the death penalty applied by a court, namely, stoning, burning, decapitation, and strangulation.

P.   How did he accomplish it? He brought a beam and stuck it into the ground, and put up a wall of stones around it, then tied a cord to it. He made a fire in front of the beam and put a sword in the middle of the post. He first hung himself on the post. The cord burned through, and he was strangled. Then the sword caught his body, and the wall of stones fell on him, and he burned up.

Q.   Yosé b. Yoezer of Seredah dozed off and he saw the bier of the other flying through the air. He said, "By a brief interval he reached the Garden of Eden before me."

The main point remains the same as before: the ultimate return of the sages' body to Heaven, along with the return of the Torah to its point of origin.

iv. The Latest Midrash-Compilations: Song of Songs Rabbah, Ruth Rabbah, Esther Rabbah I, and Lamentations Rabbah

A. BIRTH. FIRST PUBLIC APPEARANCE AND ORIGINS

Study of the Torah transforms all relationships; the normal course of a lifetime is changed. A single example, in the context of advent stories, registers this point: the grace that made of an unlettered adult a major authority. The story before us underscores the points at which Aqiba's entry into Torah study contradict the natural course of events:

A.   How did R. Aqiba begin [his Torah-study]?

B.   They say: He was forty years old and had never repeated a tradition. One time he was standing at the mouth of a well. He thought to himself, "Who carved out this stone?"

C.   They told him, "It is the water that is perpetually falling on it every day."

D.   They said to him, "Aqiba, do you not read Scripture? *The water wears away stones* (Job. 4:19)?"

E.   On the spot R. Aqiba constructed in his own regard an argument *a fortiori*: now if something soft can wear down something hard, words of Torah, which are as hard as iron, how much the more so should wear down my heart, which is made of flesh and blood."

F.   On the spot he repented [and undertook] to study the Torah.

G.   He and his son went into study session before a children's teacher, saying to him, "My lord, teach me Torah."

H.   R. Aqiba took hold of one end of the tablet, and his son took hold of the other end. The teacher wrote out for him *Alef Bet* and he learned it, *Alef Tav* and he learned it, *the Torah of the Priests* [the books of Leviticus and Numbers] and he learned it. He went on learning until he had learned the entire Torah.

I.   He went and entered study-sessions before R. Eliezer and before R. Joshua. He said to them, "My lords, open up for me the reasoning of the Mishnah."

J.   When they had stated one passage of law, he went and sat by himself and said, "Why is this *alef* written? why is this *bet* written? Why is this statement made?" He went and asked them and, in point of fact, reduced them to silence.

Once more the origins of a sage, meaning, how he undertook to study the Torah, are specified; the story is remarkable, so the narrator wishes us to notice, because, like Eliezer, Aqiba undertook Torah-study only in his mature years. Contrary to the natural order of things, he and his son went together; his wife was left alone. Once more, then, the use of biographical anecdote is shaped by paradigmatic interests: the relationship between the Torah and the natural world, even more, the negotiation that is required, case by case, to bring the world of ordinary doings into alignment with both nature and the Torah.

B. DISCIPLESHIP AND STUDY OF THE TORAH

While attractive and engaging, the stories pertinent to this rubric add nothing fresh to our survey.

C. VIRTUE

Rather than concluding with an account of the Torah's virtues, we turn to the picture of the sage who left the fold yet retained acknowledged learning. Here again, we note the range of the negotiable. A sage who has abandoned the faith retains vast and vital learning; his greatest disciple, loyal to the band of Torah-sages, with dignity encourages him to return to the fold and to the faith. The apostate-master with dignity declines:

Ruth Rabbah LXII:ii.1

A. "...and in the morning, if he will do the part of the next of kin for you, well; let him do it; but if he is not willing to do the part of the next of kin for you, then, as the Lord lives, I will do the part of the next of kin for you. [Lie down until the morning]":

B. On the Sabbath R. Meir was in session and expounding in the school of Tiberias, and Elisha, his master, was passing in the market riding a horse.

C. They said to R. Meir, "Lo, Elisha your master is passing by in the market."

D. He went out to him.

E. He [Elisha] said to him [Meir], "With what were you engaged?"

F. He said to him, "'So the Lord blessed the latter end of Job more than his beginning' (Job 42:12)."

G. He said to him, "And what do you have to say about it?"

H. He said to him, "'blessed' means that he gave him twice as much money as he had before."

I. He said to him, "Aqiba, your master, did not explain it in that way. This is how he explained it: "'So the Lord blessed the latter end of Job more than his beginning': it was on account of the repentance and the good deeds that were in his hand to begin with."...

J.   "And there is this case [which illustrates Aqiba's view]: Abbuyah, my father, was one of the leading figures of the generation, and when the time came to circumcise me, he invited all the leading men of Jerusalem, and he invited R. Eliezer and R. Joshua with them.

K.   "And when they had eaten and drunk, these began to say psalms, and those began to say alphabetical acrostics.

L.   "Said R. Eliezer to R. Joshua, 'These are engaged with what matters to them, so should we not devote ourselves to what matters to us?'

M.   "They began with [verses of] the Torah, and from the Torah, they went on to the prophets, and from the prophets to the writings. And the matters gave as much joy as when they were given from Sinai, so fire leapt round about them.

N.   "For was not the very act of giving them through fire? 'And the mountain burned with fire to the heart of heaven' (Dt. 4:11).

O.   "[My father] said, 'Since such is the great power of Torah, this son, if he survives for me, lo, I shall give him over to the Torah.'

P.   "But since his true intentionality was not for the sake of Heaven [but for the ulterior motive of mastering the supernatural power of the Torah], my Torah did not endure in me."

Q.   [Meir said to Elisha,] "Turn back."

R.   He said to him, "Why?"

S.   [Elisha] said to [Meir], "Up to here is the Sabbath limit [and within this space alone are you permitted to walk about]."

T.   [Meir] said to him, "How do you know?"

U.   [Elisha] said to him, "It is from the hooves of my horse, for the horse has already travelled two thousand cubits."

V.   [Meir] said to [Elisha], "And all this wisdom is in your possession, and yet you do not return?"

W.   He said to him, "I don't have the power to do so."

X.   He said to him, "Why not?"

Y.   He said to him, "I was riding on my horse and sauntering past the synagogue on the Day of Atonement that coincided with the Sabbath. I heard an echo floating in the air: 'Return, O backsliding children' (Jer. 3:14), 'Return to me and I will return to you' (Mal. 3:7)—except for Elisha b. Abbuyah.

Z.   "'For he knew all my power, but he rebelled against me.'"

It would be difficult to identify in the Rabbinic compilations a more singular or individual portrait than this one, which has no counterpart or parallel in these documents. So long and elegant a narrative surely shades over into biography—or invites us to. And yet the story underscores a variety of familiar propositions. First, learning by itself is nothing; the master who apostatized no longer exercises authority, even though he does, to be sure, possess accurate traditions. The correct motive in mastery of Torah defines the value of learning; here too, a range of negotiation is undertaken. The ultimate virtue of Israel must be submission to God's will, reconciliation with the nation's destiny as an expression of the nation's complete acceptance of the Torah. The private person must exhibit the same virtue, and the worst sin, social or personal, is the same: "he knew all my power, but he rebelled against me." Whether speaking of Israel led by Bar Kokhba or of Elisha, the judgment is the same. And the challenge to Israel is to accept and submit, conciliate and be reconciled, no matter what happens; Israel and individuals alike are forbidden to say, "Now where is the goodness and the long life of this man?" The concluding components of the tale approach the sublime in their working out this perfectly commonplace motif of the governing model.

D. DEATH

The death-scene of Ishmael conforms to the message that Israel is always welcome to repent; submission to God's will, by the nation or by the private person, is invariably welcome and effective. A single set of martyr-stories, abbreviated as before, suffices to register the main point throughout:

The Fathers According to Rabbi Nathan XXXVIII:V.2

A.   When they seized Rabban Simeon b. Gamaliel and R. Ishmael on the count of death, Rabban Simeon b. Gamaliel was in session and was perplexed, saying, "Woe is us! For we are put to death like those who profane the Sabbath and worship idols and practice fornication and kill."

B.   Said to him R. Ishmael b. Elisha, "Would it please you if I said something before you?"

C.   He said to him, "Go ahead."

D.   He said to him, "Is it possible that when you were sitting at a banquet, poor folk came and stood at your door, and you did not let them come in and eat?"

E.   He said to him, "By heaven [may I be cursed] if I ever did such a thing! Rather, I set up guards at the gate. When poor folk came along, they would bring them in to me and eat and drink with me and say a blessing for the sake of Heaven."

F.   He said to him, "Is it possible that when you were in session and expounding [the Torah] on the Temple mount and the vast populations of Israelites were in session before you, you took pride in yourself?"

G.   He said to him, "Ishmael my brother, one has to be ready to accept his failing."

H.   They went on appealing to the executioner for grace. This one [Ishmael] said to him, "I am a priest, son of a high priest, kill me first, so that I do not have to witness the death of my companion."

I.   And the other [Simeon] said, "I am the patriarch, son of the patriarch, kill me first, so that I do not have to witness the death of my companion."

J.   He said to him, "Cast lots." They cast lots, and the lot fell on Rabban Simeon b. Gamaliel.

K.   The executioner took the sword and cut off his head.

L.   R. Ishmael b. Elisha took it and held it in his breast and wept and cried out: "Oh holy mouth, oh faithful mouth, oh mouth that brought forth beautiful gems, precious stones and pearls! Who has laid you in the dust, who has filled your mouth with dirt and dust.

M.   "Concerning you Scripture says, *Awake, O sword, against my shepherd and against the man who is near to me* (Zech. 13:7)."

N.   He had not finished speaking before the executioner took the sword and cut off his head.

O. Concerning them Scripture says, *My wrath shall wax hot, and I will kill you with the sword, and your wives shall be widows, and your children fatherless* (Ex. 22:23).

v. The Paradigmatic Person

This survey has demonstrated that the function of—not biography but— episodes individual's lives is to show the union of nature and the social order through the person of the sage. This union takes place within the medium of the Torah, which corresponds to nature and lays out the governing rules thereof, but also encompasses the social order and defines its laws as well. Anecdotes about the master of the Torah then serve to convey principles of the Torah, with the clear proviso that anecdotes about events may equally set forth precisely these same principles. The paradigm describes regularities without regard to considerations of scale, whether social or private, any more than matters of earlier or later, past or present or future, make any difference at all.

This explains also why the paradigm really excludes not only biography but personality in any form. Individuals make a difference, so as to warrant the writing down of components of personal lives, at that point at which they lose all individuality and serve in some way or other to embody and exemplify a detail of the paradigm best set forth in the dimensions of private life. We then identify no difference between the social entity and the private person, because the paradigm works out indifferent to matters of scale or context.

If at the end we take up the question postponed at the outset, how does the paradigm emerge, having received a richer and more nuanced definition, out of the encounter with individual lives? the answer is now clear. A paradigm that proposes to present a single, coherent, and cogent picture of the life of Israel under the aspect of the timeless Torah has to make its statement about not only the social order viewed whole, but the individuals who comprise this order. The paradigm requires the counterpart to biography, as much as the counterpart to history, for its own reasons; it cares about individuals for the same reason that it cares about the social entity, Israel.

Biography does for history what personal anecdotes do for the paradigm at hand. Just as the one renders the large conclusions of its companion manageable and in human scale, so the other expresses the statements of the paradigm in a form accessible of human imitation and identification. But anecdotes about people also deepen our perception of the paradigm. For the issue of time is recast, now, as the span of a human life enters consideration. Paradigm in place of history yielded the narrative of the cult and the story of the Temple.

❧ *Part Five* ❧

TRANSCENDING
THE BOUNDS OF TIME

CHAPTER VIII

ZAKHOR: IS RABBINIC JUDAISM
A RELIGION OF MEMORY?

For the rabbis the Bible was not only a repository of past history but a revealed pattern of the whole of history, and they had learned their scriptures well. They knew that history has a purpose, the establishment of the kingdom of God on earth, and that the Jewish people has a central role to play in the process. They were convinced that the covenant between God and Israel was eternal...Above all, they had learned from the Bible that the true pulse of history often beat beneath its manifest surfaces, an invisible history that was more real than what the world...could recognize....Ironically, the very absence of historical writing among the rabbis may itself have been due in good measure to their total and unqualified absorption of the biblical interpretation of history. In its ensemble, the biblical record seemed capable of illuminating every further historical contingency.

Yosef Hayyim Yerushalmi[1]

i. Marking Time: Memory or Dream

As the dance is the physicalization of music, and memory, the immediate realization of history, so is the lived dream the here-and-now embodiment of paradigm. The marriage of music and motion yields dance; the monument and rite of commemoration, history; the serene sense of familiarity with the new put forth in response the lived paradigm: Purim in Patagonia, Exodus in America: "...as if we were slaves to Pharaoh." As essential to historical modes of thought as is memory, so critical to the paradigm that identifies event out of happenings, consequence out of the detritus of everyday affairs is the dream (in sleep) or the intuition (when awake). Then everything is changed. When the model takes shape and takes place in the acutely-, radically-present moment, past and future meet in neither past nor future but paradigm. And then the mode of thought through paradigm accomplishes its enchantment: Paradigm or pattern or model then forms an alternative to

---

1. *Zakhor: Jewish History and Jewish Memory*, pp. 21-22.

historical knowledge, a different way of thinking about the same things and responding to the same questions: O Lord, why? O Lord, how long?

People who see time in the framework of history, past, present, future forming distinct spells, experience the passage of time through the medium of memory. They look backward, into an age now over and done with. Affirming that that was then, and this is now, they evoke memory as the medium for renewing access to events or persons deemed or set forth as formative in the present moment. A religion that frames its statement out of the conception of historical time—one-time events, bound to context and defined by circumstance, but bearing long-term effects and meaning—will evoke memory as a principal medium for the recovery of sense and order out of the chaos of the everyday and here and now. By remembering how things were, or how they have been, moving beyond the barrier of the present moment, people institute a certain order.

Israelite Scripture certainly qualifies as a religion of memory.[2] It recognizes both the pastness of the past and also invokes its ineluctable power to explain the present. But then, what are we to make of a religion that insists upon the presence of the past and the pastness of the present, instructing the faithful to view themselves, out of the here and now, as living in another time, another place: "Therefore every person must see himself or herself as slave to Pharaoh in Egypt," as the Passover Haggadah-narrative phrases matters. But the same invocation of the present into the past also serves to convey the past into the here and now. Once a religious obligation imposes past upon present, shifting the present into a fully realized, contemporary-past, rites of commemoration give way to the reformulation of the ages into a governing paradigm that obliterates barriers of time as much as those of space.[3] Rules of structure and order apply without differentiation by criteria or time or space. These rules comprise a paradigm. The paradigm not only imparts sense and order to what happens but also selects out of what happens

---

2. This is not to suggest the Authorized History of Genesis to Kings tells us what really happened; at stake here are modes of thought, issues of the social construction of reality, conventions and protocols of interpretation, that are ordinarily classified as historical.

3. I am sure that considerations of space and its divisions are at least as important as those of time, which have defined the work of this book. It seems to me necessary that our sages treat as null boundaries of space as much as those of time, but I have not worked on this problem. I should anticipate that Rabbinic Judaism will emerge as not only paradigmatic, not historical, but also utopian, not locative. But the shift from bounded space to utopia is to be traced in its own terms.

what counts—and is to be counted. The paradigm is a distinctive way of marking time, telling time.

Rites of reenactment with clear focus upon times long gone will form a principal expression of a religion of memory: we do this now in commemoration of that singular ("unique") event long ago, so that we may remember, so that we may draw the right conclusions for today. It is this defining barrier between present and past, that insistence on the uniqueness of events, but also on their linear and teleological character. We recall in this context the statement of LeGoff, "The opposition between past and present is fundamental, since the activity of memory and history is founded on this distinction."[4] The work of historical imagination, then, is, through the processes of narrative shaping thought, sentimentality and emotion, to move people from here to there, from now to then. The governing proposition of imagination is easily framed: we are here as if we were there; then is as if it were now. The "as if" then embodies in language the working of imagination transcending the barrier of time. Historical imagination forms a powerful tool for the reconstruction of the every day by appeal to the model of another, long-gone but still living age. Memory then is the chosen medium for imagining.

If for our purposes Scripture has supplied the definitions of historical thinking,[5] then the traits of paradigmatic thinking will take shape in their opposites and counterparts, and these we have found in a few, clear and unmistakable ways in the Rabbinic documents we have surveyed. We simply took the opposites of the indicators of the presence of historical thinking: linear history, sustained narrative, differentiation of present from past, contrasted against episodic story-telling but no linear, sustained narrative, and the fusion of times into one time.[6] The traits of paradigmatic thinking characteristic of our sages of blessed memory emerge in both what we do not find in those documents and also in what we do find by way of counterpart: how do Rabbinic writers deal with those same themes out of Israel's (alleged) past as are laid out in historical terms in Scripture? Having denied

4. Jacques LeGoff, *History and Memory* (N.Y., 1992: Columbia University Press). Translated by Steven Randall and Elizabeth Claman, p. xii.

5. As Chapters Two through Four have shown.

6. Which is not to be called "eternity." This would represent a profound misunderstanding of the conception of time in Rabbinic Judaism. It is only in the context of history that I have dealt here with the conception of time; the much more interesting problem of time viewed in its own terms in the Rabbinic document remains to be addressed.

the distinction between present and past, paradigmatic thinking for its part finds the past to be ever-present, and deems the present to form a chapter in the past. The very dilemma of history—bridging the imagined gap between present and past—finds no comprehension at all in thought that finds the principle of order in the model or the pattern that pertains at any time and any place; in that setting a distance between here and there, a spell between now and then—both allude to a separation none perceives. That atemporality derives from a different conception of marking time from the historical one.

A religion that organizes experience by appeal to enduring paradigms will find no more use for memory than it assigns to the concept of "history." Memory matters only to those who organize affairs historically; the barrier between present and past removed, memory is assigned no task at all. Other questions take priority: identifying the pattern, whether in large things or in small, without reference to scale, but with acute interest in the model or the pattern replicated in no special context. Once we are obligated to see ourselves as if we were not now but then, not here but somewhere else, paradigmatic thinking takes over; and as soon as the subjunctive that expresses a state contrary to fact or condition falls away, so that the "as if" loses its taxonomic power, the paradigm takes over and excludes all considerations of historical specificity: now, not then, but like then. Rabbinic Judaism celebrated Purim not once but many times—everywhere Israel outlived its enemies. This it did, not through a process of spiritualization nor through rites of reenactment. Without regard to considerations of scale, the same model applied, giving meaning and depth to incident.

But how does this take place, and what medium corresponds in the experience of paradigm to the medium of memory for history? If we wonder when or where we compare ordinary affairs with an enduring paradigm, it is in dreaming or free-ranging imagination or instinct. Nostalgia is to historical thinking what realized dream is to the paradigmatic kind. Our sages of blessed memory never look back with longing, because they do not have to; nor do they look forward with either dread nor anticipation either; theirs is a different model for perceived experience. Paradigms or models take over and replace the sense of history with a different sort of common sense.

Dream and fantasy select, as much as history selects, out of a range of happenings a few incidents of consequence, history's events, paradigm's models. But in dreaming there is no earlier or later, no now or then, no here or there. Things coalesce and disintegrate, form and reform, in the setting of a few, highly restricted images. In the realm of dreams, paradigms (of experience, real or imagined) come together, float apart, reassemble in a different pattern, unrestricted by considerations of now or then, here or there. Whatever is chosen, out of the chaos of the everyday, to be designated a pattern imposes its order and structure on whatever, in the chaos of the here and now, fits.

History strings together event after event, like cultured pearls matched with precision in a necklace. Paradigm's sea-nurtured pearls impose no order or natural sequence in ordered size; being made by nature, they do not match exactly. This is why, in one combination, they make one statement, in another, a different statement. Our sages formed their conception of time out of the materials of the everyday perceptions of people, for whom past, present, and future give way to the recapitulation of patterns of meaning formed we know not how. Dreams, fantasies, moments of enchantment, occasions or circumstances or places that invoke the model or fit it—these form the medium for the organization of experience. To it time bears no meaning, memory no message. But, as I shall suggest, sages saw matters the way they did because they took the measure of history, not because they ignored it. They formulated another and different reading of history from the historical one; aware of the one, sentient of the other, they transcended history and cast off the bounds of time.

Our sages of blessed memory identified in the written part of the Torah the governing models of Israel's enduring existence, whether past, whether future. And this is precisely why they formed the conception of paradigm, and whence they drew the specificities of theirs. They knew precisely what paradigms imparted order and meaning to everyday events, and their models, then selected and explained data and also allowed prognosis to take place. In place of a past that explained the present and predicted the future, sages invoked a paradigm that imposed structure on past and future alike—a very different thing. And what, precisely, was the paradigm?

Images, in dreaming, form the counterpart to the paradigm's formulations: dream of Eden, dream of Land, nightmare of Adam, nightmare of Israel—and the waking at Sinai.[7] In that dream world formed of the paradigms of Scripture matched against our own immediate and contemporary experience, time stands still, its place taken by form. And in the world of paradigms set forth by Scripture and defined in simple, powerful images by the documents of Rabbinic Judaism, imagination asks of itself a different task

---

7. I allude to both Freedman's brief and ample formulation of the Authorized History, cited above, and also the formulation given in Song of Songs Rabbah.

from the one performed in a religion of history through the act of memory. Imagination now forms an instrument of selection out of the here and now of those particular facts that count, selection and construction out of the data of the every day a realm of being that conforms to the model that is always present, waiting to be discerned and, not recapitulated once again but, realized—as always, whenever. Seeing the dream in the setting of the everyday defines the task of imagination: not "let's pretend," but rather, "look here...." In this particular vision lies the power of this Judaism to make of the world something that, to the untrained eye, is scarcely there to be seen, but, to the eye of faith, evokes the sense of not *déja-vu* or *temps perdu* but—self-evidence.

ii. *Scripture's Memory and Tradition*

A document, such as Scripture, that formulates its statement in historical categories will negotiate data through the medium of memory, on the one hand, and through the doctrine of tradition, on the other. Remembering what was done, handing down the memory—these will formulate the rules for composing the social order in the unfolding present. Memory forms an act of prayer, an effort to overcome the separation from God, as Childs' statement at the head of this chapter formulates matters. For at stake in the historical as against the paradigmatic reading of the everyday in the context of Judaism is the encounter with God: where do we identify the "divine reality...imprinted"?

Childs' formulation of what is at stake in memory and in its theological companion, the concept of tradition, carries us to the heart of the matter, which is, Scripture's understanding of memory, concomitant with its selection of the medium of history:

> To remember was to call to mind a past event or situation, with the purpose of evoking some action...To remember was to actualize the past, to bridge the gap of time and to form a solidarity with the fathers. Israel's remembrance became a technical term to express the process by which later Israel made relevant the great redemptive acts which she recited in her tradition. The question of how to overcome the separation in time and space from the great events of the past become the paramount issue.[8]

---

8. Childs, pp. 74-75.

The premise of Scripture's historical framing of Israel's situation—the pastness of the past—then generates the question that this same framing of matters satisfactorily answers.

Once we recognize that great events belong to the past, we undertake to remember them so as to realize them once more, in Childs's language, "to overcome the separation in time and space...." If we do not conceive of time in a historical manner, we also should not have to overcome this barrier, to close this separation.[9] First comes the here-and-now conception of "exile" and "return," then comes the utilization of the category, history, to frame matters by explaining them. The insistence on the pastness of the past that defines the concept of history in the Scriptural setting then forms a way of stating that sense of distance or separation—whether from Land, whether from God—that is to be recognized and overcome. "History" then makes a statement that from the perspective of "here," a separation has taken place, and from the viewpoint of "now," there is a then. And "tradition" forms the medium by which that statement's tension is resolved: how to overcome the gap. This is not accomplished by a return to that moment of the past, as Childs says, "...Old Testament actualization cannot be correctly identified with a return to a former historical event."[10] Such a return would violate the first law of historical thinking, as we have noted many times; we can never go back.

Then what kind of history does this thinking yield in Scripture? Childs answers in these terms:

> The Old Testament witnesses to a series of historical events by which God brought the people of Israel into existence. These events were placed in a chronological order within the tradition and never recurred in Israel's history. There was one Exodus from Egypt, one period of wilderness wanderings, one conquest of the land. These events were determinative because they constituted Israel's redemption. in other words, they became the vehicle for a quality of existence, redemptive time and space.[11]

9. In this context I need hardly attempt to explain this powerful sense of the pastness of the past that animates the Hebrew Scriptures. But it seems to me to derive from the perspective of the return to Zion, which conceives of an "Israel" once separated from the land but now restored to it, thus conception ("myth") of a return after an interval of time begins with the notion of the separation of space, and this then provokes the sense of the separation in time. A rich account of what is at stake here is set forth in Philip R. Davies, *In Search of Ancient Israel* (Sheffield, 1993: Journal for the Study of the Old Testament Supplement Series 148), especially pp. 113-33.

10. Childs, p. 83.

11. *Ibidem.*

Then, we ask ourselves, what task is assigned to memory, that is, the medium for the actualization of the statement of history? Childs' reply serves us well:

> Our study of memory has indicated that each successive generation encountered anew these same determinative events...It means more than that the influence of a past event continued to be felt in successive generations...there was an immediate encounter, an actual participation in the great acts of redemption....[12]

Memory then serves as the medium for overcoming the barrier between present and past, opening the way for the present to participate in what happened long ago. By remembering, people were able to relive, regain access to, that time and that event that they knew was once upon a time. How, precisely, does that working of memory craft the world? Childs' final contribution completes this exposition of history, memory, and tradition in ancient Israel's Scriptures:

> Actualization is the process by which a past event is contemporized for a generation removed in time and space from the original event. When later Israel responded to the continuing imperative of her tradition through her memory, that moment in historical time likewise became an Exodus experience. Not in the sense that later Israel again crossed the Red Sea. This was an irreversible, once-for-all event. Rather, Israel entered the same redemptive reality of the Exodus generation. later Israel, removed in time and space from the original event, yet still in time and space, found in her tradition a means of transforming her history into redemptive history. Because the quality of time was the same, the barrier of chronological separation was overcome.[13]

It would be difficult to imagine a more concise statement of the religious experience of the historical mode of organizing matters than Childs's, since he touches on every element critical to the description of history—the pastness of the past, the singularity and irreversibility of events, but also the power of events in times past to affect the present moment and to effect change therein.

The touchstone, then, is simple: that sense of separation that precipitates the quest for reconciliation, restoration, renewal of relationship. Childs defines the final question to be taken up here: if historical thinking begins with a sense of separation of present from past, then what accounts for the

12. Childs, pp. 83-84.
13. Childs, p. 85.

datum of paradigmatic thinking, which forms the union of present and past and abandons any notion that the one is distinct from the other? Where present and past meet, there paradigmatic thinking commences.

iii. *Zakhor: Is Rabbinic Judaism a Religion of Memory?*

On the face of matters, Rabbinic Judaism defines itself as a religion of tradition and formulates its authorized medium for the transmission of tradition through processes of memory. How can the following famous allegation yield any other conclusion?

Tractate Abot 1:1-2

A.   Moses received Torah at Sinai and handed it on to Joshua, Joshua to elders, and elders to prophets.

B.   And prophets handed it on to the men of the great assembly.

C.   They said three things:

   (1) "Be prudent in judgment.

   (2) "Raise up many disciples.

   (3) "Make a fence for the Torah."

1:2 A.   Simeon the Righteous was one of the last survivors of the great assembly.

B.   He would say: "On three things does the world stand:

   (1) "On the Torah,

   (2) "and on the Temple service,

   (3) "and on deeds of loving kindness."

Here is an explicit allegation that the Torah, which is the native category for "Judaism," is formulated through a process of receiving and handing on, that is, of tradition. Implicit, further, is the claim that there is a Torah besides Scripture, since what is assigned to the named authorities are statements that neither cite Scripture nor go over points in Scripture but formulate propositions autonomous of statements of Scripture. The order of liturgy adopted and sponsored by, if not original to, Rabbinic Judaism, contains ample reference to "a memorial to the Exodus from Egypt," and paramount liturgies make reference to the past in the medium of memory.[14] None may doubt, therefore, that indicators of the presence of historical thinking—appeal to memory and to tradition—form an ample presence in Rabbinic Judaism.

Yet statements such as the ones at hand hardly require us to juxtapose "tradition," which we do have, with "memory" and "history." A statement that our sages of blessed memory stand in the line of tradition—receiving, handing on—that commenced at Scripture need not be read to convey a historical fact, that is, the facticity of a barrier between past and present, a wall of separation penetrated by a process of tradition out of the past and into the present.

That reading of matters—the historical way, with a clear distinction between present and past—in fact contradicts the sense of the passage, and it does so because it misses the character of what is transmitted in this process of tradition. The examples given above suffice to make a simple point: the substance of what is transmitted as tradition in no way recognizes the authority of the past, in no way claims to hand onto the future what has been received out of the past, in no way represents itself as a historical process at all. Why not? Because what is transmitted as tradition is not a citation of ancient Scripture, e.g., writings of Moses or Jeremiah, nor, yet, an amplification thereof. What is transmitted as tradition is the opinion of the named sage himself. "Be prudent in judgment" is set forth not along with, "as it is written...," plus a proof-text; "make a fence for the Torah" clearly belongs to the generation that makes the statement; and at every point thereafter, the joining of a name and an ethical or theological statement yields a clear, anti-historical claim: this is what this particular sage said on his own account, not what he said out of a received, ancient, historical tradition. Indeed, the

---

14. One example well attested for sages is the Remembrance-verses (*Zikhronot*) for the Additional Service of the Day of Atonement, to which reference is made explicitly in the Mishnah and Tosefta. Precisely what is meant by "Remembrance-verses" however derives from the purpose for which they are invoked. This is to beseech God to "remember" the acts of memory that he performed in the past and to "remember" Israel now in the same way. The recitation of acts of memory then forms the counterpart to the recitation of acts of revelation (*Shoferot*) and acts of sovereignty (*Malkhuyyot*); in all three cases we assemble the evidences to construct a paradigm of God's actions: this is how things are. The *Zikhronot*-verses are no more commemorative in a historical, past-tense sense than the *Malkhuyyot*-verses are commemorative, that is, allude to past moments when God ruled; for at no point do sages in the liturgy concede that there was a time in which God did not rule. So too with the *Shoferot*-verses, the acts of revelation are not commemorative but recapitulative, a very different thing, since in recapitulation the pattern is realized once again, a presence that takes place.

very formulation, occasionally, of a saying in the setting of a narrative, bears the same signal:

> Also: he saw a skull floating on the water and said to it, "Because you drowned others, they drowned you, and in the end those who drowned you will be drowned."

> *Tractate Abot 2:6*

Not only do we find no union of "traditionality" with history, we find an explicit statement that what a given sage "says" in the chain of tradition is his own, not what he has received out of the legacy of history. Tradition here is not conceived as a historical category at all, and the chain of tradition to Sinai forms not a medium for transcending the barrier of history, but for making a different statement altogether from a historical one. In a circle that denies that historical categories are native to the Torah—"considerations of temporal priority or posteriority do not apply in the Torah"—the category, tradition, simply serves in a structure that assigns to that category a quite ahistorical meaning. This is why what a sage "says," not "said," stresses the all-timeness of the statement, and it explains, also, why it seldom is necessary to specify the circumstance in which, or for which, a given statement is made.

iv. Yosef Hayim Yerushalmi, Zakhor. Jewish History and Jewish Memory Revisited

In the past two centuries, dominated as they have been by historicism, the tractate's "chain of tradition" has been read in a narrowly-historical framework, with the clear recognition that memory and commemoration form the foundation of common-sense interpretation and realization of the category, "tradition." On this basis, Yosef Hayim Yerushalmi, formulating "a number of issues concerning the place of historiography within Jewish civilization generally,"[15] alleges that "...memory of the past was always a central component of Jewish experience."[16] Yerushalmi leaves no doubt that he means history, and his criterion for the presence or absence of history, or

15. Yosef Hayim Yerushalmi, *Zakhor. Jewish History and Jewish Memory* (Seattle and London, 1982: University of Washington Press), p. xiii.

16. Yerushalmi, p. xiv.

what we should prefer to call simply "historical thinking," derives from the writing of narrative history and its surrogates or the absence of that writing.

Yerushalmi quite properly asks how people wrote history or why they did not do so, and, it follows, he takes for granted the normative status of this barrier between past and present that marks the presence of his "history" (inclusive of "memory") and my "historical thinking." I disagree with Yerushalmi's understanding of the thinking of our sages of blessed memory, characterizing as historical a mode of thought that rejects every premise of history and invokes a mode of explaining the social order that is—and by others has been characterized as—a temporal, anti-historical, and utterly out of phase with Scripture's historical thinking.

By "Jewish memory" Yerushalmi refers to "transpersonal memory": "... even individual memory is structured through social frameworks ...collective memory is not a metaphor but a social reality transmitted and sustained through the conscious efforts and institutions of the group."[17] Yerushalmi explicitly carries us from the category, "civilization," to that of religion, namely, Judaism, that in this context is defined by the documents examined here.

It is specifically to Rabbinic Judaism that Yerushalmi devotes part of his initial formulation, which he calls, "Biblical and Rabbinic Foundations: Meaning in History, Memory, and the Writing of History."[18] In Scripture, "meaning in history, memory of the past, and the writing of history...are linked...overlap...are held together in a web of delicate and reciprocal relationships. In post-biblical Judaism...they pull asunder."[19] Specifically, "unlike the biblical writers the rabbis seem to play with Time as though with an accordion, expanding and collapsing it at will. Where historical specificity is a hallmark of the biblical narratives, here that acute biblical sense of time and place often gives way to rampant and seemingly unself-conscious anachronism."[20] Anachronism by itself, Yerushalmi admits, need not exclude from the category of historical writing the reformulations of Scriptural stories in the Rabbinic compilations. But even though the rabbis did not write the history of times beyond Scripture's or try to preserve events in their own day,[21] Yerushalmi argues, rabbis still were interested in history.

17. Yerushalmi, p. xv. Yerushalmi's views are shared by LeGoff, who uses similar language to argue the same proposition.

18. Yerushalmi, pp. 1-27.

19. Yerushalmi, p. 14.

20. Yerushalmi, p. 17.

21. Yerushalmi, p. 20.

He is explicit about what he means by "interested in," the ambiguity being resolved in so many words; clearly, the documents we have examined would sustain the generalization, "rabbis were interested in" the ancient Israelite Scriptures' historical narratives. But what this interest in those writings led sages themselves to write is, of course, quite another question; they did not receive and comment upon the Scriptural history except in their own terms and for their own purposes, as we have seen in abundant evidence, and they also did not write history of their own. It is this fact, so ominous for Yerushalmi's thesis that, in our language, Judaism is a religion of memory, that Yerushalmi has to address in his terms.

A complete statement of his characterization of Judaism, made explicit at the end, begins as follows:

> For them, history was no less meaningful, their God no less the ultimate arbiter of historical destinies, their messianic hope no less fervent and absolute...If the rabbis, wise men who had inherited a powerful historical tradition, were no longer interested in history, this indicates nothing more than that they felt no need to cultivate it. Perhaps they already knew of history what they needed to know. Perhaps they were even wary of it.[22]

The important language here is the allegation that the rabbis "were no longer interested in history."

However, the documents we have surveyed leave no doubt that sages *were* deeply interested in ancient Israel's historical writings. Yerushalmi's confession that in the failure to write history, sages indicated "they felt no need to cultivate it," and "perhaps they already knew of history what they needed to know" form a striking admission that Yerushalmi faces a phenomenon he cannot explain and wishes to explain away. This is to say, here he has to confront the enormous exception to his ethnic rule: the sages whose documents mediated Scripture to Judaism through the processes of Midrash did not write any history. His thesis is the opposite; *zakhor*, for him, is the key-word for Judaism, and he even alleges that the ethnic group imposes historical consciousness upon all its members. He has therefore either to explain, or explain away, the fact that the principal documents of Judaism attest to a conception of history that can in no way be characterized as historical.

22. Yerushalmi, p. 21

Yerushalmi notes that sages did not write history, but he does not tell us whether the indicative traits of historical thinking characterized sages or did not characterize their modes of thought. If sages did not write history but thought historically, then Yerushalmi's repeated allegation that sages knew of history what they needed to know would bear some plausibility. But as we have seen, sages did not think historically; the rules of the ordering of data and explaining them that govern in Scripture history do not apply in Rabbinic literature. Rather, they thought in another way altogether, the paradigmatic way. And the way of paradigm, model, or pattern excludes the way of history; it does not accommodate historical thinking but contradicts that mode of thought at its indicative premises and generative problematic alike.

Yet Yerushalmi has observed precisely the phenomenon that Chapter Five showed here: the paradigmatic mode of thought. He says so in so many words (I have italicized language critical to what follows):

> For the rabbis the Bible was not only a repository of *past history* but a *revealed pattern of the whole of history*, and they had learned their scriptures well. They knew that history has a purpose, the establishment of the kingdom of God on earth, and that the Jewish people has a central role to play in the process. They were convinced that the covenant between God and Israel was eternal...*Above all, they had learned from the Bible that the true pulse of history often beat beneath its manifest surfaces, an invisible history that was more real than what the world...could recognize.*...Ironically, the very absence of historical writing among the rabbis may itself have been due in good measure to their total and unqualified absorption of the biblical interpretation of history. In its ensemble, the biblical record seemed capable of illuminating every further historical contingency. No fundamentally new conception of history had to be forced in order to accommodate Rome...[23]

The italicized words prove jarring; once we speak of "not only...past history," we invoke the conception of a barrier between past and present; but then the language of "pattern of the whole of history" tears down any such barrier. The further italicized language, beginning with "above all," once more signals the presence of an other-than-historical, temporal, linear, sequential conception of time and rationalization of events. Apart from the final sentence, the statement at hand serves very nicely to express the thesis of this book, as my presentation of the same statement at the head of Chapter

23. Yerushalmi, pp. 21-22.

Five has already indicated.[24]

In stating the results of paradigmatic thinking, Yerushalmi did not recognize the ahistorical, atemporal character of his statement. Once Scripture contains not the record of the past but the pattern of all time, Scripture is no longer read as a historical work at all. The following statement is important because it shows that Yerushalmi takes for granted precisely those minimal indicators of historical thinking that I identified at the outset and demonstrated definitive in the Scripture's Official History:

> The biblical past was known, the messianic future assured; the in-between-time was obscure. Then as now, history did not validate itself and reveal its meaning imminently...They obviously felt they had all the history they required...[25]

Any claim that I have imputed to Yerushalmi a mode of thought he does not, in fact, utilize—the historical one— is excluded by the statement at hand, which articulately recognizes the boundaries that separate between past, present, and future. The "in-between" between past and future corresponds to that sense of the present and its difference from past and future that LeGoff, among many, identifies as the first requirement of historical thinking.

Yerushalmi alleges that while sages did not write history, they continued to think historically, or, in his language, "belief in the meaning of history remained." At one and the same time he recognizes that sages' modes of thought were ahistorical. But he does not then explain what these same modes of thought produced in place of the historical ones:

> ...in rabbinic Judaism...historiography came to a long halt even while belief in the meaning of history remained. We can freely concede...that

---

24. I could not improve upon Yerushalmi's formulation of what is, in fact, paradigmatic thinking: *In its ensemble, the biblical record seemed capable of illuminating every further historical contingency.* Yerushalmi's failure lies not in his characterization of the facts, but in his incapacity to explain them. In his defense, we should note, the power of "the biblical record" to "illuminate" what happens in the future may certainly derive from the notion of precedent, yielding an appeal to the past to explain the future. But, as we realize full well, that is not at all what our sages meant when they worked out their paradigms, formulated through Scripture, for addressing everything that would take place. Once more, the difference lies in whether or not the past forms a chapter of the present, the present, the past, or whether a distinction between past and present is drawn. Yerushalmi does not address this critical point, because he assumes the historical mode of thought and identifies no other.

25. Yerushalmi, p. 24.

much in the rabbinic...heritage inculcated patterns and habits of thought
in later generations that were...if not anti-historical, then ahistorical.[26]

Yerushalmi finally insists that the distinction that he has drawn, between
historical and ahistorical thinking, simply makes no difference:

> Yet these factors did not inhibit the transmission of a vital Jewish past from
> one generation to the next, and Judaism neither lost its link to history nor
> its fundamentally historical orientation.[27]

Yerushalmi claims that sages' ahistorical thinking did not "inhibit the
transmission of a vital Jewish past." But what sages handed on was a paradigm
that ignored most of the "Jewish past" altogether, including the sages' own
past; its paradigmatic quality passed the bounds or selectivity in historical
narrative; its episodic character denied the very continuity that forms the
premise of all narrative; the Judaism of sages acknowledged no connection
to the kind of writing Yerushalmi has in mind as "history," and it is not
historical in orientation but, in its rejection of the premises of historical
thinking—the difference between present and past, the coherence of events
in narrative—nothing short of anti-historical in fundamental character.

Sages handed on no record of their own part of this supposedly "vital
Jewish past." They left the generation no history of their own day; their
tangential allusions to events permit us to understand nothing of the consequential history of their time. A simple comparison of Josephus's writings
to any Rabbinic document tells the story; if the one is history, the other is
not. If the one transmitted a "vital Jewish past" to coming generations, the
other did not do so. If the Judaism of the one exhibits tight links to history
and evinces a fundamentally historical orientation, the other simply did not.
Yerushalmi's allegation ignores his own correct understanding of the main
traits of Rabbinic writing. For Yerushalmi knows full well that sages did not
add a chapter to the Jewish past, one that recorded what happened in their
own day. Even though Rabbinic literature utilizes materials that appear,
nearly verbatim, in Josephus's histories and have been shown to recapitulate
and depend upon Josephus's formulations, being incomprehensible without
point-by-point review in Josephus's counterpart formulation, sages did not
preserve Josephus's writings or any other historical documents; they did not
make chronicles; they did not preserve records of the past. Indeed, out of
sages' records, we could not write a history of the Jews in late antiquity.

26. Yerushalmi, pp. 25-26.

27. Yerushalmi, pp. 25-26.

Take one enormous event for example: Julian's edict permitting the Jews to rebuild the Temple, ca. 360. We know, as a matter of fact, the story of what happened. We also know that the failure to rebuild the Temple was broadly known and entered into the Christian polemic against Judaism, for a quarter of a century later, John Chrysostom (among many) pointed to the fiasco as evidence that the Temple would never be rebuilt, the Jews would never regain their self-government in Jerusalem. But a thorough examination of Rabbinic literature of the fifth through seventh centuries, encompassing both Talmuds and many of the largest and most powerful midrash-compilations, yields no narrative of events, nothing more than the possibility of a veiled allusion, or inchoate response, to that amazing calamity. And this is only one example among many, contradicting Yerushalmi's claim that "these facts did not inhibit the transmission of a vital Jewish past." Sages transmitted nothing of the kind, if in that "vital Jewish past" was supposed to be encompassed the chapter of their own life and times.

The opposite is the case. Sages in fact left accounts of events of their own day—out of which no sustained historical narrative is to be constructed. They provided anecdotes of lives—but neither biography nor even the raw materials thereof. They set forth episodes—but no intelligible sequences, stories—but nothing approaching a continuous narrative. They persistently represented the present within the framework of the past, not only the past within the setting of the present, and that constitutes a far more gross offense against historical thinking than mere anachronism. Bringing the past into the present means denying the pastness of the past, and that, in turn, represents not the absence of history but the repudiation of its generative premise. What sages transmitted was an account of a "vital Jewish present," one that in no way acknowledged the pastness of the past or the autonomy, either, of the present moment but insisted upon their fusion.

Had sages wished to deliver the statement that they acknowledged as worthy of transmission to the future no "vital Jewish past" at all, what they did not address would have provided ample evidence of this fact. Most of the turning points in contemporary history, e.g., the war of Bar Kokhba, the rise of Christianity to the position of the state-religion of Rome, the world-historical significance of Sasanian Iran, counter-weight to Rome, and the meaning, for the Jews, of Iranian hegemony—none of these enormous and formative facts of life could have been reconstructed out of the Rabbinic writings. Out of the Rabbinic literature we should know nothing at all about Rome and Iran, and little enough about Israel beyond the framework of sages' own circles and circumstances.

Out of those same documents we cannot even write a history of the Jews' institutions, nor can we explain the archaeological records of the synagogues by appeal to what sages have to say about them. So of precisely what components did this "vital Jewish past" consist, that sages are alleged to have handed on as "link to history"? And what evidence, out of paradigmatic writings, permits us to claim that sages persisted in a "fundamentally historical orientation"? Since Yerushalmi is explicit about what he means by a historical orientation, we may answer very simply: by his criteria (as by mine), sages in no way exhibited a "fundamentally historical orientation."

CHAPTER IX

EXPLAINING THE EXPLANATION

i. Why Here? Why Now? So What?

Since our sages of blessed memory subverted the historical thinking they inherited and substituted for it an altogether different kind, recasting the essential of history, the definition of time, in anti-historical terms, we have to wonder how and why sages whose minds were shaped in Scripture and whose souls were cast in its models utterly rejected what Scripture clearly said—and said to other Jews—and substituted modes of thought and patterns of reading of a kind quite alien to the written part of revelation. Here in the Rabbinic documents we have surveyed[1] we have sustained and systematic thought that shows an alternative to history as a mode of accounting for how things are; that treats as null the most fundamental datum of the historical thinking to which we are accustomed; and that served Judaism (and Christianity) for nearly the whole of its history. If I had to explain why paradigmatic rather than historical thinking predominated, I should have to revert to that very mode of explanation, the historical and contextual, that Scripture set forth but our sages abandoned. Precisely where and when, in the context of Israel's life, did historical thinking emerge?

First, whence the source of the sense of separation of present from past? To answer that question (which is a historical one), we turn to the setting in which, in Israel, history first was set down in a sustained narrative about times past. The Official History of ancient Israel set forth by Genesis through Kings recognizes the pastness of the past and explains how the past has led to the present. That Official, Authorized, or Primary History, came to literary formulation (whatever the state of the facts contained therein) in the aftermath of the destruction of the first Temple of Jerusalem, in 586. Faced with decisive closure, looking backward from the perspective of a radically

---

1. And in all of the others, the two Talmuds providing ample instantiation of the same theses as I have documented out of the Mishnah, Tosefta, and earlier, middle, and later Midrash-compilations.

different present, the thinkers who put together the Primary History took up two complementary premises, the definitive pastness of the past, its utter closure and separation from the present, and, alongside, the power of the past to explain the present and of its lessons, properly learned, to shape the future.

The historical thinking that produced the Authorized History took place at a very specific time and responded to an acute and urgent question by taking account of the facts of the moment. An age had come to a conclusion; the present drastically differed from the now-closed past. History might begin, the sense of closure having taken hold. Since the Official or Primary History represented by Genesis through Kings came to closure at just this time, the allegation that historical thinking in Israel in particular[2] reaches literary expression in the aftermath of the catastrophe of 586 rests upon solid foundations. Here is when people wrote history-books; here is why they wrote them; here, therefore, is the circumstance in which, for Israel, historical thinking took place.

In this context, we recall Childs's formulation, "The question of how to overcome the separation in time and space from the great events of the past became the paramount issue." The advent of historical thinking and writing became possible precisely when great events from the past receded over the last horizon, and those responsible for the books at hand recognized a separation from those events and so produced a history of how things had reached their present pass. Our sages of blessed memory, however, evinced no sense of separation that precipitates the quest for reconciliation, restoration, renewal of relationship between now and then; therefore they thought in a different manner about the same events. That is the starting point of matters, and it also brings us to a conclusion: why did they think in a different way, what, in particular, led them to this other mode of thought?

---

2. We are not concerned with the advent of historical thinking in other contexts or in defining historical thinking in Israel by comparison with, or contrast to, historical thinking in either the Near Eastern or Hellenic worlds. Historical thinking in Israel has defined itself in its own writings, and those who received those writings and so radically recast them have responded to the historical thinking they learned in Scripture with this other kind of thinking of their own. Hence I explain not the origins of history or historical thinking in general, or even what is special about Israel's historical thinking, whether in the sixth century B.C.E. or in the fifth century C.E., but only the circumstances in which in this setting historical thinking took shape, by contrast with the circumstances in which, later on, another mode of thought took precedence.

Our sages of blessed memory recognized no barrier between present and past. To them, the present and past formed a single unit of time, encompassing a single span of experience. Why was that so? It is because, to them, times past took place in the present too, on which account, the present not only encompassed the past (which historical thinking concedes) but took place in the same plane of time as the past (which, to repeat, historical thinking rejects). Why? It is because our sages of blessed memory experienced the past in the present. What happened that mattered had already happened; an event then was transformed into a series; events themselves defined paradigms, yielded rules. A simple formulation of this mode of thought is as follows:

Mishnah-tractate Taanit 4:6

A. Five events took place for our fathers on the seventeenth of Tammuz, and five on the ninth of Ab.

B. On the seventeenth of Tammuz

> (1) the tablets [of the Torah] were broken,
>
> (2) the daily whole offering was cancelled,
>
> (3) the city wall was breached,
>
> (4) Apostemos burned the Torah, and
>
> (5) he set up an idol in the Temple.

C. On the ninth of Ab

> (1) the decree was made against our forefathers that they should not enter the land,
>
> (2) the first Temple and
>
> (3) the second [Temple] were destroyed,
>
> (4) Betar was taken, and
>
> (5) the city was ploughed up [after the war of Hadrian].

D. When Ab comes, rejoicing diminishes.

The paradigm, from marking time, moves outward to the formation of rules concerning the regularity and order of events. In the formulation just now given, we see the movement from event to rule. What is important about events is not their singularity but their capacity to generate a pattern, a concrete rule for the here and now. That is the conclusion drawn from the very passage at hand:

Mishnah-tractate Taanit 4:7

A. In the week in which the ninth of Ab occurs it is prohibited to get a haircut and to wash one's clothes.

B. But on Thursday of that week these are permitted,

C. because of the honor owing to the Sabbath.

D. On the eve of the ninth of Ab a person should not eat two prepared dishes, nor should one eat meat or drink wine.

E. Rabban Simeon b. Gamaliel says, "He should make some change from ordinary procedures."

F. R. Judah declares people liable to turn over beds.

G. But sages did not concur with him.

Events serve to define paradigms and therefore, also, to yield rules governing the here and now.

This brings us back to our question: how an event turned into a series, how a seemingly singular event can continually reoccur. The answer lies in the correspondence (real or imagined) of the two generative events sages found definitive: the destruction of the first Temple in 586 B.C.E. and the destruction of the second Temple six hundred years later. The singular event that framed their consciousness recapitulated what had already occurred. For they confronted a Temple in ruins, and, in the defining event of the age just preceding the composition of most of the documents surveyed here, they found quite plausible the notion that the past was a formidable presence in the contemporary world. And having lived through events that they could plausibly discover in Scripture—in Lamentations for one example, Jeremiah another—they also found entirely natural the notion that the past took place in the present as well.

When we speak of the presence of the past, therefore, we raise not generalities or possibilities, but the concrete experience that generations actively mourning the Temple endured. When we speak of the pastness of the present, we describe the consciousness of a people who could open Scripture and find themselves right there, in its record—not only in Lamentations, but also in prophecy, and, especially, in the books of the Torah.[3] Here we deal with not the spiritualization of Scripture, but with the acutely contem-

---

3. The paradigm of course also would govern the way in which Scripture would be read and responded to, the way in which historical events would be identified and defined and responded to. That is a point that scarcely requires amplification in this context.

porary and immediate realization of Scripture: once again, as then; Scripture in the present day, the present day in Scripture. That is why it was possible for sages to formulate out of Scripture a paradigm that imposed structure and order upon the world that they themselves encountered.

Since, then, sages did not see themselves as removed in time and space from the generative events to which they referred the experience of the here and now, they also had no need to make the past contemporary. If, as Childs insists, the Exodus was irreversible, a once and for all-time event, then, as we see, our sages saw matters in a different way altogether. They neither relived nor transformed one-time historical events, for they found another way to overcome the barrier of chronological separation. Specifically, if history began when the gap between present and past shaped consciousness, then we naturally ask ourselves whether the point at which historical modes of thought concluded and a different mode of thought took over produced an opposite consciousness from the historical one: not cycle but paradigm. For, it seems to me clear, the premise that time and space separated our sages of the Rabbinic writings from the great events of the past simply did not win attention. The opposite premise defined matters: barriers of space and time in no way separated sages from great events, the great events of the past enduring for all time. How then are we to account for this remarkably different way of encounter, experience, and, consequently, explanation? The answer has already been adumbrated.

Sages assembled in the documents of Rabbinic Judaism, from the Mishnah forward, all recognized the destruction of the Second Temple and all took for granted that that event was to be understood by reference to the model of the destruction of the first.[4] A variety of sources reviewed here

---

4. Then heirs to the same Scriptures who did not attach to the Temple any consequence at all, and did not assign to its destruction a central place in their consciousness, also would not look in Scripture for a paradigm to interpret that particular event. Their modes of paradigmatic thinking—and among Christianities the paradigmatic, not the historical, hermeneutic would reach full articulation—would continue to compete with historical ones, so that biographies—Gospels concerning Jesus, lives of the later sayings—and sustained histories, beginning with that of Eusebius, would come forth, right alongside writings of a paradigmatic kind. The question Yerushalmi does not raise has, in fact, a clear response: what mattered to one set of heirs did not make much difference to many among the other. One could, after all, draw the conclusion that the destruction of the second Temple represented the penalty for "the Jews" rejection of Jesus as Christ and not then abandon all manner of historical modes of thought. The origin of paradigmatic, as against historical, thinking in among Christianities requires an explanation in its own terms and context, but, I should claim, the explanation will conform to the model of explanation that is offered here.

maintain precisely that position and express it in so many words, e.g., the colloquy between Aqiba and sages about the comfort to be derived from the ephemeral glory of Rome and the temporary ruin of Jerusalem. It follows that for our sages of blessed memory, the destruction of the Temple in 70 did not mark a break with the past, such as it had for their predecessors some five hundred years earlier, but rather a recapitulation of the past. Paradigmatic thinking then began in that very event that precipitated thought about history to begin with, the end of the old order. But paradigm replaced history because what had taken place the first time as unique and unprecedented took place the second time in precisely the same pattern and therefore formed of an episode a series. Paradigmatic thinking replaced historical when history as an account of one-time, irreversible, unique events, arranged in linear sequence and pointing toward a teleological conclusion, lost all plausibility. If the first time around, history—with the past marked off from the present, events arranged in linear sequence, narrative of a sustained character serving as the medium of thought—provided the medium for making sense of matters, then the second time around, history lost all currency.

The real choice facing our sages was not linear history as against paradigmatic thinking, but rather, paradigm as against cycle. For the conclusion to be drawn from the destruction of the Temple once again, once history, its premises disallowed, yielded no explanation, can have taken the form of a theory of the cyclicality of events. As nature yielded its spring, summer, fall and winter, so the events of humanity or of Israel in particular can have been asked to conform to a cyclical pattern, in line, for example, with Qohelet's view that what has been is what will be. But our sages obviously did not take that position at all.

They rejected cyclicality in favor of a different ordering of events altogether. They did not believe the Temple would be rebuilt and destroyed again, rebuilt and destroyed, and so on into endless time. They stated the very opposite: the Temple would be rebuilt, but never again destroyed. And this represented a view of the second destruction that rejected cyclicality altogether. Sages instead opted for patterns of history and against cycles because they retained that notion for the specific and concrete meaning of events that characterized Scripture's history, even while rejecting the historicism of Scripture. What they maintained, as we have seen, is that a pattern governed, and the pattern was not a cyclical one. Here, Scripture itself imposed its structures, its order, its system—its paradigm. And the Official History left no room for the conception of cyclicality. If matters do not repeat themselves but do conform to a pattern, then the pattern itself must be identified.

Paradigmatic thinking formed the alternative to cyclical thinking because Scripture, its history subverted, nonetheless defined how matters were to be understood.[5] Viewed whole, the Official History indeed defined the paradigm of Israel's existence, formed out of the components of Eden and the Land, Adam and Israel, Sinai, then given movement through Israel's responsibility to the covenant and Israel's adherence to, or violation, of God's will, fully exposed in the Torah that marked the covenant of Sinai. Scripture laid matters out, and our sages then drew conclusions from that layout that conformed to their experience. So the second destruction precipitated thinking about paradigms of Israel's life, such as came to full exposure in the thinking behind the Midrash-compilations we have surveyed. The episode made into a series, sages' paradigmatic thinking asked of Scripture different questions from the historical ones of 586 because our sages brought to Scripture different premises; drew from Scripture different conclusions. But in point of fact, not a single paradigm set forth by sages can be distinguished in any important component from the counterpart in Scripture, not Eden and Adam in comparison to the land of Israel and the people Israel, and not the tale of Israel's experience in the spinning out of the tension between the word of God and the will of Israel.

The contrast between history's time and nature's time shows that history recognizes natural time and imposes its points of differentiation, upon it. History knows days, months, years, but proposes to differentiate among them, treating this day as different from that because on this day, such and such happened, but on that day, it did not. History's time takes over nature's time and imposes upon it a second set of indicators or points of differentiation. History therefore defines and measures time through two intersecting indicators, the meeting of [1] the natural and [2] the human. As is clear in the foregoing remarks, the context in which "time" is now defined is [1] the passage of days, weeks, months, and years, as marked by the movement of the sun and the stars in the heavens and [2] the recognition of noteworthy events that have taken place in specific occasions during the passage of those days and months and years. By contrast, paradigmatic time in the context of Judaism tells time through the events of nature, to which are correlated

5. Here—for the wrong reasons to be sure—Yerushalmi is right in saying, "In its ensemble, the biblical record seemed capable of illuminating every further historical contingency" The important language is "in its ensemble."

the events of Israel's life: its social structure, its reckoning of time, its disposition of its natural resources, and its history too. That is, through the point at which nature is celebrated, the Temple, there Israel tells time.

Predictably, therefore, the only history our sages deem worth narrating—and not in sustained narrative even then—is the story of the Temple cult through days and months and years, and the history of the Temple and its priesthood and administration through time and into eternity. We now fully understand this fact. It is because, to begin with, the very conception of paradigmatic thinking as against the historical kind took shape in deep reflection on the meaning of events: what happened before has happened again—to the Temple. Ways of telling time before give way, history's premises having lost plausibility here as much as elsewhere. Now Israel will tell time in nature's way, shaping history solely in response to what happens in the cult and to the Temple. There is no other history, because, to begin with, there is no history.

Nature's time is the sole way of marking time, and Israel's paradigm conforms to nature's time and proves enduringly congruent with it. Israel conforming to nature yields not cyclical history but a reality formed by appeal to the paradigm of cult and Temple, just as God had defined that pattern and paradigm to Moses in the Torah. Genesis begins with nature's time and systematically explains how the resources of nature came to Israel's service to God. History's time yielded an Israel against and despite history, nature's time, as the Torah tells it, an Israel fully harmonious with nature. At stake in the paradigm then is creation: how come? So long as the Judaism set forth by our sages of blessed memory in the Mishnah, Tosefta, Talmuds, and Midrash-compilations governed, Israel formed itself in response to the eternities of nature's time, bringing into conformity the ephemera of the here and now. That answers the questions, why here? why now? so what? When and where this Judaism lost its power of self-evidence, there history intervened, philosophy and theology, including normative law, gave way to narrative, and the lines of structure and order took a new turning. But that was only recently, and, it now appears, for only a brief spell.

GENERAL INDEX

Augustine, Saint, 111

Barr, James, 27, 36, 63
Biography
    anecdotal one-time discourse in biographical historical thinking, 63-93
    lives of sages, 87
    narrative of person named in sustaining narrative of history, 77-79, 86-87, 92

Cassuto, Umberto, 28
Childs, Brevard S., 47, 145, 202-4, 216, 219
Chrysostom, John, 213
Communal life of Israel
    historical vs. paradigmatic thinking, in Judaism, 13-38
    from historical time to time Cyclical and time Paradigmatic, 47-50

Davies, Philip R., 26

Freedman, David Noel, 26, 36-38, 94

Halpern, Baruch, 13-15, 17, 37, 59
Hebrew scriptures
    as history of Israel, 1-10
    paradigmatic vs. historical thinking in Judaism, 13-25
Historicaal thinking and scriptural writings
    one-time event as factor in historical thinking, 65-77, 79-86
    absence of history in Rabbinic literature, 6-7, 93
    of ancient Israel, 25-38
    exempting Torah from secular order, 94-107
    of one-time event or one time biographical anecdote, 63-99
History
    absence in Rabbinic writings, 6-7
    from historical time to time cyclical and time pardigmatic, 47-50
    historical writing and conception of time, 39-47
    paradigmatic thinking in history of Israel, 113-16
        and time and paradigm in scripture, 4-6

INDEX TO
BIBLICAL AND TALMUDIC REFERENCES